More praise for Coming Home to Eat

"[A] perspective that is at once ecological, economic, humanistic and spiritual. In his eloquent, richly evocative book, [Nabhan] offers a fascinating, enlightening and moving account of his own experiences . . . prompting us to think twice about everything from the value of so-called 'health foods' to the decline in the percentage of American families who have dinner together at home."
—*Los Angeles Times*

"Knowing where your food comes from can change your life. In this amazing and eloquent book, Nabhan makes us understand how finding and eating local foods connects us deeply and sensually with where we are [and] why the everyday choices we make about food are the most important choices we make."
—Alice Waters,
chef-owner of Chez Panisse in Berkeley, California

"Gary Paul Nabhan is reawakening in modern America that inalienable need to delve deeply, sensually into its sustenance. . . . He offers an elegant, inspired and eloquently detailed account of becoming a 'direct participant' (to use his words) in the food that sustains him, and the lives of those around him."
—Rick Bayless,
founding member of Chefs Collaborative
and host of Public Television's *Mexico—One Plate at a Time*

"Nabhan explores the seasonal resources of his regional food shed in an attempt to understand the full meaning of eating well. Indulging a joyful taste for wild food . . . leads him to an enriched sense of community and to better ways of eating that are delicious to the palate and easy on the land. . . . This timely and thoughtful book suggests a different path toward health and responsible living."
—*Audobon*

"A practical primer on how to 'eat locally, think globally' (and enjoy it more) wherever you are. Nabhan explores one of the greatest sources of global despoliation and tells us exactly what we can do about it: eat consciously, and eat foods grown close at hand."
—Stanley Crawford,
author of *A Garlic Testament: Seasons on a Small New Mexico Farm*

"Weaving together the traditions of Thoreau and M. F. K Fisher, Nabhan challenges the wisdom of buying into the planetary supermarket and offers his personal journey to eat locally as an alternative. A rare combination of the sensual and the intellectual, *Coming Home to Eat* is a soul food treatise for our time."
—Peter Hoffman,
chef-owner of Savoy Restaurant in New York City
and national chair of the Chefs Collaborative

"[A] tale certain to inspire gardeners, cooks, and others eager to replace convenience with flavor."   —*Country Living Gardener*

"A profound and engaging book, a passionate call to us to rethink our food industry and to return when possible to our own locale for the sources of what we cook and eat."   —Jim Harrison,
author of *The Beast God Forgot to Invent*

"Dr. Nabhan's adventures with food wove through my day. . . . [A] good book for gardeners to read this winter, as they dream of what to order from that avalanche of catalogs [and] a reasoned primer on the risks of bio-engineered crops."   —Anne Raver, *New York Times*

"Nabhan is a brilliant scientist (ethnobotany) and remarkably successful social activist. In *Coming Home to Eat* he weaves ideas about eating right into his interest in the pleasure of caring for ecosystems and communities. His stories are often funny and always invaluable."
                    —William Kittredge, author of *The Nature of Generosity*

"[Nabhan] writes with a passion for those of us who still see and trust the wild in our land. His stories celebrate the sense of place that belongs in all our foods."   —David Mas Masumoto, organic farmer
and author of *Epitaph for a Peach* and *Harvest Son*

"[A] global meditation on finding sustenance in your own backyard."
                    —*Tucson Weekly*

"A purist at heart, Nabhan questions the world-at-your-fingertips approach to eating adopted by many Americans. . . . [H]is narrative will change the way that readers look at their meals forever."   —*Natural Home*

"[T]his book is about communion. It describes a sacred relationship to food and place. . . . The author celebrates the sensual pleasures of food while giving the reader an education about global food politics in a savory blend of personal story, research, and reflection, all served up in delicious prose."
                    —*Earthlight*

"An eloquent and trailblazing writer. . . . Warmhearted, innovative, and respectful of life, Nabhan inspires readers to think twice about corporate domination of the food supply and the old adage You Are What You Eat."
                    —*Booklist*

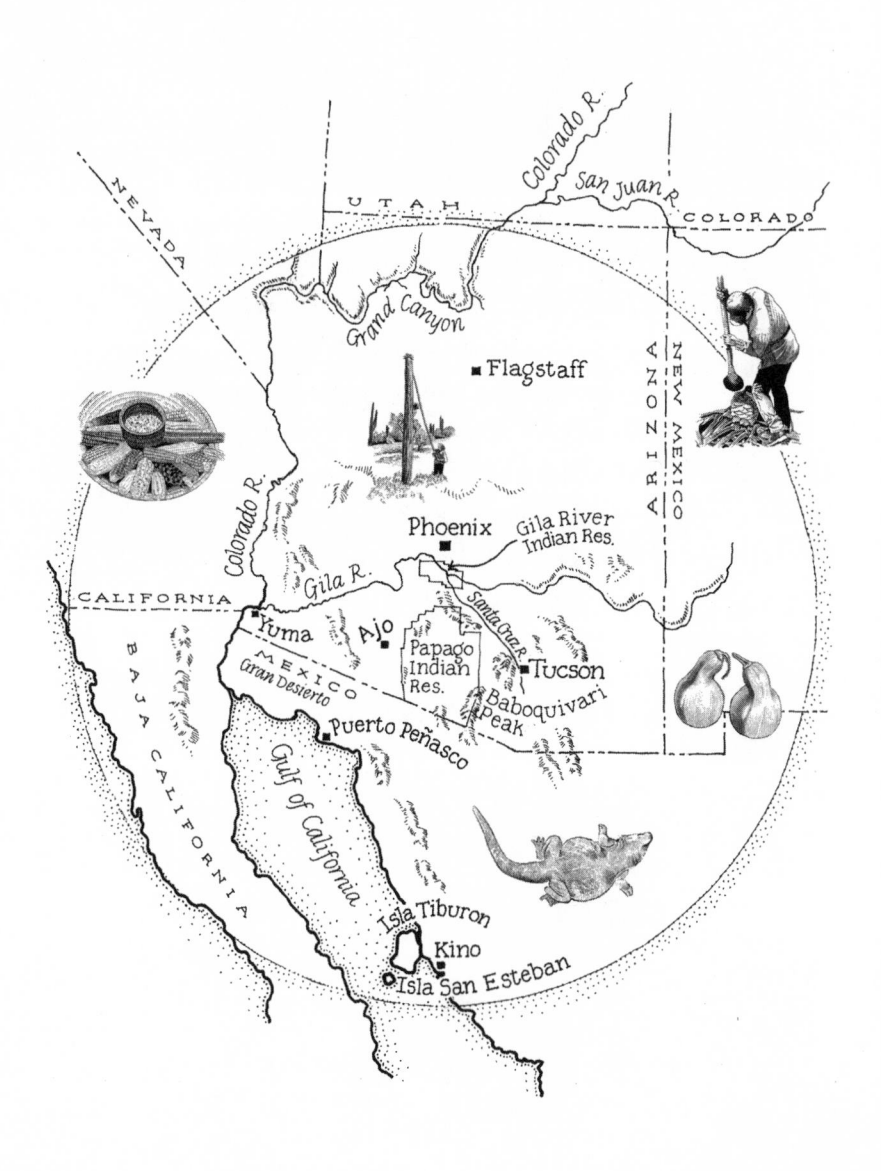

Coming Home to Eat

The Pleasures and Politics of Local Foods

Gary Paul Nabhan, Ph.D.

W. W. NORTON & COMPANY

NEW YORK   LONDON

Copyright © 2002 by Gary Paul Nabhan

For information about permission to reproduce selections from this book, write to
Permissions, W. W. Norton & Company, Inc., 500 Fifth Avenue, New York, NY 10110

The text of this book is composed in Times New Roman
with the display set in Nueva Bold Extended
Composition by Adrian Kitzinger
Manufacturing by The Maple-Vail Book Manufacturing Group
Book design by Mary A. Wirth
Drawings by Hannah Hinchman
Production manager: Andrew Marasia

Library of Congress Cataloging-in-Publication Data

Nabhan, Gary Paul.
Coming home to eat : the pleasures and politics of local foods / Gary Paul Nabhan.
p. cm.
Includes bibliographical references and index.
ISBN 0-393-02017-7
1. Gastronomy. I. Title.

TX631 .N33 2001
641'.01'3—dc21   2001034556

ISBN 0-393-32374-9 pbk.

W. W. Norton & Company, Inc., 500 Fifth Avenue, New York, N.Y. 10110
www.wwnorton.com

W. W. Norton & Company Ltd., Castle House, 75/76 Wells Street, London W1T 3QT

1 2 3 4 5 6 7 8 9 0

For my wife, Laurie;

my brothers, Norm and Doug;

and my mother Jerri, the hearth for us all

The whole of nature is a conjugation
of the verb *to eat,* in the active
and in the passive.

—WILLIAM R. INGE, *Outspoken Essays,* First Series

Nature is a damp place
over which large numbers
of ducks fly, uncooked.

—OSCAR WILDE

Contents

IV Winter: The Reflective Months

Preface and Acknowledgments

This book is about a year of eating locally, a year that also happened to be a watershed in the history of global food politics. It is the story of finding kindred food-loving souls within a 250-mile radius of my home in Arizona, and sharing with them the pleasures of gardening and gathering, pit roasting and fermenting, feasting and frolicking. But it is also a book of juxtapositions: about how the remaining farmers, fishermen, and foragers within my "foodshed" struggle with challenges, insults, and absurdities different from the ones their ancestors faced a century ago. Wherever I foraged with my neighbors for wild greens, hunted for quail, or sowed heirloom crops, we have seldom been out of earshot of the global vending machine. It can still be heard dropping its hermetically sealed packages of textured soy protein, genetically engineered tortillas, and artificial spices no matter how hard you or I try to get away from its noise.

Fortunately, I am not the only one wondering what kinds of ancient culinary melodies are being drowned out by the noise of that transnational vending machine. One defining moment—the equivalent of a Boston Tea Party—can fittingly be said to have taken place at the turn of the twenty-first century. Farmers refused to grow certain patented seeds foisted upon them by transnational corporations, and students destroyed experimental fields and labs where genetically engineered crops were being developed. Consumers demanded that the contents of foods be labeled on their packages, and boycotted companies whose advertising was deceptive. Mobs attacked McDonald's and Starbucks as part of the protests against the annual meeting of the World Trade Organization in Seattle. Groups in other countries fought against the corporate control of farmlands, seeds, and genes, and banned U.S. agricultural products potentially harmful to butterflies and babies. The launching of the Slow Food Movement in the United States made me aware that there are at least 100,000 like-minded souls in Europe and Latin America. This book celebrates the sensual pleasures of food without ignoring its global politics, for we will hardly be able to savor such pleasures any longer if we do not decide how to disconnect that omnipresent vending machine.

My brother Douglas first encouraged me to undertake this project, and although his busy schedule kept him from joining me in my explorations, I remain indebted to him. My sweetheart (and now wife), Laurie, lived through the hare- (and turkey-) raising parts of this experiment, as did my daughter, Laura, and my mother, Jerri. I promise them plain, palatable meals for many years to come. My heartfelt thanks go to Victoria Shoemaker, my agent, and Alane Salierno Mason, my editor, for believing in this project from the beginning and improving it along the way. Agnese Haury, Hillary Oppmann, Patti West, and Yajaira Gray kept in front of me the fast-breaking news of food politics, and supported this effort in innumerable ways. Danny Lopez, Delores Lewis, Stella Tucker, Andrew and Nina Hipps, José-Juan Moreno, Beto Cruz, Rick Bayless, Dick Nelson, the late Dana Meadows, Hope Shand, Vess Quinlan, Tom Orum, Nancy Ferguson, Anne Raver, Sandy Tolan, Kent and Diane Whealy, Diann Peart, Jane Rissler, Paul Hawken, David Cavagnaro,

Becky and Don Routson, Gary Snyder, Enrique La Madrid, and Jack Loeffler offered guidance, inspiration, or example. Special thanks go to all the participants and donors supporting the Desert Walk for Heritage and Health, as well as the Comcaac (Seri) and Tohono O'odham (Papago) communities that hosted us. In gratitude to my fellow desert walkers, I am setting up scholarship and intern funds, including one in honor of the late Sally Pablo, a pioneering O'odham native foods and diabetes educator.

A percentage of royalties from this book will go into those funds held by the Center for Sustainable Environments and Native Seeds/SEARCH in Tucson, but I encourage your donations to them as well.

Finally I am deeply grateful to the Lannan Foundation, its founders, board, and staff, for a literary award that made working on this book possible. Blessings to all of you.

Introduction

There are moments in this life that I recall not as visual snapshots but as tastes and fragrances. They make sense to me, to who I am, in ways that I suppose are profoundly rooted. At the same time they are blessedly involuntary; for I cannot control when they spring up within me and take me over. They are truly re-membered, that is, those moments seem as deeply etched into the matter of my body now as anything can be.

One such set of visceral recollections came from my first visit to eat and drink and walk on my grandparents' home ground in Lebanon. Like almost everyone else I know, I had eaten food of sorts and drunk various beverages all my life, and yet I am like that proverbial fish who had no clear concept of water. At last, in Lebanon, it became poignantly, perhaps painfully, evident to me that the kinds of food I eat and who I've shared them with say more or less everything tangible about how I've lived. They mark how ethereally remote or how bodily close I've been to the land, to the sea, and to the labors of the harvest at various points in my life.

If food is the sumptuous sea of energy we dive into and swim through every day, I have lived but one brief moment leaping like a flying fish and catching a glimmering glimpse of that sea roiling all around us. And then just as quickly, I splashed back beneath its surface, to be evermore immersed in what effortlessly buoys us up.

That brief moment of leaping came by way of juxtaposition in Lebanon. It sprung me loose from ever again being complacent about not knowing where true nourishment comes from.

Over the quarter century prior to that leap, I had dreamed of making a pilgrimage to taste Lebanon. I had grown up eating Lebanese American among my father's clan, as my mother and aunts adapted the recipes of their foremothers to fit the availability of *materia prima* in our newfound home. I craved to compare the kibbe, koosa, tabbouleh, labneh and hummus bi tahini of my youth to that of the motherland, and to reconnect with relatives while doing so.

Fortunately my younger brother, Douglas, had the generosity and wherewithal to arrange a reunion with our distant cousins in the Bekáa Valley. Douglas had worked as a lawyer in Riyadh, Saudi Arabia, and on a brief business trip to Beirut the year before, had hooked up with the Nabhan clan for a glorious but emotionally exhausting twenty-four hours. He came back home sighing like a guy who had fallen in love for the first time in his life. He had been smitten by the shower of genuine affection poured onto him by our long-lost cousins, by their lovely children, and by the tangible sense of reconnection with our own heritage.

"You just can't believe it. . . . I don't know what to do. . . . I cried all the way back across the ocean." Douglas immediately proposed that he take me and my older brother, Norman, back with him to Beirut and the Bekáa Valley, even though the three of us had never traveled together as adults. Seeing how deeply Doug had been moved, Norm and I dropped everything else in order to join him. Douglas knew far more Arabic than we did, but he had also persuaded his Lebanon-born friend Sam Habboush to accompany us, just in case words failed him during his next venture into the surf of emotion.

"You might want to think about fasting for a few days before we arrive." Sam warned us. If your cousins are anything like mine," he moaned, "they'll ask you if you're hungry every twenty minutes."

Doug concurred. "Get ready for an all-night feast. I swear our cousins won't let you leave the room until you've had every traditional dish they can fit on the table."

When we arrived at the Beirut airport, we were immediately met by a distant cousin in government services who had somehow positioned himself as the first official just outside the arrival gate. Our family from the Bekáa Valley had insisted that he guarantee our safe passage through customs. He led us straight to our other cousins and uncles, who not only escorted us but constantly held, hugged, and kissed us from the very moment we set foot on Lebanese soil. They tried to feed us immediately, but, seeing how tired we were, they graciously granted us a day to recover from jet lag. They would then drive us over the mountains to the Bekáa Valley, where they said the rest of our kin were already preparing for our arrival.

Lebanon was "in recovery," trying to break its twenty-two-year addiction to internecine strife that had been doped up by external political, economic, and religious forces. Beirut was not a pretty sight. It was a little like seeing someone who had just had plastic surgery after a car accident, but was still bandaged, bruised, and battered. "You're looking better," you offer optimistically, painfully aware that your reaction might be considered a bit premature.

Our cousins nonchalantly drove us past bombed-out buildings where, three stories up, families were trying to shape a refuge for themselves, despite the tons of twisted steel, crumbling plaster, and blasted concrete walls hanging above them. Shell-pocked buildings dotted the neighborhoods surrounding the airport, although more than a few edifices were being intentionally demolished to make way for new ones to go up in their stead. The city was struggling to regain its stature as an international trade center, even though its reputation as an intellectual and cultural forum remained badly crippled.

At the end of our day of rest in Beirut we were invited to dinner by a Lebanese Maronite businessman whom my brother knew. He urged us to join his entourage at the exclusive Club Du Lubnan before we headed for the hinterland, so that we could sample the finest the "New Beirut" had to offer. Although we were anxious to get out of the city to devote ourselves to our relatives, we accepted the invitation anyway. It would allow us a few more hours to restore our emotional energy before full immersion in family passions, politics, and personalities.

A taxi wound down narrow streets to the edge of the city not far from the ancient ports of Juniye and Byblos, and dropped us off at the glass-and-marble entranceway of an elite casino. Suddenly a wave of disorientation crashed around me, and when I resurfaced from it, I felt something had gone awry. I had a vague, unsettling feeling that I had been in that space before, not in the Club Du Lubnan per se but in some other hall of gambling with the same essential character.

We were escorted through double doors into an immense but disturbingly quiet lobby, decorated in marble, and mirrors. I glanced around feverishly, embarrassed to be having a déjà-vu moment in the presence of my brothers. Was this place reminiscent of a governor's palace I had once visited in central Mexico? A now-abandoned mansion of the Rockefeller family in western Massachusetts, or a recently erected resort hotel in Las Vegas? I could not put my finger on it.

Meanwhile, we were asked to present photo IDs and credit cards, put through financial and security checks by computer, and then given lifetime membership cards to the club. (Now *that* was something that gave me a false sense of "eternal belonging," as much as anything I'd ever received!) Next we were ushered into an exclusive dining room overlooking blackjack tables where Saudi oilmen, English gaming professionals, Russian prostitutes, Egyptian merchants, and French diplomats quietly gambled amid sheer opulence.

We never saw a menu or wine list, for our host generously ordered for us all drinks, appetizers, and dinner courses with a mere whisper to

the waiter: French champagne, caviar from failing black sturgeon populations of the Caspian Sea, jumbo Guaymas shrimp from the Gulf of
California, Sicilian capers, Argentine beef, French and Italian wine,
Cuban cigars, and on, and on. Our host, a regular visitor to the club, had
favorites that were well known to the waiters and chefs. One brief word
from him and another dish or bottle suddenly appeared before us, as if it
had been flown in fresh from another continent.

Perhaps because I too had just flown in and was still jet-lagged, it
took several courses before I realized the simplest of facts: Not a single
item being served to us came from Lebanese soil. No matter that I had
arrived with an eagerness to learn of the traditional foods rooted in my
grandparents' natal grounds, the casino's other clients were apparently
there to partake of something altogether different. Perhaps they came
merely to sample the riches of the global marketplace, perhaps for the
sake of status alone. The fare on the table, the marble on the walls, and
even the conversation among the Saudi oilmen and their Russian whores
reinforced a single message to all who were present: The entire world
was at our disposal.

At one moment during dinner, I realized how parochial, how distant
I felt from the other guests. I tried in vain to listen with open ears and an
open heart to our modest, but charming companions. They were courte-
ous and cosmopolitan, well educated and widely traveled. Our hosts
were erudite Christian businessmen, who constantly expressed how
devoutly religious and family-oriented they were. But as their dinner
conversation with my brothers turned to the current advantages of offshore banking and tax havens, I floated away for good.

What was it that sprung me loose from my comfort zone? Although
I did not doubt the honesty of these men, I did become more and more
skeptical of their implicit assumption that tax-free havens were "safe
and politically neutral ground," an unquestionably ethical place for the
wealthy to harbor their hard-earned riches.

They debated only whether the Isle of Man, the Seychelles, or Malta provided the most confidential tax-free bank accounts for the wealthy, or at least for those among the wealthy who wished to remain unconstrained by national allegiances. They spoke in detail of various arrangements these islands had for allowing anyone banking there to maintain complete anonymity and protection from extradition or "political vagaries." They were clearly convinced that tax-free, nonextradition savings accounts for international investors were essential assets for their own futures. I was amused that none of them expressed any fear that money laundering and Internet investment hoaxes might be aided by the rise of tax-free, extradition-free, scrutiny-free investing venues. It didn't matter that offshore financial meccas were just the ticket for venture capitalists the likes of international terrorist Osama bin Laden, brother of former Mexican president, Raul Salinas de Gortari, or former Chilean dictator Augusto Pinochet.

Of course, there was a good reason that such an issue did not emerge among "polite company." It was well known that Salinas had illicitly moved $100 million out of Mexico with the help of an ethically lax banking firm, one that has fortunately shored up its policies since its embarrassing lapse in appropriate levels of oversight was reported in newspapers around the world. Businessmen such as our dinner companions were not prone to discuss the plight of millions of Mexican peasants, most of whom had been ignorant of the fact that their future was being stolen from them by the Salinas brothers. Instead, they spoke casually and somewhat proudly of their personal encounters with Saudi capitalist Prince al-Waleed bin Talal, as if this man were simply one more savvy investor who had a right to do anything he wanted to do with his money, regardless of whether it might challenge the laws of the many countries from which he had derived his income.

As the last sip of French cognac was sipped and the last Cuban cigar smoked by our party, I realized that the conversation and the cuisine had come into perfect alignment. They both reflected a desire for a life unsoiled by local, regional, cultural, or even nationalistic constraints, where one could pick and choose from the planetary supermarket without any contact with local fishermen or farmers, let alone any responsibility to them.

I did not sleep much that night, letting jet lag and disjointed dream fragments take their course. There were jets taking off and landing in a bombed-out neighborhood of Beirut. Suitcases were being dumped open by customs officials, suitcases full of broken bottles of wine and spoiled food. And then there were roulette wheels, turning, turning without stopping on any particular number. My dreams, I later decided, were all disjointed echoes of a fact I had recently read: *The food we put into our mouths today travels an average of thirteen hundred miles from where it is produced, changing hands at least six times along the way.*

The next afternoon we drove over the snowcapped mountains in to the Bekáa Valley. With two carloads of cousins we passed through several roadblocks of Shiite Muslim militia, Syrian and Lebanese forces, Hezbollah guerrillas, and local police. Crossing the ancient croplands of the Fertile Crescent, the Bekáa's orchards, vineyards, grainfields, vegetable gardens, and pastures—I grew more and more heartened.

Suddenly our cousins' beat-up old cars careered around a curve into a side canyon where a cluster of cobblestone and concrete houses filled the canyon bottom. They glittered in the sun beneath eroded limestone slopes stippled with fig and olive trees. I could hardly absorb what the Kfar Sibad landscape felt like, for the cars were slowing to enter a street swelling with kinfolk. "You really have no idea how long they have been waiting for you," our cousin Shibley explained.

It went into slow motion then: I had never seen so many people with the same bulging eyes and beaked noses as me, my brothers, uncles, and aunts. They mobbed the street under a banner proclaiming WELCOME HOME NABHANS. As we tumbled out of the cars, our cousins engulfed us, wrapping us in hugs and in camel hair *abeyas,* the robes of princes. Aunts, uncles, cousins kissed us on the tops of our heads, on our cheeks, on our mouths. They held on to us as if they finally had us back—back from some unimaginable placeless exile where each of us had become the *muhajjar,* "the ones that had been forced to depart." But now we had returned to the ancestral home, *ca biladna,* back in the safety of the family haven, our *laji.* Older women began trilling the *zalgrita,* keening the song of homecoming as they accompanied us indoors.

We came across the threshold into a home emanating the warmth of jovial men bringing out their home-distilled arak and women warming up foods shaped all day by their own hands. We were conjoined in a feast a world apart from the one we had been offered in the Club Du Lubnan. It exuded the aroma of our aunts' and cousins' hands, the musk of goats and sheep grazed on the slopes above us, the salt and the bitter herbal bite of the alkaline earth itself. We were given a meal I shall never forget, for ever since I've carried it homeward, into every one of my body's cells.

Our aunts presented each of us with a dish of kibbe nayyi, raw ground lamb shaped into a loaf, with our names spelled in piñons: WELCOME HOME NORMAN, WELCOME HOME DOUGLAS, WELCOME HOME GARY PAUL. Our uncle Najiim's arak was mixed with springwater until it turned perfectly milky, and an anise-scented glass of this distilled essence was passed among us, amid greetings and questions in Arabic and English, French and Spanish. We were then moved from the living room into a makeshift dining room retrofitted to accommodate some thirty-six of us. We were seated around card tables piled with platters of food: home-cured olives and pickles; hummus bi tahini and baba ghannouj; freshly baked pita, fatyr, and sfiha; sliced scallions, tomatoes, and eggplant; smoked fish; fried kibbe, grilled liver, and boiled bone marrow.

Suddenly the local butcher, Eli Abu Anton Bourjailly, began to sing a cappella an impassioned *zajal* folksong, and my older cousins carried in a whole roasted lamb atop an enormous platter of pilaf, piñons, and peas. As Eli sang verse after stirring verse, his eyes growing wider, wilder, and more melancholy with each couplet, a few of my cousins began to chant along, punctuating each rhyme with a shout, and then clapping, at first sparingly, then faster and more fervently until the song climaxed in a rousing chorus that everyone sang.

The singing, the shouting, the toasts, the tears, the bread, and the wine did not cease for hours. Even when my aunts were not putting more food on my plate, they were instructing me in how each breadstuff, each vegetable, and each distillate had been brought to fruition. Najiim painstakingly explained the many steps in distilling arak at home, including his complex means of flavoring it with only that aniseed. He uses only seeds obtained from a sandy valley in Syria where the family had lived centuries before; regrettably, he explained, anise didn't grow well on the heavier rocky soils here in the canyon, so it had to be imported from across the Syrian border. Later Shibley showed me how to pluck, butterfly, and grill a dozen little game birds he had hunted in the canyon over the previous week, saving them for our arrival. And when we went hiking up to where my grandfather had once planted fields of his koosa squash varieties, we hailed a couple of his Bedu (Bedouin) neighbors, out herding their sheep and goats, in order to get milk the next day to make cheese.

"They use our upper pastures high in the mountains during the summer, when the wild thyme, the one we call *zahtar,* is blooming. They give us milk in exchange for the use of high pastures. Late summertime, our yogurt and cheese, they taste like wild *zahtar.*"

One afternoon I had the time to sneak away from the feeding frenzy to accompany my cousin Nicolas to visit his fields of squashes and his poultry shed full of laying hens. As we were leaving his shed, I asked him if he had any herb or vegetable seeds that had come down through the family. He nodded and opened a cabinet full of hand-lettered seed envelopes and bags. I then asked if he might spare enough for me to plant in my garden in Arizona as well.

"Of course," he said and in a matter of minutes, he had wrapped and labeled for me little seed packets of eggplant, cucumbers, gherkins, peppers, parsley, zucchini, and tomatoes. After we had looked at the seeds and he had given me testimony on their specific features and planting needs, I tried to explain to him that I had worked a few years as a seed saver and plant explorer on contract for the UN Food and Agriculture Organization and for the U.S. Department of Agriculture. He listened quietly but looked puzzled. Finally, as we were leaving his henhouse, he hesitated for a moment, then said to me in broken English: "Gary Paul, we read something about your work in the Beirut paper one time. Was it an article reprinted I think from that ARAMCO magazine? It told what you just said—about being what you call it, seed saver."

He was quiet for a moment, then said in halting English: "We were proud because this article, it was about our own cousin. But one thing, we didn't understand it, well, because *all of us,* we save seed for family gardens here. Gary Paul, how come they pay people to be seed saver? Everyone in America, don't they make garden, save seeds?"

It was at that point in the homecoming that I realized how deeply, how desperately most Americans needed to go home. I had to count myself among such desperadoes. Ohhh, I moaned to myself, to go home farther than I had ever gone home before, to hunt and to hoe, to saw and to sickle, to smoke and to cure, to sup, to imbibe and to dine on what was divinely local!

In the twenty-five years I had wandered the world as a seed saver, I had never been so deeply moved by a people's devoted relationship to food as I was then among my own kin. And yet even there in the Fertile Crescent, there had never been another time in history when such relationships were under such stress. One fact from our time is so blatantly obvious that even to repeat it is to pretend that it is not immediately self-evident: More people than ever before in history have absolutely no involvement in producing the foods that sustain them. Most children are so laughably clueless about the origins of their food that they are just as likely to mention Safeway as the Garden of Eden as the place where the first apple came from. Eve, honey, please forgive us for our sins, the freeze-dried ones, the ones we have spiced with MSG, and all the others we heave into our shopping carts.

While the younger generation's relative lack of historicity has always been an easy target, there are in fact a few things new under the sun. The markets are being flooded with nutraceuticals, transgenic foods, irradiated grains, and other such marginally edible gobbledygook. A handful of companies control the bulk of the global food economy, perhaps fewer now than ever before. Most of them are unwilling to tell us whether our food crops have been sprayed with toxins in the old-fashioned way, or ingeniously modified genetically to produce the same toxins, with no easy way to discern whether the results of such slippery engineering feats have been put in our mouths.

Still, we have become a nation of food worriers more than food savorers. We fatalistically concede that we hardly know anything about who grew our food and how, but we are fixated on whether today's fare is more nutritious or less so, more tasty or more toxic, higher in fiber, folic acid, fat, and antioxidants or less so. As conscientious consumers, we are told that we should be preoccupied with issues regarding the chemical composition, the days since initial packaging, and the densities of insect parts and fecal coliform found in the grains ground down to make our daily bread. Nonetheless we don't much fathom from whom or from whence they came.

Flying in the face of such ironies, I resolved myself to entertain a modest proposal on my return from Lebanon to my Sonoran Desert home. It was not so much to adopt or imitate my cousins' diets in Kfar Sibad, but to emulate their efforts by filling my larder as much as possible from the foodstuffs found in my own backyard, within my own horizons. My mouth, my heart, my belly, and my brain began ruminating over the same simple few questions:

Just what exactly is it that we want to have cross our lips, to roll off our tongues, down our throats, to fill our nostrils with hardly described fragrances, to slide to a brief halt within our bellies, to mix with our own gastric juices to be transformed and conjured into something new by the myriad microbes in our guts, to migrate across our stomach linings, to surge into our bloodstreams, and to be carried along with insulin for one last ride, and then to be lodged within our very own bodies? What do we want to be made of? What do we claim as our tastes? And what on earth do we ultimately want to taste like?

I

Spring

The Cruelest Months

Chapter One

Eating My Way through House and Homeland

Spring equinox: A day of turning over the earth—churning up dark garden soil buried beneath the winter's leaf litter—to replenish it with sunlight. A day of humus-stained hands and hopeful hearts. Laurie and I passed the daylight hours weeding, tilling, watering, and planting. We worked to make a fertile place for vegetables, herbs, and beans in all the unsown garden beds around our desert home.

I took a pick known as a Pulaski and loosened the dry, compacted alkaline soil. Laurie, a few feet away from me, wisps of blond hair streaming into her face, turned it over shovelful by shovelful. I sifted the decomposed matter rescued from our compost pit of food scraps and clippings until I had separated out the smaller grained particles, returning the larger chunks to the pit. We folded in leaf litter and organic soil gleaned from beneath mesquite trees and poured this mixture into the beds, establishing a new blend of local earth.

Down on the soiled knees of our jeans, we planted one heirloom seed stock after another, watering them, covering them with netting, and then placing larger meshed frames over them to deter the birds. I mouthed the names of the seeds as we buried them snugly in their beds: Mesilla Valley *pasilla* chiles, O'odham pinto tepary bean (a dry legume that has been cultivated in the desert for centuries), Mrs. Burns' lemon basil, Zuni tomatillos. It was a canticle of desert seeds, sung into darkness in hope that they would rise again into light. Once one bed was done, we moved to the next, then the next. Between beds, we would drink from our canteens, and Laurie would tuck her long blond hair back under the brim of her felt cowboy hat. She hummed to herself, nodding occasionally, while I blathered on about the history of each of the seeds.

Even when we ducked inside the house for a moment to get a drink or to bring out more seeds, we were never far from the musky fragrance of soil bathed in warm sunlight.

This day of toil marked the first phase of a fifteen-month ritual, one involving my sweetheart Laurie as well as many of my kin and old friends. The ritual extended beyond the planting of vegetables in our backyard; it included the tending of a small orchard and some terraces of agaves and prickly pears in front; the gathering of desert greens, yucca blossoms, and cactus buds and fruit in the wildlands beyond our fence; the hunting of game birds and the capture of other creatures out where the desert wilderness seems boundless. We searched for other food producers hidden in our own neighborhood, discovering those who locally grow vegetables, dress game, or can fruit that complements our own.

The ritual then moved indoors to the drying rack, chopping block, the hand-cranked grinder, the stove, and the dinner table. It had no single name. It might be termed "a communion of neighbors." It might be thought of as a "return to the old ways" of subsisting on native resources at a time when globalization is all the rage. My friend Jack Kloppenberg called it "coming into the foodshed." In some kind of shorthand to myself, I've decided to call it "coming home to eat." I've lost my interest in those "movable feasts" or "global smorgasbords" that have been the most pervasive secular rites celebrated by humankind since the Industrial Revolution began.

Let me try to be more precise about what this ritual entails, for precision is not my inclination.

I have initiated an extended communion with my plant and animal neighbors, the native flora and fauna found within 250 miles of my home.

I have chosen to eat with them, as well as eat them. I've decided to join them in what Italo Calvino calls "the ecstasy of swallowing each other in turn, as we were aware, in our turn, of being swallowed." Calvino suggests that we must swallow our pride and "erase the lines between our bodies and *sopa de frijoles, huachinango a la Veracruzana,* and *enchiladas. . . .*" For the moment I pick up a clod of clay, roll it into a marble-size ball, and tuck it into my cheek. Let me stick to this earth a while longer. . . .

As the end of this first day arrived, I was still many turns away from seeing this modest proposal bear fruit. But blisters had blossomed on my palms, and my fingernails had filled with grains of granitic grit. At last I felt that I had tangibly begun *something* in earnest, although Laurie kept pressing me to articulate just what this something might be.

"You know we can't begin to eat out of that garden tomorrow, don't you?"

"I know . . . but we do have all that stuff in the pantry that we stashed away last season. It'll tide us over until this grows up," I replied, trying to exude optimism while remaining humbled by what little lay before us. "I guess this is just our warm-up exercise."

I glanced at the garden. There were a few rows of multiplier onions that had resprouted earlier in the winter, a few transplanted chilies, and quite a number of recently planted but empty-looking rows in the vegetable beds. The seeds that we had buried there might not germinate for another week or two.

I had to keep telling myself that this would be an *extended* ritual, like some marathon run, one that lumbers slowly forward at first, replete with aches and pains and even a bit of queasiness, until it gains momentum.

Still, this ritual is simple in its intent: to make me a direct participant, as fully and as frequently as possible, in the making of the bread and wine that sustain not only my life but the lives surrounding me as well. At last I want fully to bear the brunt of what my own eating of the living world entails. I want to escape the trap that I, like most Americans, have fallen into the last four decades: obtaining nine-tenths of our food from nonlocal sources, with shippers, processors, packagers, retailers, and advertisers gaining three times more income from each dollar of food purchased than do farmers, fishermen, and ranchers. I want to reduce the distance that my food travels before it reaches my mouth and my mind, so that I can reduce the ignorance my friend Jim Harrison describes with such devastating simplicity: "The majority of our population that eats beef, pork, and chicken has never known an actual cow, pig, or hen."

However straightforward my intentions have been, the road back home has been chock-full of holes, and marred by curves, bumps, and sudden diversions. It has taken me more than a year to get to this point of beginning in earnest. What I had hoped this ritual might do, as most rituals eventually do, was move me beyond abstract intention into the unanticipated peculiarities of practice. Each day's bread, each season's batch of wine, might rise and take shape in its own weird way. The folks that I make and break bread with are surely part of the communion as well; every mouthful I take will be flavored by their presence.

Bread and wine. Whenever I have extended the offerings beyond bread and wine, to include the other forms of nourishment found in the larder, Laurie reminds me that *killing* fish and quail is much more gruesome than reaping grains and harvesting grapes. However local my endeavor has become, Laurie remains unconvinced that all my food getting will necessarily be noble. Laurie has found herself among my family members, friends, and neighbors who have been maintaining a healthy skepticism about my current project. They ask me over and over again to explain "the rules."

The rules. Although they never come out and say it, my friends have been convinced that I will force them to join me in suffering through some horrendously restrictive diet. Each of us, they have hinted, will surely lose dozens of pounds if only because the desert offers so few foods each season. Alternatively they have worried that I am about to make them "human subjects," testing some new harebrained theory of nutritional ecology I have conjured up.

Worse yet, they have all heard about the time I offered aflatoxin-laced mesquite pods in pudding form to my children at Thanksgiving. Fortunately Laura and Dusty declined to sample the pudding, leaving me the only victim. My digestive tract did not recover for another couple of weeks; meanwhile my near-fatal pudding recipe was sent off to be published in *Organic Gardening*. (Once it was in print, I regretted that I had not reminded others to avoid moldy mesquite.) My daughter, Laura, recently admitted to me that even when she was a little girl, she was already suspicious of my cooking, aware that whenever she sat down at the table, she was literally being asked to be party to a half-baked experiment.

Rules? I clear my throat and try to state my position. "I have no rules," I assert, "other than Thoreau's advice to 'live each season as it passes, breathe the air, drink the drink, taste the fruit, and resign yourself to the influences of each.'" Unfortunately all my listeners hear is "resign yourself." This comment immediately brings out all their worst fears: I will be asking them to join me in eating any plant or animal, living or dead, that comes within my grasp.

"Will we have to eat turkey vulture if you find one rotting on the roadside? Will you remove all the cactus spines from the prickly pear fruit before you put it into the salad? Do we have to eat that wild chili pepper ice cream you invented?"

I try to say something reassuring, but it all sounds so *defensive*. The trouble is, I don't have any hard-and-fast rules, only a few tentative hypotheses about what "eating locally" and "coming into the food shed" might ultimately mean. I may change my mind about some of the provisional guidelines over the coming year, or change them several times. This is no *diet,* and it has no defined *zones,* other than a 250-mile loop around my home that I drew this morning on an old *Arizona Highways* map.

I must also explain that I am not "doing food therapy," as if I have joined a support group where we gather weekly to admit how long we have been addicted to buying junk foods from the global marketplace. That addiction is real, even though the psychosis of believing that hauled-in surrogates can fill in for what is homegrown has not attracted the attention of many therapists. But I don't need their outside help; I must simply try to stumble homeward, setting my hunger on what has nurtured me longest.

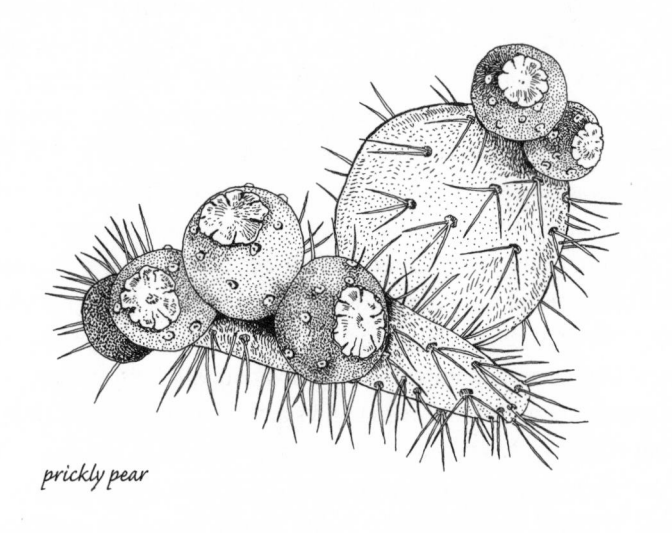

prickly pear

At first I was inclined to give most of my culinary attention to native vegetables and heirloom turkeys—that is, seeds and breeds that had adapted to the blistering heat, the pathetic-looking, alkaline earth, and the scant, brackish waters of our desert homeland. But the decision I made was not without its detractors, most of whom were my freeze-dried-Stroganoff-eating, instant-cappuccino-drinking, wilderness-backpacking buddies. They questioned me relentlessly, wondering how any home garden in the desert could ever be economical and ecologically benign, given that water was so scarce and costly here.

That point was true: Most of the vegetable crops I was sowing required irrigation with two to three times the amount of water that naturally fell here as rain, which was a meager twelve inches a year. The water that flowed out of my backyard hose into my beds was fossil groundwater pumped to my house with fossil fuel, so that even my most locally grown food drew on water and energy supplies from a distant place—the Pleistocene. In other words they were lain down in the earth tens of thousands of years ago when mammoths and mastodons still romped around these parts. Still, I asked these skeptics, what was the lesser evil: growing my own or having Cargill, ConAgra, and SYSCO bring me foods from thousands of miles away, grown and transported in ways that require even more energy and water than what I could locally squander?

Fortunately for me and other Arizonans, three of our neighbors in Tucson painstakingly answered that question more than fifteen years ago, when they measured all costs and returns from their two home gardens for three years running. While doing so, Tom Orum, David Cleveland, and Nancy Ferguson undoubtedly spent more time weighing and counting vegetables than most of us will do in our entire lifetimes.

Although Tom, Dave, and Nancy liberally irrigated their desert gardens, the market value of the vegetables they produced was more than ten times what they paid for tap water, and three times their total costs for water, manure, tools, and seeds. Even though water was their largest single gardening expense, they reaped between $7 and $9 worth of vegetables for every dollar they spent on water. Devoting just two to three hours a week to sowing, manuring, watering, weeding, and harvesting, they produced $150 to $180 worth of vegetables each year, harvesting a broad mix of greens, beans, beets, fruits, or shoots no matter what the season.

I had shared some community garden plots with Tom, Nancy, and other friends a few years before, so I knew that they were religious gardeners, devoted to their daily practice of getting dirt under their fingernails and fresh greens in their mouths. However, their diligence in keeping up garden accounting day after day for a full three years was altogether flabbergasting. To my relief, in the final year, as Tom placed some newly harvested squashes on the scale, I finally heard Nancy admit just how strenuous the whole ordeal had become. Not gardening itself, mind you, but the accounting that went along with it: the weighing of all the produce, the measuring of manure piles and water use, the jotting down of seasonal market prices for vegetables.

In the end my friends had proved that even in the desert, where water was ecologically and energetically costly, home gardening consumed far fewer resources than did the production of trucked-in food. Large-scale production is typically far more wasteful of water and energy in the field, in the warehouse, in transport, and in the supermarket. Somehow the return on the water, time, and energy invested in gardening is always recouped. The toil involved in tilling the soil and hand-picking the harvest is infinitely more satisfying than fighting the mobs in the grocery store for periodically misted, ethylene-gassed fruits and vegetables transported from fields and orchards a thousand miles away from our dinner tables. Nancy and Tom have retired from weighing all their veggies every day, but they have not grown tired of gardening.

A little less ambitious than my buddies Tom and Nancy, I currently hoped to wrest four out of every five of my meals from locally grown foodstuffs. Unlike them, I refused to count calories, kilowatts, or acre-feet. Instead, I decided to count species. I hoped that nine out of every ten kinds of plants and animals I would eat over the coming months would be from species that were native to this region when the first desert cultures settled in to farm here several thousand years ago.

Mind you, that was a *hope,* not a *rule.* I would prefer to feel the tension between lofty goals and realistic choices than to never hope at all, even if I risk being called a hypocrite for failing to accomplish those goals.

It was at this point in my elaboration that most of my friends sensed that there still might be some rough edges to my modest proposal.

"What *kinds* of crops are you willing to eat?" they asked.

"Oh, you know: chilies, squashes, tomatillos, beans, prickly pears, century plants, and amaranths, ones that have close relatives growing wild around here."

"You didn't mention corn."

"Well, it's just a seminative. I mean, the closest patch of its wild ancestor, teosinte, is more than five hundred miles south of here. Besides, I think I can do without Frito-Lay's chips made from genetically modified corn for a while."

"And how about animals? Which are kosher for you?"

The term *kosher* had currency for me even though I have Arabic rather than Jewish roots; I had recently been reading the Old Testament to try to understand the logic of its food taboos.

"Well," I mused, "no factory chickens, no pond-grown trout or salmon, no feedlot anything. But I'm all for free-range turkeys, and quail and doves. Fish and shellfish from the Gulf of California, wild 'pork' from jabalina, maybe a few caterpillars and grasshoppers . . ." I tried to recall the ancient list of clean and unclean beasts writ in Leviticus, and realized that it sounded as though I had gotten the two mixed up. I began to falter: "Maybe some fat lizards, and a snake or two . . ."

Whenever any of my friends or neighbors listened to any of this, their discomfort became more and more obvious; sooner or later they shuddered with disgust and walked away. They had already concluded that they would be exposed to cactus spines, jimsonweed poisons, as well as all sorts of plant mucus and root microbes over the coming months of sitting down at my table, whether they ate anything or not. Although not a vegetarian, Laurie had seen far too much muscle, blood, and bone over her twenty years of nursing to look forward to any home-butchering events. She had begun to imagine with horror the various animal innards that would be sticking to the cutting board, and had tried to remind me why Yahweh set up a series of food taboos for Moses and Aaron.

I finally had to give up trying to rid Laurie and the others of their fears; some of their anxieties were no doubt justified. They had already seen Calvin Schwabe's *Unmentionable Cuisine* and Richard Sterling's *Dining with Headhunters* among my cookbooks piled up next to the stove. Before the year was out they would indeed find an errant cactus spine in their prickly pear punch, or a little rattlesnake meat in a fritter. If life itself is inherently dangerous, then surely eating to stay alive must involve some risks.

Now that I had scared off a few more potential dinner guests, I decided to retreat once more into the garden. To rake, to hoe. I toiled long enough and hard enough to work up a modest lather. As a Spam-colored sunset blanketed the western sky, the sweat on my back chilled. I paused for a moment to catch the light's decline, to let my own heartbeat slow. I was heading toward the back door to go inside but suddenly changed directions. Without much forethought I wandered out the back gate and planted summer squash seeds in the satellite dish perched just outside my garden wall.

I had never used it for what most people use satellite dishes for anyway. There had been a hookup and a standpipe for one long before I moved into this burnt-adobe home in a desert valley west of Tucson, Arizona. The winter solstice of 2000, I had a friend help me make the dish into the roof for what I call the Minstrel Hut. The hut is where I sit as I write to tell you of my plantings.

Back to the dish. The dish is perched eight feet off the ground on a metal ring welded to four upright metal poles that are anchored in a concrete slab. The dish is painted pale green, and its mouth opens wide to the dry desert sky. Beneath its rim it is surrounded by a circular wall of living ocotillo branches.

Do you know ocotillo? Ocotillos are multistemmed desert plants that look like bunches of gangly TV antennas sticking out of the alkaline earth. They are most commonly found on limestone but also frequent the granitic slopes of the Sierritas, which rise above my home. Their awkwardly long branches, barren as rebar much of the year, miraculously sprout tiny leaves after the most meager of desert thunderstorms.

You can prune the straightest branches off the mother plant of an ocotillo, stick them in desert soil, and bind them together as a living fence or as a permeable wall. If you are lucky they will forget that they've been cut off from their mothers, and they will sprout new roots and grow new branchlets. Since the very first time I saw them used in Mexican fence construction, I had always dreamed of making a house with living walls. If I planted summer squash seeds in their midst, I figured that the ocotillo branches would serve as a living trellis for the vines, which could further buffer me from the desert sun during the heat of July and August.

I had gone out into the garden at the end of the day to plant a few squash seeds at the base of the newly rooted ocotillo walls. And yet I was tired enough that I hesitated for a moment before planting. Another possibility emerged from that momentary mental vacuum. I could also plant squash seeds *above* the reach of the ocotillo branches, in the satellite dish that was then yawning at a gaudy desert sunset. As the last daylight faded all around me, I tossed shovelfuls of peat, sand, and compost into the dish and watered them thoroughly, for the next morning I would plant a dozen squash seeds in the moistened soil within the rim.

Over the next fifteen months I would have a chance to sit in the Minstrel Hut knowing that squash seedlings had not only germinated just above my head, they had sent roots down into the soil within the dish. Their vines would cascade down from elevated heights like Rapunzel's hair as she let it down from the tower.

I remembered that old adage for peacemakers: "swords into plowshares." Perhaps I could offer an amendment for today's place makers: satellite dishes into squash planters. We could let the local seeds grow where we had once placed our hope for "keeping in touch with the outside world."

Chapter Two

Purging the Canned, Making Room for the Fresh

After our planting was finished by dusk, I went into the house to complete one last chore for the day. It was a cleansing, one cognizant of the fact that the average American brings home nearly 3,300 pounds of foodstuffs each year for his or her own consumption. Of course, much of this is never eaten. It is nearly two-and-a-half times the weight of what most of our contemporaries in other regions of the world consume, and much of it comes from *their* farmlands. While hoping to curb my own excesses in eating and wasting, I had also decided to purge my kitchen cabinets of all foods whose origins were distant from here or whose presence would distract me from my mission. Instead of eating them myself, I would take them to a drop-off box for the Community Food Bank of Tucson, in the hope that they would find some use by those without the slack to buy them, waste them, or give them away.

As I rummaged through the cupboard, I felt two simultaneous emotions: embarrassment over the kinds of food I'd been residing with, and relief that I lived in a community with a food bank that could make the best of such orphans. The Community Food Bank of Tucson was both a food orphanage and adoption service, an opera of loss and reconciliation, a caloric ballet. Its director, Punch Woods, was as creative as any choreographer I had ever met, orchestrating and coordinating the movement of 14 million pounds of food each year. That meant that daily his staff had to rescue perishable foods from dozens of restaurants and wholesalers, and accept countless donations of nonperishables from individual citizens like me. By doing so the Food Bank was able to offer 25,000 meals a day to the many hungry, elderly, homeless, or calamity-stricken people who fall within 50 miles of our home. At the same time they kept millions of pounds of nutritious food from going to waste.

Like most kitchen cabinets I have known, ours was filled with many cans and boxes that had not been opened since their purchase months before. Even if they stayed around here, it seemed unlikely that most of them would be opened and used in the near future. And so I began to read labels, deciding what to purge from my own larder and pass on to someone else.

If you think exposing your underwear drawer to the public would be embarrassing, imagine what it would be like giving a tour of your pantry to all the food activists and farm reform folks you've ever known. As I opened the cabinet, knowing that I would have to "tell all," a box of Betty Crocker's Pudding in the Mix Supermoist White Cake Mix fell out onto the counter.

Although I could not recall buying it or, for that matter, ever baking a white pudding cake in this house, there it was, thanks to General Mills in Minneapolis. I blamed the pudding cake's presence on a recent visit from my mother. Whether we wanted them or not, she always brought with her a grocery bag full of mainstream American foods, perhaps as a counterpoint to all the weird dishes I placed on the table.

Nevertheless, other items that I found in the pantry were just as mysterious to me.

For instance, the jar of Ferrero's Nutella, a hazelnut spread with skim milk and cocoa, which was made in New Jersey, with more peanut oil than hazelnuts. I couldn't tell whether the product was made from the wild hazelnut native to America, or from the larger cultivated "filbert" first imported from England by the colonists of Massachusetts in 1629. Chances were that they were from a variety cultivated in Turkey, where most filberts are farmed today.

Next, I said good-bye to a couple of unopened boxes of breakfast goodies. My daughter's favorite was Kellogg's Marshmallow-Blasted Froot Loops, a sweetened multigrained cereal with some fifty ingredients (including six dyes) that made almost everything else look wholesome by comparison. Alongside the Loops I had another cereal, factory-designed for the more mature, weight-conscious adult: Post Selects Low Fat Cranberry Almond Crunch Cereal, featuring real Ocean Spray cranberries.

I stared at this box as if I had Alzheimer's. Had I ever seen its airbrushed cover photo of a giant bowl tipped toward me, overflowing with flakes, nuts, and fruits, kindly captioned to assure me that the serving suggestion had been "Enlarged To Show Texture"? Perhaps it was harmless compared to the marshmallow-blasted product next to it, but while it might claim to be "low fat," it was not "low hype." Post Cereals come to us from Kraft Foods in Tarrytown, New York, where, Kraft's spin doctors tell us, their employees have "a passion for food" and a deep love for the taste of "home-baked" fruits. It made me imagine all the Kraft employees running home each night with bowls full of bananas, cranberries, and blueberries to bake in ovens in their very own kitchens. That way they could return in the morning to insert their "home-baked fruits" into the thousands of boxes moving along the conveyor belts in front of them.

If this year could resolve anything for me, perhaps it would rid me of the desire to ever again buy any packaged food that boasted of its homemade flavor. I distrusted these foods even more than I did the industrially processed beverage mixes next to them, such as the Hi-C 10 Percent Orange Drink with 100 Percent Vitamin C made by a subsidiary of Coca-Cola, or the Quik Mix for those who need a chocolate fix, provided by Nestlé.

After I cleaned out the breakfast and baked-goods section of the cabinet of its exotics, its puddings, and its hyperboles, I moved on to the canned goods. They sat on my shelf proclaiming to the world that I had unwittingly sanctioned the movement of food from one corner of the earth to the other.

I had never noticed how far the foods in my cabinet had traveled in order to have the honor of being eaten by an American. For instance, the brand of boiled baby clams I bought now and then at the corner store was packaged in California but grown in aquaculture farms off the coast of Thailand, or what's left of it. Similarly, the Miso-Cups on my shelf were products of Japan, but these "Savory Soups with Seaweed" have been distributed worldwide since 1978 by California's Edwards & Sons, which claims that the cups were the first "convenience health food." The label on the bottle of capers in my pantry claimed that the pickled flower buds were made in Mexico, although I had been assured that this odd little condiment was only grown in Sicily, France, and Spain. In fact, some claim that Sicilian mafiosi perfected their smuggling skills with capers before they went on to bigger and better things.

I winced when I realized I had several cans of tuna doused in chipotle sauce. They were canned in Mazatlán, Sinaloa, near where Mexican fishermen were notorious for killing dolphins in the process of netting tuna. I wondered if the blood of those playful mammals had mingled with that of fish inside these cans.

Next to the tuna was a can of Alaska pink salmon boasting that it had "quality you can see." And yet there was one quality the label did not identify: whether this meat had been taken from the bodies of free-living or farmed salmon. Because some free-living salmon were endangered, and some farmed salmon genetically engineered, the canning company did not see any advantage to proclaiming the distinction. I wondered whether any company now using genetically engineered salmon was bragging about how fast its fish could grow in captivity, as if it was keeping wild salmon from further endangerment. Unfortunately most farmed salmon are still fed fish meals derived from wild populations, diminishing the foods available to free-ranging salmon.

As I completed my kitchen-cupboard food inventory, I discovered that I had unknowingly purchased foods from six of the world's top ten food and beverage companies: Nestlé, Philip Morris, ConAgra, Pepsi-Co, Coca-Cola, and Mars. The ten titans of the food and drink business collectively sell more than $220 billion of processed agricultural products in the global marketplace each year. In other words trademarked products from these multinational corporations now generate about one-tenth of all retail sales of foods and beverages across the face of the earth. That amounts to the annual equivalent of thirty-three dollars' worth of processed food or canned drinks for each of the six billion people living on this planet or orbiting around us in satellites. Together with forty-one other transnationals, these ten global food giants are among the largest one hundred economies in the world. In other words, only forty-nine countries generate gross national products on the same order of magnitude that these global food barons do.

However eclectic I thought my tastes in food had become, this inventory revealed that the bulk of my diet had been brought to me by just a handful of food processors and distributors. The contents of my cupboard, fridge, and pantry in Arizona were dominated by agricultural commodities that had been bred, produced, processed, and distributed by the same companies, active everywhere from Argentina to Zaire. And these companies—while dominating more and more countries' commerce—were becoming fewer in number, as mergers and acquisitions in the food industry recently topped a trillion dollars a year.

I remembered that when I was in agricultural school, none of my teachers ever commented that fewer and fewer people controlled the companies that brought our society most of its food, fiber, beverages, and medicines. Years later at an agricultural symposium, one of those professors chastised me and my old friend Hope Shand for implying that the food industry's fate was in the hands of too few corporations. The next morning, as I drove home from the symposium, I heard a National Public Radio reporter introduce an executive from Cargill, the world's largest grain exporter. The executive announced Cargill's intent to buy the cereal crop assets of its only major competitor, the Continental Grain Company. If the merger went forward as predicted, we were told, Cargill would control at least 45 percent of the world's grain trade, and 30 percent of the soybean exports from the United States. Where in the world, I wondered, would ag students find employment in the future if they did not wish to work for a transnational like Cargill? There were fewer and fewer options left for those of us who loved agricultural sciences, and that ultimately meant fewer food options remaining for our communities as well.

The only can I hesitated sending away was one of Natural Value 100% Natural Pumpkin. It contained but one ingredient: pumpkin. Apparently it was organically grown somewhere near Sacramento, California (at least a thousand miles beyond my food shed), by farmers who identified themselves as "lovers of the Planet Earth." But should lovers of planet Earth assume that it is okay to distribute their products from one corner of the earth to another? And should I assume that I have a God-given right to access the entire earth's bounty, however far away some of its produce is grown? Just because it was organically grown and contained no additives, was this nationally distributed pumpkin product any more benign than Nestlé's Quik, Hi-C orange drink, or Betty Crocker's pudding cake? As nutritionist Joan Gussow has reminded me, "*Organic* does not necessarily mean that the food was grown in an ecologically, energetically, or socially sustainable way." If you send it halfway around the world before it is eaten, an organic food still may be "good" for the consumer, but is it "good" for the food system?

I paused for a moment, then tossed this can in with the others. I was ready to invest my time in remembering what pumpkins and squash taste like when they are grown on my own home ground.

The next day I chose to sow two different kinds of squash seeds in the satellite dish, beginning an experiment of sorts. The experiment would help me determine whether or not all squashes were equally suited to being grown in this particular place. Did native varieties always do better than introduced ones? Or could I grow my Arab clan's heirlooms with the same ease that I could grow squash from the tribes here in this desert?

In this season's comparison, the seeds of one kind of squash came from my O'odham Indian neighbors, who have grown them in this valley for many centuries. The other kind came from my cousins in Lebanon, who have grown them at roughly the same elevation in a similar climate. While these squash seeds were germinating, I went back through old horticultural texts to refamiliarize myself with the origins of squash.

Five species of squashes were native to the Americas, but once Columbus and other explorers began to take crop seeds from one continent to the next, their cultivation spread to Africa, Asia, and Europe. Squashes and pumpkins had been in my neighborhood a long time, sixteen hundred to two thousand years, maybe. Their wild relatives, the coyote gourds, grew all around my yard. They attracted scads of stingless squash and gourd bees, which assured me that most of my squash blossoms would be pollinated to balloon into juicy green and yellow fruit. By belonging to a group of plants native to my region, squashes were guaranteed pollination by wild creatures also native to this ground. Domestic honeybees, on the other hand, have been declining throughout North America, but they have been in the American deserts for less than three centuries, so their absence has little long-term effect on squash as long as the stingless bees remain present.

But there was another level of nativity involved here. I could gain tips about squash growing from some of my neighbors, whose families were the oldest continuous inhabitants of this desert land. My O'odham friends who lived nearby had always guided me in my planting times, my methods of pest control, and in the way I prepared the squashes themselves. The O'odham families I knew loved to pick the tender young squashes for early-season eating. They called them *ha:l mamad,* which means "baby-girl squash" in their language.

This season I decided to nurture the peculiar variety of O'odham baby-girl squashes given to me years ago by my Indian neighbors, one that has sturdy, bristly vines. I would test them against the bush-forming zucchinis that have been known to be in cultivation in the Mediterranean for more than 120 years. This particular heirloom, *koosa biladi,* was adapted to the semiarid climate and limestone-derived soils that nurtured my grandfather when he still lived near the present-day Lebanon-Syria border.

When I was four or five years old, I watched my grandfather as he took a young cylindrical squash in one hand, a grooved aluminum blade in the other, and cored the unripened seeds and pith out of the middle of the squash. My mother and my aunts stuffed it with ground lamb, tomatoes, onions, and nutmeg or cinnamon, and occasionally, pine nuts. They then steamed it in a big kettle with dozens of other squash babies.

At the time I did not think much about origins—that is, whether squash originally came from the Old World or from the New. I just assumed that squashes were part of my family—that is, something familiar to us that I didn't see much of elsewhere, in my friends' homes. Whenever we ate Sunday dinner with our Lebanese kin during the tail end of summer, the fragrance of steamed, nutmeg-laden squash would invade my nostrils. My nostrils would tell me that my mother and my aunts had fixed something for my grandfather that made him moan with love and appreciation for his "American daughters," my married-in Irish mother included. These women knew that the mere sight of platters piled high with stuffed squash and grape leaves made him feel reconnected with the "old country," the Bekáa Valley of his birth.

Long after my father had died, and my mother had moved to Arizona to live close to me and her grandchildren, she went shopping for squash in a food market one day. While she was selecting zucchini for making *koosa mishwi,* a lanky Westerner passing through the produce section noticed how carefully she chose which squashes she was putting into her shopping cart.

"Ma'am, excuse me, could I ask you what you do with those zucchinis?"

"*I stuff them!*" she replied, startled, as if everyone should know that.

Eight months later that man, Chuck Buxton, became her husband. Over the following fourteen years, he had the pleasure of eating *koosa mishwi* with my family dozens of times, even though he had never eaten Lebanese food before meeting my mother.

After planting my two kinds of squashes, one from my current home ground and the other from my grandfather's, I prepared the sole remaining squash from my previous season's harvest for dinner. The girth of that winter squash was too big for me to core it as my grandfather had once demonstrated to me. Instead I layered its steamy slices between piñon nuts, onions, and spices, then sautéed them in sunflower oil. And as I took the first mouthful of this meal, I closed my eyes to see if it tasted of home.

After pondering the phrase for a few days, I have decided that "the taste of homemade food" was not simply the soup your parents made from scratch at your house when you were sick as a child, the carrot torte you won at the cakewalk at the grade school across the street, or the fresh tortillas sold door-to-door by the Mexican widow from the next block over. It was an oral pleasure that rose from the flavors, the minerals, the sourness or sweetness of the very ground we walk on, the very soil the seeds break through as they take in the air we ourselves have recently breathed.

I've often wondered about the characteristic taste of my current homeground, the Sonoran Desert, a place where pregnant women once craved the mineral-rich clay flavor of the dry earth itself. To calm their craving, native women here once practiced geophagy, eating the very earth beneath their feet, after a bit of sifting and washing to purify the clay.

cutting mescal heads

Another flavor characteristic of the desert was that of its succulents, for they were among the oldest forms of sustenance in this region. One of them was known as mescal, the pit-roasted heart of the century plant, or desert agave. Its fibers have been found in human feces left behind in the caves in the desert borderlands as long ago as 8,500 years. Although its roasted leaf bases were eaten and its fermented beverages were drunk for millennia, mescal processing in the United States was brought to a close during Prohibition, when most mescal harvesters were arrested on suspicion of bootlegging tequilalike moonshine from the agave's fermented sugars. Even after Prohibitionist fervor subsided, the pit-roasting tradition never recovered in the U.S. border states, although it persisted just south of the border despite the refusal of most *mescaleros* to pay taxes to the Mexican government. In Sonora hundreds of cowboys continue to dedicate a few weeks each year to pit roasting mescal, a little of which they eat, more of which they ferment, and most of the fermented juices they distill into mescal called *bacanora* or *lechuguilla*.

The week of April Fool's, I invited two cowboys from Cucurpe, Sonora, to show me how to roast *mescal lechuguilla,* the sword-leafed agave that occurs around my home as well as theirs. They were only sporadically involved in bootlegging nowadays, and a little rusty at roasting agaves, since electricity had come to their village a decade or so before, allowing ice-cold beer to be drunk with more frequency than home-brewed hooch. Nevertheless, when we found big blushing rosettes nearly ready to send up their flower stalks, they were adept at harvesting the succulent plants. They rapidly trimmed the leaves down to nubbins, using special tools called *coas* that I had once purchased in Tequila, Jalisco. When we were done the plants looked like giant pineapples and were ready for roasting.

Chano, one of the Sonorans, who was of Opata Indian descent, guided us through the construction of the *barranco* where the agaves would be roasted. Because I had known his sidekick Beto for twenty-five years, Beto had insisted that Chano also be invited along, because he knew that Chano was a master at the art of mescal roasting. He then crawled down into the *barranco,* a hole in the ground that looked like a dry well. It was six feet deep, and we had made its circular walls out of cracked-up slabs of concrete piled into a cylinder. Chano asked for some kindling, lit a match on it down around his toes, waited for the fire to be hot enough to melt his boot soles, then popped out of the hole like a jack-in-the-box. We tossed in three armloads of mesquite wood, let it burn for four hours, then heaved basketball-size agave heads into this oven and covered the well-like hole with tin and dirt. We checked on temperature of the *barranco* every few hours, but sat around telling stories and making quail traps for forty hours before we finally opened it up to sample the baked mescal.

We shoveled off a six-inch cap of dirt, removed a tin sheet from the mouth of the *barranco,* then let our noses do the rest of the work. We were overwhelmed by a musky fragrance, that of caramel. The smoky hearts of agave had turned sweet and amber in the process that Beto and Chano called *la tatemada,* "the earthen roasting." We pitchforked the roasted heads and lifted them out of the *barranco.* I pulled a few caramelized leaf bases off the largest and handed Chano one of them to

roasted mescal

sample. He ran the leaf fibers through his teeth, skimming the roasted sugars off the fiber, chewing the smoky pulp. Then he closed his eyes to compare the taste with that of roasted mescal he had sampled at other times in his life, clear back to his childhood.

Chano opened his eyes and smiled, then signaled me with hand jive, "Thumbs up." A dozen of our friends poured in around the pit-baked agaves, and one by one, they tasted mescal for the very first time.

"It's like baked yams. . . ."

"You eat it like sugarcane."

"It's sorta like blackstrap molasses. . . ."

Although we all ate our fill as soon as we unearthed the roasted agaves, we were left with 150 pounds of the mescal to share and savor over the coming months. It was perhaps the first traditional-style *tatemada* of agaves in the Tucson basin in more than a half century, renewing a custom that had been practiced here for millennia. The oldest baked good known from the desert borderlands had come home.

Chapter Three

Coping with Death, and the Life Thereafter

aster came a few days after the mescal roast, and with it an unseasonable snow. Those of us who dwell in the Sonoran Desert seldom get snow for Christmas, let alone at Eastertime. The snow quickly melted, but it put the desert's thin-furred critters and heat-loving cacti out of kilter for a while, for they had been behaving as though spring were already in full swing. Antelope jackrabbits huddled together, shivering, unprepared for playing a bit part as snowshoe hares. Desert lilies and other wildflowers were nipped in the bud, ice burned before they could fully bloom. The nesting places typically considered high and dry were now wet and muddy. Some burrows full of fledglings or half-furred babies were flooded, others iced up—everything seemed to be caught out of sync.

I normally take my time cruising down the Sierrita Mountain foothills, sloping down to the flatter stretch called La Abra, and climbing up over the Tucson Mountains to get to Laurie's house in town. But this morning my slack time disappeared when I went out to quickly water the garden, and saw how many plants had been ice burned by the freak storm. I began culling the damaged ones out of the rows, until I realized I had barely enough time to drive the fifty miles into the city without being late for Laurie's departure to a medical clinic where she was training her nurse-practitioner students. I tossed together a little lunch to take with me but skipped putting out anything for dinner. Heck, I'd better not be late for a visit with a *nurse,* I thought—*her* time is at premium. I jumped into my beat-up old Blazer and scrambled toward town.

Just before I reached the Tucson city limits, I saw feathers fly up above the truck in front of me. A split second later, I saw the body of a bird on the road in front of the Blazer, and swerved to avoid hitting it. Despite being late already I pulled to the side, walked back, and found a Gambel quail. Its neck was broken, but its body was still intact, bloodless.

Not wanting to carry it on the dashboard all day, I arrived at Laurie's door with bird in hand, hoping she would let me keep it in her refrigerator until we had dinner that night.

"This is how you greet your girlfriend at seven in the morning? You hand her a roadkill bird?"

"Well, it's worth two under the tire, you know. . . . Haven't you always wanted a shaggy bird dog like me to fetch you game birds?

"It's hard enough training a boyfriend to be a boyfriend, let alone training one to be a bird dog. Can't you put it on ice and take it to work with you?"

That evening, after plucking and gutting the quail, I stuffed its cavities full of garlic and wild oregano from my garden and basted it in a prickly pear syrup glaze. Laurie made a salad of wild greens, and we sat down to eat around seven-thirty. After a prayer we each sampled the quail—a rich taste of dark juicy meat, faintly sweet and spicy. Laurie loved it as much as I loved her salad, a complex of slightly bitter and somewhat sour, almost lemony greens.

We were just cleaning up the dishes when the phone rang. It was my mother's voice, trembling. I instantly knew that something had happened to Chuck Buxton, her already ailing husband of fourteen years.

"Gary Paul, come up here as soon as you can, I need you. I've been trying to reach you for the last hour or so. Chuck just died at the hospital."

As soon as I could pack my clothes and cancel immediate commitments, I was out the door, while Laurie began making plans to follow me as soon as she could. I was on the road to my mother's home in Glendale, Arizona, two and a half hours north of my own. I would stay with her for several days, for she sorely needed someone to listen to her stories, hold her in her grief, and help her with errands, airport shuttles, and cooking for visitors. I needed that time with her as well, to feel some solidarity with family, and slowly to begin a meditation on what Chuck's life meant, a meditation I would stay with for months. I am slow in knowing how to deal with such passages, and have a habit of holding on to life through little gestures and rituals when I feel the floods of change rushing all around me.

In a moment such as this, I did not think to pack even a single home-grown food for myself or for others to eat over the following days. But once I got on the road, I realized how desperately I would need a few locally produced foods to fortify me, and to anchor me to the tasks at hand. Whenever I took a break over the next few days, I would seek out some local reminder that the world was not entirely composed of highways, airports, and funeral homes.

En route to Glendale I picked up a dozen turkey eggs near the gas station in Abra Valley. I snatched two bags of Sonoran acorns in a Mexican minimarket at Casa Grande, where I made a bathroom stop. A Pima man sold me a bag of roasted piñon nuts at a street corner while I was crossing the Gila River Indian Reservation. I munched on a few acorns and piñons as I drove, brooding about the ways I could best help my mother.

As soon as I arrived at her house, we spent several hours talking and making calls to our kin. Later she dispatched me to do errands for her, including a grocery run. As I picked up the items on her grocery list, I threw into the basket some chilies, damiana tea, prickly pear pads, and tomatillo salsa. Next door to the Southwest Supermarket, a Mexican restaurant had fish and shrimp from the Gulf of California. I took a half-hour reprieve there before returning to help my mother deal with all incoming calls from those who wished to attend the funeral.

The next morning I picked up folks at the airport and went with my sister-in-law KC to a couple of florist shops nearby. On the way back from Sky Harbor airport, I stopped by the Farm at South Mountain to say hello to my former student Diann Peart. Diann, a biologist who now runs the Farm Institute, which promotes food production in urban areas, gave me fresh flowers as well as a bunch of I'itoi's onions, a desert-adapted scallionlike shallot I had brought back from near extinction twenty years before.

For years this desert heirloom had been kept alive by just one O'odham lady, Ida Lopez, who lived out in the middle of the Papago Indian Reservation. Since that day when I took the gift of green scallions away from her yard, my colleagues at Native Seeds/SEARCH had propagated and distributed tens of thousands of them for planting in urban and Indian reservation gardens around southern Arizona. Since four of us founded Native Seeds in 1982, we had rescued dozens of Native American vegetable varieties from extinction, had multiplied their seeds, and distributed them free to more than one hundred Indian communities in our region. Their progeny have been nurtured along by scores of desert gardeners, including Diann.

I left after my brief visit with her replenished by her generosity, with a box full of greens, scallions, and some freshly cut flowers for my mother—something live and luscious as a salve after Chuck's death. At least *some* things I love don't die, I thought. They just get reincarnated as vegetables.

Despite the pressing need to spend four days dealing with funeral arrangements and family regroupings in the most urbanized area within the entire Sonoran Desert, I found a way to keep my diet dominated by locally grown or regionally harvested native foods. On the way back to Tucson I stopped at Ramona Farms in Sacaton and bought fifty pounds of tepary beans.

Twenty-three years earlier I had worked my way through a master's in agricultural sciences at the University of Arizona by selling hundred-pound bags of this "Indian bean" to trading posts on a dozen Indian reservations. I had been interested in it because it required so little water compared to other crops being grown in the desert; a pound of edible hybrid corn, for example, was seldom grown in the desert without consuming two hundred gallons of water, whereas a pound of tepary beans required a fraction of that. I was grateful that Terry Button and his Akimel O'odham wife, Ramona, had made sure that this ancient, drought-tolerant foodstuff had persisted. Fortunately I didn't even have to call ahead when I showed up at the storage shed where Terry keeps his sacks of beans.

While the globalized food economy clearly dominated Phoenix as it does other big cities, an almost-invisible informal food-exchange network could still be found there. Urban gardeners cared for tiny plots in their backyards, on balconies, and in vacant lots, the likes of which provide one-seventh of all the vegetables eaten worldwide. Medicinal herb and spice peddlers worked out of camper trucks and double-width trailers. Part-time farmers rented land, tractors, and harvesting equipment to work vacant lots in the middle of the metropolitan area, just as a third of all remaining U.S. farmers did. Street-corner vendors of nuts, fruits, and acorns remained unaccounted for in agricultural statistics, and they often went untaxed. And nationwide, farmers' market coordinators like Diann ensured that more than a billion dollars' worth of produce is purchased from their outdoor stands during the growing season.

They knew where they could find one another, even though they didn't much use cell phones, faxes, or electronic directories posted on the Internet. Their own informal networks went back a long time, perhaps as far as the ancient Chichimecans who once traded turkeys, seeds, and macaws back and forth between Mesoamerica and the desert southwest—an area then regarded to be the northernmost margins of the great civilizations of the Americas.

Much of that old-time way of living and trading had recently died in the desert borderlands. But enough of it survives to remind me of how the world once worked.

How *did* the world work in terms of the flow of food from one family to the next? As some of the most detailed oral histories of farming cultures have demonstrated, about four-fifths of what any family ate would come from its own labors and those of friends and neighbors living in the same valley. The other fifth might come from trade—oranges from more tropical climes, or cranberries from the north. Seeds would be traded in from elsewhere as well, but they would be carefully grown and evaluated before they were allowed to hybridize with time-tried local stocks. And so most traditional farming societies were curious about foods from other landscapes, but justifiably skeptical that they could fare as well under local conditions as their family heirlooms did after decades of fine-tuning. Few members of traditional cultures were still so self-sufficient that they could afford to be isolationist. Most were not so foolhardy as to believe that they could depend predominantly and indefinitely on "exotic foods," those from beyond their own watershed.

Chuck and my mother had both grown up with a semblance of such "foodshed logic" still embedded in their families' lives and livelihoods. But during their own lifetimes, those who adhered to such a logic all but disappeared from public view. While processing native foods with hand tools, screens, and roasting pits, I thought about all the labor-saving devices I had seen at my mother's house, and the conveyor-belt dream. The night before the funeral, I had decided to make a potato salad for the potluck to be held at the church, but I lacked a few ingredients. My mother was already sleeping, emotionally exhausted from the day, so I was on my own in her kitchen and pantry, hoping to find some pickles, capers, and onions to add to the salad.

When I entered her pantry—perhaps for the first time in more than two years—I was surprised to find that it had very little food stored in it, other than a second refrigerator filled with canned beverages. Instead it was filled with boxes of all sizes. I suddenly realized that my mother and Chuck no longer stored several weeks' worth of food in the back room as they had done for most of the years of their lives since the Great Depression. Instead their larder was stuffed with boxes holding various electrical food-processing technologies, from the simplest blender to the most complex espresso machine.

It was a dazzling display of so-called labor-saving devices. A Wel-bilt Bread Machine. A Deco Sonic Convection Roaster. A Dazey Seal-a-Meal II. The Hot Spot II Coffee and Hot Beverage Warmer. A Rival Crock Pot Slow Cooker. Two toasters and a toaster-oven. A waffle iron, a juicer, a deep-fryer, a vegetable peeler, an iced-tea brewer, a dicer, and an electric meat-carving knife.

Perhaps these machines were the trophies that Chuck and my mother offered one another for having survived the depression. They no longer had to do stoop labor, or peel and dice vegetables by hand. They were finally freed from the menial chores that had been associated with food getting and food processing for more than ten thousand years. With these tools, with the Minute Rice that was premeasured into plastic bags, ready for boiling, and with the Kraft Macaroni and Cheese Dinner poured out of a box into the microwave, they had gained the leisure time that their own parents never knew. They had joined the 90 percent of American families that keep microwaves in their homes, who no longer had to "slave away" for hours in the kitchen or the barn. They could relax, and watch TV, which encouraged them to be more insatiable consumers, convinced that there would always be producers of anything they needed out there somewhere. Chuck could rest in peace, for his widow would never again be constrained by laboring in the food chain that had imprisoned his own mother most of her life.

I closed the pantry, forgetting about pickles, capers, and onions, and hand chopped the boiled potatoes for another ten minutes before I set them aside for the morning. I dreamed of cogs and gears and conveyor belts for most of the night. It was not until I was back at work on the potato salad that I realized how the conveyor belt had lopped around and around with nothing at all upon it. As I mourn Chuck's death, I also mourn the passing of a way of life he had known, and wondered why it had gone.

The season that brought fluke snows was surely behind us, and Chuck's ashes had been scattered in the desert. I awoke this morning to realize that I might miss another desert harvest if I didn't watch out. Up until now Laurie and I had done our foraging together, sharing the efforts with a friend or two at most. But I had begun to realize how most desert harvests had historically been *communal* activities, so I sent out an open invitation for others to join us, arranging for four different afternoons of gathering and processing a particular wild food.

"Close your eyes," I told the uninitiated who came out to join us. "Imagine that someone put a delicate vegetable the size of a marble into your mouth. You could not put your finger on it exactly, but its taste

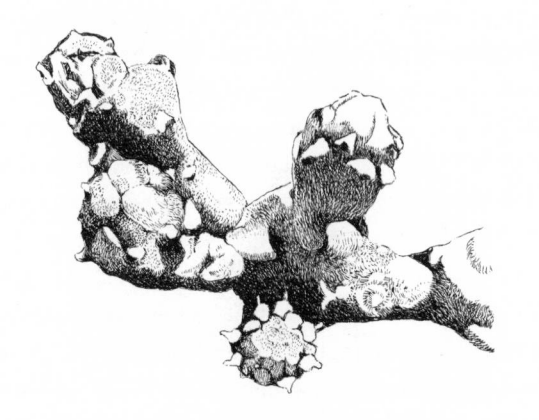

cholla bud

reminded you of asparagus tips, artichoke hearts, and capers. You tasted an initial lemony burst as your teeth and tongue crushed its tenderness, followed by the lingering smokiness of mesquite, perhaps because the vegetable had been steamed over mesquite coals in a *horno,* or a roasting pit. You open your eyes and see a bowlful of the vegetable you had savored, spines and all, sitting menacingly on the table before you."

I was describing cholla cactus flower buds—a little-known delicacy of my Tohono O'odham neighbors and their Akimel O'odham kin in the Phoenix area. Over the last five hundred years or more, these tribes have shaped a diet out of the flora and fauna of southern Arizona. About twenty years ago, as a green-behind-the-ears transplant from the Midwest, I had learned to pit-roast cholla buds from gracious Akimel O'odham families living along the Gila River just south of Phoenix. Today I spent time with some of the sons, daughters, and grandchildren of those same families, guiding them through the cactus patch below my home. Some of them had forgotten how to process cactus buds, and had decided to drive down and join a number of Tohono O'odham, Latino, and Anglo families who annually harvest cholla together.

By cactus patch, I mean the long stretch of desert slopes lying below the Sierrita that is filled with flat-padded prickly pear and cylindrical cholla. A century ago it was badly overgrazed, then further injured by a four-year drought. Most cattle, grasses, and trees died off, but two hardy kinds of prickly pears and four tenacious species of cholla quickly colonized these degraded lands. That was bad news for future ranchers in the valley called La Abra, but good news for cholla cactus pickers like me.

Although I have picked cholla buds here for several years, I was perplexed by the patterns of cactus I found this season. April is typically the time for cholla bud picking in the desert, but this year's snow on Easter must have knocked off many of the emerging flower buds of the staghorn cholla. Some plants had dozens, while others had few or none to pick. The snow may have sat longer on the north-facing branches of the cholla, leaving fewer buds on those particular branches, but I could hardly find any other correlation: altitude, plant height, size, or partial protection by shade trees.

My companions from the Gila River began to wonder why they had driven two hours to pick buds with us, when there were similar patches on their tribal lands. Besides, the wind was howling like a harsh nanny, forcing us to huddle around the few prolific chollas to keep our spirits up.

"I remember when you came and helped our Aunt Sally with her cholla bud roast," one young O'odham woman called out to me over the wind. We paused for a moment, silent, since Sally was bedridden and blind from diabetes, no longer able to join in such efforts. (She has since passed away.) Then Sally's niece added shyly, "I guess I was just a little girl then."

The wind raged. We were silent for a minute or two, hearing only the wind and the sound of our tongs brushing one thorny cactus branch against another, making a tinny, scraping noise like that of an out-of-tune fiddle.

"Do you remember if our people up on the Gila River pick these a little differently than the Tohono O'odham do it around here? All I can remember is what I would do when I would go out and pick some with the other kids, but I can't recall picking the buds when they were this small. I thought we got them just as the flowers were ready to pop open."

"Well, it's probably not exactly the same up there," I replied, trying to recall the details of the process for myself, "because you have the cholla they call *ha:nam* there by the Gila. Here by the mountains, it's mostly *ciolim*. Some Tohono O'odham say that the smaller and more compact the *ciolim* buds are, the sweeter they taste. I guess I've gradually gotten used to doing it their way because they're my neighbors now."

The wind made us weary, so we took refuge in my backyard. I had earlier started to roast coals in an earthen pit, and prepared an eight-foot-long box lined with window screen for removing the spines. We poured out bucketfuls of cactus buds into the box and used brooms to sweep them across the screen, knocking most of their spines off. We picked up the despined buds with our tongs and refilled our buckets with them, pouring half the loads into the roasting pit, and half into big pots of boiling water on the stove.

Once we rescued the pit-roasted cholla buds, we returned indoors to where my dining room table was full of traditional foods the cactus crew had brought along: tepary beans, posole, acorns, piñon nuts, and a wide variety of other foods. Just before everything was put out on the table, a quiet Akimel O'odham elder among us asked if he could offer a blessing in the Pima language. I nodded and called everyone into a circle.

Suddenly we were quiet, hearing only the wind howl outside. The elder then whispered a blessing he had crafted in his heart for us, for the food, and for the land, thanking the Creator, Earth Maker, reminding us of all we had been given. We huddled in my living room, relieved to be out of the wind, while the remaining cholla buds huddled under the earth, in the roasting pit. I felt some holy sort of spirit rising up around us, in the smoke, the wind, the songs we shared. In this solemn mood, several of us took our food outside to catch the fleeting colors of the sunset.

The spicy bite of mesquite smoke inundated every plant cell of the cholla buds, and every animal cell of the humans who stood around the smoldering roasting pit. We sucked the smoky taste into our mouths as well. I recited Calvino's words once again: "I was living and dying in all the fibers of what is chewed and digested, and in all the fibers that absorb the sun, consuming and digesting. . . ."

I remembered the ancient art of roasting, of baking fibrous foodstuffs directly over red-hot coals—pit roasting, an art predating agriculture. Although I often imagined Ice Age mammoth hunters roasting freshly killed meat over the coals of blazing bonfires, it was likely that women and men of the Pleistocene roasted just as many plant foods over red-hot embers. A pit full of coals was their canned heat, the wrath of a dangerous spirit turned into useful energy.

The caloric cost of eating was not merely the number o[...]-duced by the fruit, nuts, meats, and roots we ate; it was als[...]rt expended in hunting and gathering, in processing and butchering, and most obviously, those we feel as heat while roasting, baking, grilling, or boiling our fare. Archaeologists have estimated that most hunter-gatherers directly consumed a total of some 2,500 to 3,500 calories on the "average" day—including the energy expended while carrying food to cookfires and gathering the wood used in grilling meats and tubers. Of course, averages didn't mean much to those who foraged in highly seasonal environments. And yet, when the Biodiversity Project newsletter recently published a discussion on my friend Peter Vitousek's estimate that most contemporary Americans require 46,000 calories each day to produce the food they eat, ecologist Stuart Pimm saw it and disagreed.

"Way low," he argued; Vitousek's estimate did not at all cover the many ways in which we consume fossil fuels to transport our groceries, supply our gas stoves, power our food processors and coffeemakers. What Peter and Stuart did agree on is this sobering fact: More than 40 percent of the earth's annual productivity is funneled into feeding just one species, our species, undoubtedly at the expense of the myriad other creatures trying to feed themselves on this wayward ark careening through space.

After the cholla bud harvesters left late in the evening, I walked outside, beyond my gate, and peered into the open pit where the cholla buds had been steamed, roasted, and smoked. The branchlets of desert broom in the bottom of the pit were charred, their aromatic oils reduced to a black tar. The heavy trunks of mesquite had been transformed into fluffy, grayish-white ash. The ashes and branches of desert broom rustled and stirred in the unrelenting wind. I heard in my head the echo of words said in my presence many times over the last forty years, but now I felt them etched into my muscles as well: "This is the body that has been given up for you. Take and eat it. Do this in memory of me."

Chapter Four

Riding the Dunes and Finding the Ghosts

Although summer solstice had not yet arrived, the season could hardly be called springtime anymore. It was already dry. Most spring wildflowers had already withered and died. I decided to drive out into the heart of the desolation that had taken the place of those fields of once-abundant wildflowers, out where I could feel how the world had been left after Chuck's passing. I drove my old Blazer down to the Mexican border on a bone-dry day in May, passing through the sea of sand called the Gran Desierto de Altar.

Mexico's Highway 2 had hardly any traffic in the hour before dawn, and I went another half hour without passing another car. The highway's soft shoulder was often lined with sand-adapted snowy sunflowers, but this spring dried up so early, the stalks had already turned brittle. I was alone, no radio on, drinking tea out of a thermos and munching on sunflower seeds now and then. I was thinking back over the last couple months, saddened by how bleak the world can be.

The Sand Papago who historically lived out here had a name for parts of April and May in their O'odham dialect that meant "the lean moon" or the "month of hunger weather." But the bleakness I reflected upon was not the Gran Desierto beyond my windshield. I was not thinking about the paucity of vegetative cover here, or to the incapacity of these sandy swales to support agriculture without the help of irrigation or miraculous downpours.

I had in mind that miragelike visage we call the human condition: How easy it is for us to lose who we are, to forget what we were made of, to get stuck far from where we know how best to live.

My mind wandered as I drove through blowing sand and wavering mirages. Since Chuck's death, I had been talking with my mother constantly, trying to help her recover from the loss of her partner of fourteen years. She and I both knew that you don't really recover from that kind of loss, you just go on. Chuck had already been suffering from emphysema and incurable cancer when he took a bad fall just before Easter, breaking his leg and ripping most of the skin off his forearm as he tried to catch himself. Somehow he had mustered up his old cheerfulness by the time we arrived for Easter dinner. As my mother cooked up his favorite holiday foods—sugar-cured ham, yams, green beans with almonds—Chuck kidded her about her holiday-induced forgetfulness: "It just wouldn't be right to be havin' Easter dinner without you burnin' the biscuits." He guffawed from his wheelchair. He panted heavily after letting this sentence loose, his oxygen tank hooked up at his side.

"Oh, honey," my mother sighed. "I just get too many dishes going at the same time, and I forget whether I've even put the biscuits in the oven." She handed one platter after another to me, to Laurie, and to my daughter, Laura Rose, and we tried to find room for all of them on the dining room table.

Although it remained unspoken, we collectively sensed it might be his last Easter supper. I led all of us in giving thanks for the food but also seized the moment to thank him for all the holiday hospitality he had shown members of his stepfamily over the years.

Two days later Chuck was dead; his heart had given out. That had been the last meal he shared with loved ones, for he spent his final forty hours alive on intravenously provided slurries of nutrients.

That was the prevailing bleakness that glared at me as I drove along: the very notion that a man who grew up on a farm, raising grains and stock, hunting and fishing for more than sixty years, might die in the antiseptic atmosphere of IVs, heart monitors, and oxygen tanks. Chuck had shucked corn, dressed game and filleted fish for tens of thousands of meals over his lifetime. But as his emphysema worsened, he had abandoned his fisherman's shack on the Gulf of California coast, sold off his guns and fishing tackle. He finally traded his lifelong love of hunting dogs for the keeping of lap dogs. They lounged around with him in front of the TV when the contaminated air of Phoenix kept him housebound.

In the last month of his life, as he sat weakened by radiation and poisoned by chemotherapy, unable even to walk around the block, he once caught my mother asking me about my work down on the Gulf. He lit up like he was suddenly plugged into an old connection: "Well, how's the fishing down there?"

"Not bad, Chuck. The corvinas are running again like they used to in the seventies—some real big schools over by El Gulfo."

"Oh, them corvinas are good fish!" he exclaimed, looking past the TV screen toward the south-facing window, as if he could see clear down to Mexico. Then he got dead quiet, looking down at his own hands, as if he'd realized he'd never feel the flip-flopping of a silver-finned catch within his own grasp again.

By accident and illness, his life had grown remote from the hunting, fishing, and farming that had sustained his body and soul for so long. The radiation killed his gut biota, but the chemotherapy was so toxic that he couldn't even register or savor the flavors of his favorite foods anymore. We could see how he was losing weight and losing his hair, but what concerned me was that as his appetite went, so did his will to stay connected with the living world.

"Chuck, you have to try to eat *something*," I heard my mother say one evening.

"Then just microwave me some chicken fingers or one of them frozen burritos you got at Costco. . . . Don't go to the fuss of fixin' anything from scratch; I can't taste it anyway."

Driving along the border at twilight, I sensed Chuck's passing not merely as the blinking out of a single life but as part of a widespread darkening, as shadows fall on once-brilliant means of making a living here on earth. Chuck had farmed with his family in Michigan, fished in Florida; he had even cowboyed and rodeoed and hunted elk on horseback up along the Mogollon Rim in north-central Arizona. He could talk to dogs and horses; he could shape things with tools and tractors. He had skills with boats and outboards that I could hardly learn today even if I were to devote myself full-time to such pursuits. In short, he had seaworthy and landworthy knowledge—he deeply understood how to work with a field, a river, or an ocean so that they rendered their bounty as food. He had the kind of knowledge no amount of book learning can help me recover.

And yet look what had happened over Chuck's lifetime—we went from being a country in which 15 percent of all citizens were farmers, ranchers, and full-time fishermen, to one in which fewer than 3 percent of our neighbors devote themselves to such food-producing pursuits. The U.S. Department of Agriculture considered it a miracle that so few people need to toil all day to feed our entire nation. Nonetheless we are no longer the agrarian nation Thomas Jefferson had envisioned, where fully 97 percent of the people ably "grew the vegetables they ate, and wrung the necks of the turkeys they dressed." Over the last half century we have lost one out of every five farmland acres worked in the years immediately following World War II. When Chuck returned from the war, the United States had 1.2 billion acres of farms. When he died, fewer than 925 million acres could still be called farmlands. As the number of farms in any locality decreased during Chuck's lifetime, the probability that he could obtain all his diet from local sources also diminished. When Chuck's grandfather farmed in the 1870s, roughly 5 percent of all food produced in the world moved between nations, or between distant regions within the same nation. By the time Chuck gave up farming after World War II, that percentage had doubled, and it doubled again by the time his ashes were spread over the land he loved.

As I meditated on the meaning of this detachment from working the land, I realized that many Americans were absolutely delighted that they were no longer stooping to pick rows of vegetables. While most were relieved that they would never again have to bloody their hands while butchering livestock or poultry, some others believed that we had traded away hard-earned virtues for insulated comforts.

I once talked this issue over with Vess Quinlan, a cowboy poet who grew up much as Chuck Buxton and their other rural contemporaries had done, but had never succumbed to the propaganda that our society is better off with fewer farmers and cowboys out working the land simply because feedlots and factory farms claimed higher levels of productivity per capita.

"There are a lot of people who claim they want to see ranchlands and farmlands preserved as open space, but what about taking care of the people who have made their living in a way that takes care of the land? I just hate it when I see some corporation buy a ranch and then let go some man who has fine cowboying skills, and instead of doing what he's uniquely suited to do, that man is forced to work in construction or in a hardware store or even a real estate office."

Vess was one of many folks I knew who believed that undue corporate influences on government food policy had forced many families off the land, families that had the skills to take care of it better than it is generally being taken care of today. He was the first to explain to me the odd sequence of events that changed rural life for them following World War II: "When our generation came home from the war, the military chiefs had all this stockpiled nitrogen for bombs, and at first they didn't know what to do with it. Then someone suggested that they take all the nitrogen they had contracted companies for and turn it into fertilizer to boost grain production in the U.S."

As we sat there I had no way of knowing whether Vess correctly remembered when the use of nitrogen fertilizers took off. Later, though I checked his claim against one of the Worldwatch Institute's *State of the World* annuals, in which Worldwatch founder Lester Brown confirmed "the phenomenal growth in world fertilizer use since mid-century." What began as a means to use up all the wartime nitrogen production in the United States resulted in a tenfold increase in world fertilizer use between 1950, when only 14 tons were applied to fields, to 146 tons in 1990, when global use of fertilizers peaked. World grain production climbed the upward curve behind fertilizer use, tripling from 632 million tons in 1950 to 1,780 million tons in 1990.

Vess went on: "With all that nitrogen boosting yields, we soon had a surplus of corn. I grew upon the taste of range-fed beef, but soon I was hearing food celebrities patterned after Betty Crocker touting corn-fed beef on the radio, and I couldn't figure out what was wrong with beef raised on grass."

"Well, there wasn't a damn thing wrong with it," Vess declared angrily, "except that the corn producers suddenly had a surplus, and someone got the idea of fattening up stock in feedlots to use up that excess corn. American consumers were encouraged to eat that marbled, feedlot beef, even though the grass-fed beef is less fatty and better for us." The promotion of grain-fed beef paid off for a handful of feedlot owners and meatpackers, who now capture about four-fifths of the entire beef market in the United States, where livestock consume half of all the grain now produced in the country. Each full-pound hamburger eaten at American drive-ins has a seven-pound investment of grain hidden within its grease.

"Not surprisingly"—Vess laughed darkly—"they began to overproduce beef in feedlots, and they ended up with all this excess tallow and fat that they decided to put into chicken feed. All of a sudden we had eggs with higher cholesterol content than ever before, all because of policies that favored overproduction so that big subsidized corporations could dump their products into the marketplace."

Vess contended that as small ranches grew to be less profitable, corporations bought them out, consolidated them, and fired nearly every old cowboy who truly knew how to maintain the health of the land. Ironically the health of American consumers deteriorated as well, as the overproduction of fatty foods contributed to an overweight population.

That former cowboy's words used to ring and sting in my ears whenever I thought about how poorly my own agriculture degree had prepared me for anything like farming or ranching. By the time I began college, most of my professors had already accepted the view that the only lucrative new agricultural jobs would be in the government's agricultural services, or selling fertilizers, feed, and seeds for transnational corporations. In any case, in 1910, farmers themselves gained forty cents for every dollar consumers spent on food but received less than seven cents per dollar by the time I left college in 1982. The "middlemen" of agricultural services were gaining the rest, without ever investing it back into land stewardship.

Have I lost my way? I wondered. I glanced out the window and realized that I was surrounded by dunes, swales, and cinder cones. There was not a cow, cornfield, Costco, or corporation headquarters in sight. I was out in the desert wilderness, trying to dry out from a sort of drunkenness most folks in my society had succumbed to. And yet I was seeing flashbacks, hallucinating up all the pain I had ever felt in my belly and in the land. I could see Chuck, and Vess too; there in front of me were all the other failed farmers and ranchers that I had ever known. The sickening taste of overprocessed, chemically preserved foods rose from my belly and filled my mouth.

I swallowed the last of my water and passed the ramshackle shop of a shade-tree mechanic, recognizing that I had been there before, at the turnoff for a track across twenty miles of sand, leading to the Sierra del

Rosario. I could see that pink granitic range, looking precisely like rosary beads being buried by a flood of sand.

I had spent a week out there in 1976, when I first moved to the Sonoran Desert, hoping to learn as much as I could about desert food plants. I apprenticed myself to Richard Felger, an eccentric botanist who had spent years compiling an enormous list of native species historically used as food by desert Indians. Felger needed assistants to help him collect the flora of the field dunes rimming the Gran Desierto, so I went along, assuming that we would bring edible plants into the camp each night and try them ourselves.

I was wrong. Richard was, at the time, on a strict diet of Russian caviar, Ry-Krisp crackers, and Alice B. Toklas brownies. Nevertheless, he had remarkable recall regarding the botanical history of early European encounters with edible desert plants. One night, around the campfire, he told me about a hero of his who had wandered into this same area more than a century before us. While exploring for a train route across the desert to the California coast in 1854, Col. Andrew Belcher Gray came upon a family of seminomadic Sand Papago Indians. They were eating a peculiar sand-loving plant previously undescribed in science. Although he had collected specimens of the plant, Richard had never personally eaten it, for Colonel Gray claimed that its juices had destroyed the enamel of the teeth of the young Sand Papago women he had witnessed eating this delicacy. Richard is, among other things, a true believer in the power of plants, and happily paranoid when it comes to rumors that plants might harm as well as heal him.

Over the decade following that numinous trip into the dunes, I had gone out on my own to retrace the routes of Gray and other botanical explorers through the Gran Desierto. In truth I was hoping to taste this edible underground wonder, *camote de los medanos,* known in English simply as sand food. After my first dozen unsuccessful searches at places where it had been collected previously, I conceded that it might well be as scarce as some contemporary botanists suspected it to be. But I soon learned how to find the purple flowering stalks of parasitic sand food as they rose up through several feet of loose sand. At last I relocat-

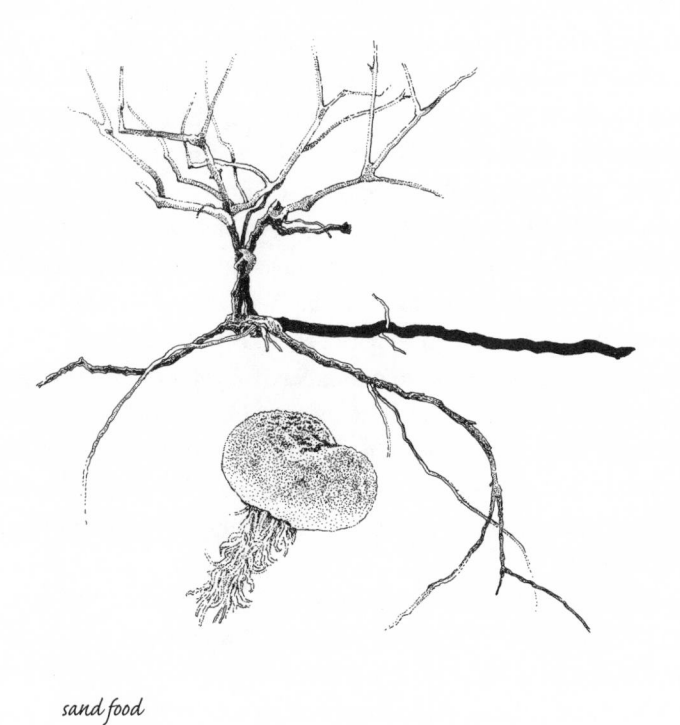

sand food

ed plants at a few of its historic localities, gradually realizing that it was rarely encountered but not truly endangered.

However, another piece of the puzzle was missing. Because most of the remaining Sand Papago families were forced to relocate away from these dunes a century ago, none of their kin were left to make a living out here as full-time foragers of wild plants and animals. Most of the knowledge of how to survive only with what this desert offered died along with the last 350 Sand Papago who had lived out amid the dunes of the Gran Desierto full-time. I doubted I would ever encounter someone who had once routinely eaten sand food as part of his or her traditional diet.

Then in the late 1980s, I was driving along this same highway, when

I pulled off onto a small patch of excess asphalt that a road construction crew had discarded amid the dunes. There, while looking around for desert wildflowers, I had stumbled on a broken-off stalk of sand food, perhaps damaged by another vehicle parking in the same spot earlier the same day. I slipped it into my shirt pocket and brought it to the oldest surviving Sand Papago elder, Candelaria Orosco, who still moved back and forth across the border between Ajo, Arizona, and Sonoyta, Sonora. She had once lived in the dunes near Yuma but refused to go back there because she was still angry about having been locked up with her grandfather in the Yuma Penitentiary when she was just a child.

Candelaria was a child no more; her 102 years of desert living had shriveled her up and left her feisty, amused by the old-time foods and medicines I would bring her. When I pulled the stalk of sand food out of my pocket, she knew exactly what I had brought her. There was no way that she could confuse it with other sand-loving plants that her people had once eaten.

"*Hia tadk,*" she murmured in her O'odham dialect. "That's why they called us *Hia Tadk Kumdam,* the Sand Root Crushers. It tastes a little like melon."

"Oh, that's what the old people compared its flavor to?" I asked in Spanish.

"That's what it tasted like to *me* when I ate it years ago," she answered to me in Spanish. Then, taking a deep breath, she added in a barely audible voice, "How could I tell you what something tastes like if I had not tasted it myself?"

Candelaria's words still echoed through me as I found myself approaching the same small patch of asphalt on the edge of Highway 2 at 8 A.M. on that blazing May morning. It was time that I found out for myself what sand food tasted like, even if I would arrive a bit late for my rendezvous with my daughter in Yuma. I pulled the Blazer onto a small patch of asphalt edging the road, turned off the ignition, and placed a reflective shade screen up against the windshield in a vain attempt to keep the car cool while I wandered around. With a canteen attached to my hip, a buck knife on my belt, and a wide-brimmed straw hat atop my head, I set out toward the border fence that lay a quarter mile north of me among the dunes and the swales.

Unlike the other times I had stopped at or near this site over the previous two decades, there were virtually no wildflowers blooming this spring. I had been fortunate before, setting out after hearing accounts that the dunes had received a torrential downpour that had sprouted a dozen kinds of belly flowers as well as helping sand food itself along. This time, even the tenacious creosote bushes looked as though they were drought stressed. I ambled up one ridge, down the other side, and into a trough like the others I had seen sand food growing in before. I spotted two shriveled-up skeletons of its flower stalks from previous years' blooms, but no new signs of life even when I dug down into the sand.

I had been humbled several times already by the difficulty of sustaining this local food-getting exercise, but the forty minutes of wandering those dunes without encountering anything edible brought me to my knees.

"If I had to live out here . . . and were always this inept," I keep on mumbling to myself, "I'd be dead by now."

I returned to the swale where the two dried-up stalks had stood to dig all around them, sure that there must be edible matter hidden underground.

Finally I began to worry about my own water balance—I had already emptied my canteen—and I despaired at all the time I was wasting. The temperature was now well over ninety degrees, so I couldn't easily gauge how much I was sweating. Any moisture reaching my skin evaporated off of me before I knew it. I had to concede that I was probably not as good a forager as Candelaria was, and that I should get back into the Blazer so that I could spend the rest of the day with my daughter.

Unlocking the car, I removed the sunshade screen and tossed the canteen on the passenger seat. Before driving on for another hour, I decided to take a pee. Unzipping my jeans and looking down at my boots, I noticed a familiar lavender color emerging from the pieces of asphalt at the road's edge. Amazing, I thought. The sand food was right there in front of me. I scanned the asphalt to the west, and there was another, and still another stalk of sand food blooming within inches of the highway itself. Perhaps some moisture had been trapped beneath the roadbed, enabling sand food and its shrubby hosts to thrive at the highway side even when they lacked sufficient water to bloom out in the open desert.

This highway had not existed when Candelaria made her living as a wandering forager, but it had saved me from complete failure in my momentary pursuit. I used my lug wrench as a pick to dig the sand food flower stalk free, and broke off just one ten-inch branch of it so that the rest could still grow. There was a certain relief to the fact that I had not accidentally urinated on it. At last the Blazer climbed back onto the road, heading toward Yuma.

My planned arrival time in Yuma was to be around ten in the morning, knowing that my daughter loved to sleep in Saturday mornings until that hour. It was already nine o'clock and I guessed that I had about forty-five minutes of driving before me, judging from where I was along Highway 2. Having been up since five, I was thirsty and hungry. The sand food could not be eaten without my scrubbing off all the grains of sand embedded in its skin. I decided to stop at the next human habitation along the highway, to ask for water and clean off the season's meager harvest of sand food.

The desert parasite sat like a special guest in the passenger seat next to me. "Do you need to wash up before breakfast?" I asked politely. I began to wonder whether the desert heat had left a few of my brain cells charbroiled.

I glanced over at my guest: a pale pinkish stalk with half-formed bracts edged with a subtle lavender hue, not unlike that of the little cup of flowers topping the entire stalk. The cup was reminiscent of a ground-hugging peyote cactus, its delicate flowers barely reaching above the surface. So this was the bizarre food that gave the Sand Papago their nickname among neighboring tribes; so this was the plant so peculiar and so pathetically hard to find by untrained eyes that it became the "needle in the haystack" of American culinary history. Its very use was discovered by accident just a few decades before an ancient foraging tradition had been entirely obliterated.

After a few miles more of talking to the sand food stalk riding shotgun with me, I spotted a truck stop on the horizon. When I stopped in front of it, I saw an elderly man watering two lemon trees alongside the small café. His hose spewed out brackish water, which left a salty white stain around the basin where the lemons grew. I asked if I could use the bathroom, and he silently pointed to an outbuilding with a sink in front of it. I used the facility, washed my hands, and then scrubbed and rinsed the sand off the succulent stalk I carried with me. Walking back past the elderly man, I asked him if he had ever seen this plant before.

"It may be what some old-timers around here call *camote de los indios,* but I don't know the desert here too well. I stay here by my garden. But there is a man who lives by himself another mile down, across the road. He is a *curandero;* he gathers herbs to sell to *yerberias* in all of the border towns. You go ask that Miguelito about your plant."

I drove another mile through the dunes, seeing only a cinder pile for highway repair, and a small shack beneath a transplanted salt cedar tree. I aimed for the shack and left the road. I idled in front of it for a minute, but no one stirred, so I declared it uninhabited and began to drive away. Just as I did, a straw hat appeared over the crest of a sand dune. A wiry man with no shirt, torn blue jeans, and thong sandals waved to me. The sand food and I got out of the Blazer. I walked over to meet him.

"I am looking for a *curandero* named Don Miguel," I declared.

Silence. Just when I thought he would not talk to me at all, his eyes focused on the stalk draped at my side.

"I am a *yerbero,* an herbalist, not a *curandero.*" I regretted that I used the word *curandero,* for in some circles it is synonymous with *brujo,* or witch. "However, my name is Miguelito, as you said."

"I was wondering if you ever see this plant growing around here."

He eyed me, then cast his vision down toward the plant, studying it carefully. At last he muttered, "Why do you want to know?"

"I wonder if there is ever enough of it in one place to really fill the belly. You know, if someone was hungry, could they find enough to survive?"

"Do you want to buy more like this or are you selling it?"

"No, no, I'm only curious. I was told about this plant by an old Papago lady, who ate it when she was a little girl, but now that she eats the white man's food, she's sick with diabetes. I just wonder if I could ever find enough to bring to her, maybe to help her diabetes."

"No, it is here, but it goes quickly. Look, it bruises just from you holding it. I can't gather it and keep it, then haul it to stores like I do the medicinal herbs. For diabetes I can give you other plants: *cósagui,* the range ratany roots; *jediondilla,* the creosote leaves; *zaramatraca,* the little tubers that grow under the night-blooming cactus. I gather them nearby. I gather *yerba de la mansa* at the Río Colorado delta. I take them back to an herb store I started in Juarez, south of El Paso. I'd rather be out here picking the herbs than back there running the store. But there is little reason for me to pick this *camote de los medanos.* It won't keep like a true medicinal herb."

We chatted hardly a minute longer. He was quick to ascertain that I had nothing to sell or much interest in buying many of his herbs. Abruptly he bade me *adios.* He trudged off into the sand, his *mochila* bag full of clippers and knives hanging from his shoulder. He dropped out of sight over the crest of a dune, and the desert appeared unpeopled once more.

After I got the Blazer back on the road to Yuma, I tried to think about other things, but my mind kept wandering back to the herbalist in the dunes. Selling herbs had recently become big business, with a retail value of $600 million for herb products in the United States alone, but this career veteran had remained poor despite the boom in international herb trade. Apparently the wealth being generated by the herbal bonanza was not trickling down to the most knowledgeable folks on the front line—the local collectors, the folk diagnosticians, and the traditionally trained healers. Don Miguel might have been the last of the old-timey *curanderos* and medicinal plant gatherers to live out in the Gran Desierto.

The Sand Papago were not extinct, as it was once thought, but few of them now lived anywhere near patches of sand food and other edible dune plants. Those who did live nearby had day jobs, other duties, other diets. Candelaria had insisted that patches of sand food plants were drying up because no one nowadays knew how to prune them back, to harvest and eat their stalks in a way that stimulated others to grow, to branch, and to proliferate.

Miguelito did not discuss the harvesting of sand food, but herbalists are not prone to offer their secrets about how they handle certain plants. If he came here season after season to gather medicines from the wild, he would periodically stumble on this curiosity, and perhaps it would speak to him. But would he be the last to know how to eat it, as Candelaria was for her Sand Papago clan? Would his children or grandchildren follow after him, gathering herbs? Probably not in this place.

I guess that Miguelito's career as an herb hunter would not appeal to most folks, let alone to his kin in booming bordertowns. Today most of the world's six billion people obtain the bulk of their medicines from just twenty transnational pharmaceutical corporations. Ten of those corporations control a third of the world market, bottling and packaging pharmaceuticals that gross more than $80 billion a year. If these companies were all exemplars of the humanitarian ideal of reducing the suffering and premature deaths associated with diseases, we would all wish them well as they take home the profits of their hard work. But when the public hears of twentyfold differences in the price of the same basic medicines, derived from the same sources, from one country to the next, frustration and anger replace good wishes. Americans today are as frustrated with the inflated prices and poor public service of the pharmaceutical industry as they are with the customer service and safety records of airlines. And that may be why some Americans have begun experimenting with medicinal herbs gathered from local or from Mexican sources: to reduce their health-care costs, and to regain some control over what bioactive chemicals go into their own bodies. For the first time in decades, many Americans are more interested in where their medicines come from than they are in acquiring another magic pill. But this renewed interest in herbs is probably not enough to keep Miguelito's tradition populated with people of his ilk.

The other name for the Gran Desierto was the *despoblado,* the "unpeopled land." It had been *unpeopled* as the result of lack of respect for the folks who truly knew how to live there. It is a stretch of desert that supported more people prehistorically than it does today. The bulk of its former residents had abandoned their homesteads there more than a century ago, destroying any sense of continuity between the plant lore of the *antepasados,* "those who came before," and the knowledge the few current colonists used to wrangle their living off skinny cows, tourists stuck in the sand, and truckers with flat tires.

Most of the desert's edible plants still persisted somewhere in small patches, but ancient knowledge about how to harvest, prune, or cook them had already wilted and withered. The time-tried ways of gaining a livelihood within this austere landscape had nearly faded from memory. If you were to put down on your Arizona or Sonora driver's license application "Occupation: Hunter-Gatherer," the state officials would have you examined for sun-induced brain damage. The very notion that someone could have garnered most of his or her annual caloric intake from a desertscape such as this would be considered ludicrous to most contemporary residents of the Sonoran Desert. If the notion was not an outright impossibility, then at least it implied that anyone who attempted such a pursuit was cursed with the most impoverished diet imaginable. If stranded, one could perhaps "eke out an existence" here for a few dreadful moments, but why on earth would anyone *choose* to live here?

I took out my pocket knife and cut off a piece of sand food. As it crossed my lips, a flavor not unlike that of a sweet jicama or near-ripe melon filled my mouth. Delicious. A texture like a freshly cut chunk of sugarcane or a slightly fibrous cucumber.

Driving past one honey-colored dune after another, I wondered whether other sand food plants lay in wait in the swales. It was a lovely undulating landscape, like hips, like lips. These dunes had left a good taste in my mouth, although I realized that I would never be a full-time hunter-gatherer, and might not even be successful enough as a gardener or farmer to gain all my foods and medicines on my own land for a year or more running.

"That's a tougher row to hoe than you even know," one of my uncles used to say to me whenever I began to speak romantically about subsistence farming or hunting during my college days. Older and perhaps a little less prone to idealize, I now accepted that both desert farmers and hunter-gatherers had inevitably suffered unremitting hardships over the centuries.

And yet, acknowledging those hardships, another part of my head, heart, and heritage kept me from writing off these food traditions as anachronisms. I could not regard them merely as obsolete pursuits. I was glad I had had a chance to hand pick cholla buds, pit roast mescal, and unearth sand food before I died, before I followed Chuck and countless others into the cremation urn, and out once more as part of the potassium cycle. I could no longer dismiss the fact that in even the most apparently barren stretch of desert, there were extraordinary flavors to savor, textures to tongue and to crunch between my teeth. That is, there are wild flavors and textures that I could never again live without for very long. The wild foods I had stumbled on during these months of witnessing death and hunger weather had been little saviors for me, reminders that life still goes on all around me, and that more often than not, *life tastes good.*

Chapter Five

Dead Chemicals or Peaches Eaten Alive

Yuma, Arizona, had been known as Salad Town for several decades. Not that the boys at the local military base consumed more salad than beef or beer. No, it's Salad Town in another way: The majority of the fields you see as you approach town were planted with salad greens and onions. Sometimes you see melons, oilseeds, dates, or broccoli. But mostly you see greens, turgid green vegetables that are shipped sopping wet all winter long across North America. They are grown with water that is pumped up out of the Río Colorado, one of several dozen rivers worldwide that no longer flows into an ocean. Today more than four out of every five gallons of fresh river water found on this planet are pumped out of riverbeds and consumed by agricultural crops.

In the days of Cesar Chávez, stoop labor in the fields near Yuma revolved around head lettuce. Lettuce growers didn't offer farmworkers many amenities in those days, but Chávez and others were successful in improving most every condition for lettuce workers that they could. A few problems persisted, however. Head lettuce was incredibly vulnerable to insect infestations. The insecticides sprayed over the lettuce fields sat thick in the cooler air above the Río Colorado floodplain, where their concentrations accumulated in the fields, homes, and roadsides situated there. If their working and sleeping hours were largely spent on that floodplain, farmworkers with allergies or other respiratory problems suffered mightily from such pesticide exposure.

But while the farmworkers were heading for the emergency rooms with pesticide-triggered respiratory problems, the insects in the lettuce patches were developing resistance to the pesticides. By the eighties, Yuma farmers felt they had exhausted their arsenal of toxic chemicals, for the whiteflies had developed so much genetic resistance that they were able to wreak havoc on any lettuce field within reach. Worse yet, the whiteflies brought with them a devastating virus—a tropical gemnivirus, to be exact—one that found Salad Town an ideal location for ushering in an epidemic.

Curiously, because most of Yuma's farmers went to the same coffee shop each morning to discuss planting and pest problems, they inadvertently made things worse by sowing their winter lettuce crops at about the same time that they heard the others would be planting. That provided the whiteflies and gemniviruses with millions of simultaneously ripened lettuce heads perfectly suited to infestation. It was like a new strain of salmonella getting a free ticket to a "factory" house full of genetically-uniform poultry. In essence the lettuce heads became sitting ducks for whitefly and virus mischief. By the mid- to late eighties, hundreds of thousands of insect-riddled, discolored heads lay rotting in the fields, showing the telltale signs of virus infections and whitefly infestations. The farmworkers were all laid off until the farmers figured out what to do, but by that time tens of millions of dollars of crop losses had already been incurred.

Gradually the remaining farmers in the Yuma, Imperial, and Mexicali Valleys have learned to desynchronize their planting times and diversify their crops. Many of them switched to growing a patchwork of salad ingredients of all shapes, colors, sizes, and species, including California-style mesclun greens. They used more and more pesticides early in the season, hoping to devastate the whiteflies before their populations ballooned. Farmworkers and their Indian neighbors now suffer from respiratory problems caused by aerial pesticide spraying, but the whiteflies no longer form the thick milky clouds over Yuma that they once did.

As I drove into Yuma that day, the last of the greens were being harvested from the fields. Summerlike heat had already become a reality in Yuma several weeks before. I picked up my daughter, and had an iced tea with her at the coffee shop where the Río Colorado Valley's farmers still love to meet. The last few baseball-capped farmers in bib overalls left the shop while we chatted. When I shuttled Laura Rose over to a Saturday practice she had for an upcoming dance recital, she reported to me the latest teenage gossip about one of the fast-food restaurants located along Yuma's main drag.

"Oh, Papa, do you know about this? My friends are saying that KFC is called that because it doesn't really have chicken in it anymore."

"KFC? You mean Kentucky Fried Chicken?"

"Yeah, but look, they hardly ever use the word *chicken* anymore in describing their foods. That's because it *isn't* chicken anymore, we think."

"What is it, turkey?"

"No! That's not what the other kids tell me. It's like they've bred chickens to be so big and added so many chemicals to them that the government won't let them call the meat chicken anymore. I don't even think it says chicken on the regular menu anymore—you just get KFC eight-piece buckets, or KFC twelve-piece buckets or . . . Here, turn in before you miss Dance Masters—I'll see you in an hour and a half."

After Laura Rose went inside to the dance studio, I sat idling the Blazer for a moment, wondering whether I had just heard the latest urban myth: Big Birds Butchered by Estate of Kentucky Colonel. So I headed back down the main drag, parked out in front of the colonel's picture, then went in to investigate.

Bad timing. It was close enough to noon that the place was loaded with Latino farmworkers and young families from the military base. The KFC staff was so occupied that I wouldn't be able to get more than an order—let alone a full sentence—in edgewise for at least another hour.

And so I stood there, looking up at the KFC menu sign, perhaps the first time I had done so in six years. (The last time I had done so was with a Seri Indian tribal chairman who had requested that we stop there in the middle of night, on our way up from his village in Mexico. Since his family still ate more rattlesnake than chicken at home, I asked if they could offer him "an eight-piece bucket that tasted just like rattlesnake" but the tired cashier didn't understand what I was talking about.)

My God, I thought, Laura Rose was right about one thing! When I came in the door, I couldn't immediately find the word *chicken* on the regular menu. I couldn't find a picture of a rooster or a hen in the entire place. There was a promotional poster that said something like "Coming Soon: Honey Barbecue Chicken," but it was as if the novelty of the new item was that it did indeed include chicken. Or perhaps they had at last engineered barbecue-sauce-making genes right into the Big Bird.

I decided to pass on purchasing anything from KFC that day, but the entire conversation with my daughter had made me realize that kids today grow up cynical about the food being produced on their behalf on factory farms. At the same time they were more vulnerable than ever to highly processed foods and beverages supplemented with pinches of herbs, vitamins, and energy enhancers. Now marketed everywhere on radio, TV, and billboards, these magical potions are collectively known as nutraceuticals. Although the food industry, in its in-house publications, prefers to call such mineral-enhanced, cholesterol-lowering, herbally flavored wonders "functional foods," I find the term a bit peculiar. It is as if that makes whole chili peppers, unadulterated apples, and fresh prickly pear cactus pads "dysfunctional foods."

While I had an hour to kill, I decided to wander over to the nearest Safeway store to see what nutraceuticals it had to offer. I had been proceeding fairly well on my four-out-of-five native foods plan, eating local legumes, greens, fruits, and vegetables, intermixed with a few tomatoes, chilies, and grains from beyond my terrain. Nevertheless, I decided that I had the slack to blow fifty dollars so that I could prepare Laurie a nutraceutical Sunday brunch the next day. But before entering the grocery store, I sat in the Blazer and scanned a couple of recent articles on nutraceuticals so that I could be sure of purchasing the real McCoy.

The first article, sent to me by friends in St. Louis, claimed that Monsanto would be helping all of us lead healthier lives by genetically engineering "functional foods" that would reduce our vulnerability to cancer and heart disease. Gary Barton, Monsanto's spokesman for biotechnology products, claimed that he was working on a fat-resistant potato chip.

"The average North American eats about 125 pounds of potatoes a year, a lot in the form of potato chips," Barton shrewdly observed. "What we're looking at with potatoes, through a genetic modification, is increasing the starch and thereby in the cooking process less fat would be absorbed in potato chips."

A Canadian nutritional chemist defined a nutraceutical as "any food or food ingredient considered to provide medical or health benefits, including the prevention and treatment of disease." By that definition whole chili peppers, apples, and cactus pads had made the grade and could be marketed as bona fide nutraceuticals. But when I delved into the appendix of the Canadian's article to see what besides peppers, apples, and cactus pads I could put on my shopping list, I didn't find any whole foods listed at all. The inventory was laced with biochemicals: lignins from flax, carotenoids from tomato products, collagen hydrolysate from gelatin, and stanol esters from wood oils. I found another feature on nutraceuticals that listed the highly cultured microorganism Lactobacillus GG, which had just appeared in a newly patented product, Culturelle. Apparently Culturelle was the first "advanced probiotic proprietary dietary supplement" to be marketed by ConAgra, the transnational manufacturer of Hunt's, Wesson, Banquet, Swift, and Healthy Choice foods. I also learned that the rage for functional foods had begun in Japan, but that the major players in these lab concoctions now included not just ConAgra but Coca-Cola, Nestlé, Kellogg, and Procter & Gamble as well. Functional foods were becoming big business, as a report for Japanese businessmen observed: "The market for nutraceuticals is growing quickly worldwide, and it is this global scope that attracts marketers. It is estimated that $250 billion—50% of the U.S. food market of $503 billion—may be attributable to nutraceutical use if taken at its broadest definition (dietary supplements, sugar substitutes, fat substitutes, fiber-enriched foods, vegetables, fatless meat, skim milk, low-calorie diets, etc.)."

With that rather broad definition in mind, I ambled into Safeway ready to see how many nutraceuticals had hit the mainstream, willing to purchase as many as fifty dollars could bring me. During my first four minutes of walking around the Safeway store, I found nutraceuticals in all twelve of the food aisles. If I had included a nutritionally balanced dog chow specially formulated to slow aging in your pet, my hit rate would have risen to thirteen aisles.

In the dairy aisle I had to choose among several of the latest margarines. Even though it was already famous the world over, I bypassed Proctor & Gamble's Olestra, recalling the early complaint from British consumers that its fat-free fat "leaks," leaving them with stained underwear and oily toilets. Anyway, Dr. Tim Lobstein of London's Food Commission believes that Olestra depletes certain vitamins and carotenoids. I opted for Benecol, the light spread that helps promote healthy cholesterol levels by way of its stanol esters, a chemical typically derived from wood byproducts. I was secretly excited that Benecol's plant stanol esters might be derived from wood oils, since I had not yet had anything like pine, wood, or fir oils on my list of items consumed since my experiment had begun at Eastertime.

Elsewhere in the dairy aisle I picked up a green bag full of Veggie Shreds, made with organic tofu, which Galaxy Foods in Orlando, Florida, had discovered to be "Nature's Alternative to Cheese." It was free of saturated fats, cholesterol, antibiotics, and rBST (recombinant bovine somatotrophin) hormones (for rapid production), but heavily laden with soybeans. Although I only knew soybeans in their solid and gaseous states, Galaxy Foods had whipped them into a liquid state to make the Veggie Shreds. The label did not reveal whether shreds were derived from genetically modified soybeans, but Galaxy did assure me that each cheddar-flavored shred "melts great on everything," just as Olestra apparently does.

Just to ensure that all my nondairy product purchases were not soy based, I selected Rice Dream, an alternative to soy beverages, which were in turn an alternative to cow beverages like milk. Rice Dream came from Imagine Foods. I shook the container to determine whether there was something wet inside or whether it was all in the producer's imagination.

Not far from the antidairy section, I found two new releases from the AriZona Rx brand of teas, produced in Lake Success, New York. The first was a Stress Relief Elixir of black and green teas enhanced with *Panax ginseng,* kava, chamomile, and valerian root, fortified with vitamins and minerals, and verified to be a "safe and certain tonic" by one James W. Lippincott. Perhaps it was safe for consumers who were not already overdosing on ginseng or valerian or kava from other sources, but was it safe for the future of these plants? Ginseng was overharvested in several states to the degree that its genetic diversity had markedly diminished outside of protected areas, and the demand for kava-kava cultivation has recently led to the deforestation of more than 70 percent of the natural vegetation that had been left on certain islands in the South Pacific. Had the popularity of Stress Relief Elixirs put these herb populations under stress?

The Energy Body Elixir's label claimed that it was "not genuine unless signed," apparently referring to James's mass-produced signature. The other Arizona Rx product was an Energy Herbal Tonic purporting to be an invigorating blend of green tea, tropical and citrus fruits, *Panax ginseng,* Siberian ginseng, guarana, schizandra, and vitamins A, C, and E. Perhaps what the labeling implied was correct: A lot of energy went into extracting and combining herbs from Siberia's boreal climes to the tropics of South America. It was beyond comprehension how the production of such a beverage could be cost effective, given the energy cost of transporting ginseng from Siberia and guarana from South America all the way to Lake Success. Unless, of course, the Energy Herbal Tonic was 99 percent water from the lake.

In case I needed some other boosts for my drive back to Tucson late that night, I tossed into the shopping cart a box of Celestial Seasonings Fast Lane Tea, containing not only black tea leaves from Java in the East Indies, but the same ginseng root that reindeer used to eat for endurance. I also grabbed twenty-one ounces of powder known as Crystal Light Body Refreshers, because it contained 20 percent daily value of ten vitamins and minerals, and had 90 percent fewer calories than leading soft drinks. Artificially flavored to taste like a mix of strawberry, kiwi, and tangerine, the label of this Kraft Foods product cautioned me that it contained phenylalanine, just in case I knew that I was a phenylketonuric. I guess I would find out whether I was or not when I dissolved the magic powder into a two-quart tub during my moonlit drive back across the desert.

I realized that I had not yet purchased any products packaged by Safeway itself, so I chose a Safeway Select Premium Quality Shiitake Mushroom Risotto, for shiitakes were reputed to boost one's immune system. Mine was now undergoing a slight dip in response to reading so many labels. My spirits were beginning to lag as well, so I began to look around for a hemp-seed granola and a damiana-laced tequila with aphrodisiac qualities that I heard about. While I was passing by the breakfast cereals, I pulled off the shelf a little cup full of sugar-free, microwavable instant oatmeal and fruit, not having much room left for the bigger boxes of high-fiber psyllium seed cereals. Still, no hemp, no aphrodisiacs.

In order to rebound from this disappointment, I headed straight for the dessert aisle, only to find that it no longer carried many products enhanced with natural fats or sugars. Instead I had to purchase a low-fat strawberry mousse mix that was rich on NutraSweet aspartames and phenylketonuric alerts, but lacking in molecules of strawberries and sug-arcane. I worried that the mousse wouldn't set up in the Blazer on the way home, so I purchased some Hawaiian Fruit Cookies. Unlike the Diabetic Coconut Cookies I also threw into the cart, they contained a few droplets of cane juice, even though the Hawaiian cookies didn't look that appetiz-ing. They brought my total purchase up over forty-five dollars.

If the taxes didn't carry me over the fifty-dollar mark, I decided that I would run back and get a can of Spam luncheon meat to go with the Hawaiian cookies. I couldn't be sure that Spam qualified as a nutraceu-tical, but I took a gamble on it because it contained no fillers, cereals, or meat by-products, only 100 percent high-quality pork and ham. I figured that it must have some outstanding nutritional benefits, or the U.S. gov-ernment would not have shipped more than a million pounds of it to nourish Allied troops during World War II. In fact, it may be the world's most popular functional food, since the Hormel Foods Corporation is close to selling its six-*billionth* can of nutritionally balanced Spammy the Pig products.

After returning to watch my daughter's group dance at the studio, then spending several hours with Laura Rose and her friends at their favorite flea market, I began the long drive back toward Tucson. The cookies were no comfort—too stale and brittle, with the fibrous after-taste of wood chips. I nearly fell asleep at the wheel after drinking the Stress Relief Elixir, so I quickly opened the Energy Herbal Tonic to see if it could keep me awake. When it didn't, I pulled off the highway at a gas station, where the attendant let me microwave a jar full of Body Refresher punch spiked with Fast Lane tea. I drank forty ounces of it over the next hour's drive and began to nibble on the Veggie Shreds.

Arriving home at midnight, I couldn't get to sleep for another two hours. As I tossed and turned, I worried that I would sleep too late into the morning to offer Laurie a surprise brunch. In the end, though, every-thing worked out all right, since I had to wake up around six in the morn-ing to pee away all the tonics and elixirs I had consumed the night before. While Laurie slept I arranged on the table the Fast Lane Tea, the

Instant Sugar-Free Oatmeal, some Rice Dream milk substitute, the Coconut and Hawaiian Fruit Cookies. I was preparing to open the meat-by-product-free can of Spam and to mix up the strawberry-free Strawberry Mousse when Laurie wandered into the kitchen, half asleep.

"What's all this?" she yawned.

"A special brunch just for you."

"Is this another experiment or is this a brunch?"

"Oh, come on now! It's just food. Most of it is organically grown and free of chemicals, except the nutritious chemicals that were added in."

"That doesn't mean I can eat it."

I looked at her, wondering if she had been sick while I was away. "You can't eat it? What's the matter?"

"Memories."

"Memories?"

"Yeah, oatmeal memories. You know, of cold winter mornings when my mother or my aunt would force me to eat slimy oatmeal sludge while I was slipping on my lime green leggings so that I could trudge through the snow to my school in Missouri. That oatmeal was so hideous that it made me want to vomit."

"But this is a different kind of oatmeal. It's microwavable and sugar-free, except for the dried fruit embedded in it. I'll pour some Rice Dream on it for you so that you won't have to drink fatty milk."

"But I like fat. And that lactose-free rice drink, what did you call it? I don't need it. I'm not lactose intolerant. Besides, rice should be rice, little white or brown grains, you know. Where did you get that?"

"Safeway. It's called Rice Dream, and it's made by Imagine Foods."

"Rice Dream? Who would want to dream of rice? Someone has a bad imagination."

"Okay, I know you like macaroons. Have a couple of these coconut cookies. They're fat-free, sugar-free, and . . ."

Laurie bit into one of them. "Taste-free! That's *terrible*. Let me try that other kind of cookie. . . . I can't believe it, it's even worse. Look, I skipped dinner last night, and really need something substantial to eat."

"Okay, I'll make you some mesquite waffles with cactus fruit syrup right away if you'll just answer two simple questions for me."

"What are they?"

"I want to know what you think of the Hawaiian cookies. First, do you detect a touch of tropical taste, as the box says they have?"

"After Missouri, I lived in the Latin American tropics as a kid, remember? Those cookies don't have a tropical taste, they have a fake taste."

"Well, then let's skip the other question." I smirked. "It had to do with whether you could detect the delicious sweetness alluded to on the package. . . ."

To make up for inflicting such an awful meal on Laurie so early in the day, I decided to surprise her with something more genuine when she came back from horseback riding late that afternoon. Before the sun had dropped behind the mountains in the west, I went out into the rangelands beyond my house, to look for wolfberries—of which there were hardly any this season—and yucca blossoms, which were bug-infested but abundant. With pruning shears I lopped off a single stalk of these blossoms from a multistalked yucca, leaving the rest for the yucca moth, this species' only known pollinator. Back at home I plucked a hundred or so pale white yucca petals from the flowering stalk, diced and washed them, then put them in a salad bowl. Adding the handful of wolfberries and a few backyard greens, I whipped up a fresh salad, then let it cool in the fridge. Hoping that Laurie would stay out on her ride a little longer, I rushed out to the backyard orchard, where dozens of freshly ripened peaches were within reach. I plucked a dozen or so fat furry peaches off the tree, took them into the kitchen, skinned and sliced them, then mixed them into a cobbler recipe I found among Laurie's stash of cookbooks. I set a timer so that the cobbler would bake a half hour. While it baked in the oven, I took a mess of newly arrived publications out with me to the orchard, and sat down to read.

The first package I opened had the fine new edition of Henry David Thoreau's *Wild Fruits* within it. It reminded me of my favorite line from old Henry, one I had quoted for years without knowing which of his manuscripts it was derived from: "Live in each season as it passes, breathe the air, drink the drink, taste the fruit, and resign yourself to the influences of each."

I chuckled to myself as I thumbed through Henry's treatise on wild fruits. I hadn't had much luck harvesting many wild fruits that day, and had ended up relying upon their distant domesticated kin. I had resigned myself to the fact that the seasons were shifting, making it more and more difficult to predict when wild fruits might be ripe. But that was the trouble with reading Thoreau. The journal notes he wrote always spoke of the elegant simplicity of life, hardly mentioning the times he came up so short that his mother, sister, or benefactor Ralph Waldo Emerson had to feed him. Whenever I tried to practice what Thoreau preached, I found myself beset with complexities, not the least of which was my somewhat skeptical family.

They simply wanted something good to eat, not much caring whether this was an era in which we desperately needed to live fully each season as it passed. They did not share my bewilderment about how spring and summer harvests were timed differently than they had been when I first came to the desert a quarter century ago. For Laurie I was unduly preoccupied with some calendar I carried around in my head: she did not see that the arrival of hummingbirds was early, or that the flowering of pomegranates and penstemons was out of sync with them, or that the peaches now had a shorter fruiting period than they did even a few years ago. She simply knew that we might as well be out on horseback watching wild plants, or out in the garden and orchard as frequently as we could, for she could see that my old assumptions about seasonality did me hardly any good.

Realizing she was right, I began to relax just as the sun went down. I reached up and pulled down a ripe peach from the branch above me, and bit into it. Its juices filled my mouth, dripped into my beard and down my chin. Within seconds of leaving the mother tree, the peach was in my mouth, and it was becoming part of my body. To merely say "the fruit was fresh" is not enough to explain the sensation I felt: this fruit was still alive when it touched my lips.

I heard Laurie's boots thump as she came into the house at twilight, calling for me, not seeing me hidden beneath the peach tree. I wiped the juices from my chin, then went in to the house and greeted her. She was dusty and sweaty, her blond hair trailing down every which way, but she seemed happy about her ride on old Sunbeam.

"Mmm, something smells good . . . ," she said as she kissed me. "Let me change out of these riding clothes, and I'll be back with you in a moment."

While she left for the bedroom, I peeked in the oven and saw that the cobbler was done, its golden brown crust stained with sizzling peach juices. I turned the oven off and let the cobbler cool on the counter under a kitchen towel. Then I grabbed another kitchen towel to take outdoors, just as Laurie was coming down the hall, dressed only in her bathing suit and a white cotton blouse.

"I'd love to cool off in the cattle tank," she said, referring to the little pool we kept filled next to the orchard.

"Sure, but as soon as we cool off, let me blindfold you and offer you a treat."

"Blindfold me? As long as you make sure it's a treat and not a trick," she smiled, wondering if she should trust her live-in prankster.

We both splashed into the pool as the last light of day diminished. I had brought to the poolside two glasses of chardonnay from the Sonoita vineyards an hour southeast of us. We sipped wine and relaxed. Soon the cool air of evening brought the fragrances of citrus, mint, peaches, and night-blooming cactus to our noses. As we told one another of the day's ups and downs, our skin chilled in the breeze, so we got out of the cool water, covered with goose bumps. I grabbed the little kitchen towel and a larger beach towel and wrapped the latter around Laurie, drying her off and hugging her at the same time.

"Okay," she said cautiously, "I guess I'm as ready to be blindfolded as I will ever be. . . ."

I took the kitchen towel and placed it over her eyes, then tied it behind her head. I lightly held her shoulders, and slowly spun her around until she did not know which direction she faced. I held her hand and placed my arm around her, then walked her in a circuitous route through all the plumes of floral fragrances in our backyard. Finally I brought her to the lawn chair under the peach tree, and helped her sit down slowly, without any of the branches brushing against her.

"Here's where you'll have to trust me. I'm going to place something to your lips that I'd like you to taste. If you don't want to, just say so, but I just tasted it myself a little while ago, and it was delicious."

"Ohhh, this better be good. Okay, I'll trust you."

I picked one of the peaches, dipped it in a bowl of water, and cut it in half, plucking out the pit. Then I placed the fleshy side of the peach up against her lips and gave it a little squeeze.

"Juices!" she squealed. "Peach? Yes, peach. I guess I knew that the fruit was nearly ripe, but I hadn't gotten around to picking any yet. . . ."

"Taste. I'll hold."

She tentatively bit into the tree-ripened peach. A smile of relief and pleasure broke across her face. I took the towel from her head. Laurie took the peach with both hands and ate it all.

"Let me do it to you. You sit here and close your eyes."

I obeyed, as she prepared a peach for me. As its taste burst across my lips, I remembered what fruits tasted like when I was a child—it was as though I tasted them with my tongue, my lips, my nose, my chin, and all the skin that their juices dripped across. Their flavors lingered inside and outside my mouth after the fruit was swallowed. It now felt—or tasted—that same way again.

I pulled up another lawn chair, brought out the rest of the bottle of wine, and moved our two wine glasses over from the edge of the pool. The sky was moonless and filled with stars. We leaned back in our chairs, sipping wine and plucking peaches from the branches above us, dipping them in the bowl of water, pitting them, and eating them on the spot. We ate one peach after another, seeking the perfectly ripe ones, but also savoring the flavors of a few musky, almost fermented overripe fruit, and a few slightly green ones. Between fruits we would clear our palates with a sip of wine.

"This one tastes piquant but fruity, with a lingering aftertaste of something that grew of a tree," I recited to Laurie, trying to parody a pompous wine taster we had once met.

"Well, this one tastes like chardonnay." Laurie smirked, and as I looked over at her, I noticed that she had dunked a piece of peach into her half-filled wine glass. She leaned over and kissed me, and wine dribbled from her mouth to mine.

"Let's sleep out under these stars," I suggested. I helped her up from her chair, and walked with her over to where we kept some sleeping bags and foam pads on the back patio. She leaned against me ever so slightly as we walked barefoot, in the dark, onto the patio. I opened the screen door to the bedroom, and rescued two pillows, while Laurie laid down the pads and unrolled the flannel-lined bags next to one another.

We slipped our feet into the bags but kept them unzipped, open to the night sky. It was an evening for smelling the aroma of night-blooming flowers, hearing night moths, and maybe even bats arriving at the palest of blossoms, and watching the Milky Way swirl, pulse, and thrum while we held on, clutching, caressing, and steadying each other. At last we gasped as two shooting stars flashed through the heavens at the same time and fell to the horizon. As we slept, the hawkmoths circled around us, visiting every silky blossom within our reach.

A few minutes before the summer's sunlight hurled itself into the backyard, I stirred with the sound of turkeys, and remembered that I had never removed the cobbler from under the towel on the counter. As I got up, Laurie pulled the pillow over her head and tried to sleep a while longer. I went inside and put on some clothes. I looked at the cobbler: It was fine.

I tucked it into the fridge, then went back outside where Laurie was still deep in sleep. I fed and watered the turkeys and surveyed the orchard.

There was a wine bottle, two wine glasses, three towels, dozens of peach pits, Thoreau's *Wild Fruits,* and photocopies of a couple of papers from *Science* magazine that someone had sent me. The papers were blowing around, unread, lodging themselves underneath the peach and apricot trees. As I picked them up and took them inside, I glanced at their contents, trying to put their pages back in order. One was about geographic patterns of endangered species: Its maps suggested that the agricultural regions that formerly supported the highest levels of wild plant diversity now have the greatest number of endangered species. As monoculture fragmented the heterogeneity of habitats in these regions, more and more wild foods and medicines had become rare.

The second article struck me as curious. It was a summary of opinion surveys querying Americans and Europeans about their acceptance of biotechnology, especially their level of comfort for genetically engineered medicines, crops, and foods. Comparing the surveys, it was clear that Europeans were much more concerned about the sudden presence of genetically modified organisms in their fields, pharmacies, and supermarkets than Americans were. The Europeans feared that these new products might be risks to their own health, to that of wildlife, and to the environment as a whole. Americans, for the most part, were not aware of potential risks—allergies or inadvertent damage to wildlife—associated with these products.

It seemed as though this issue was hardly on Americans' radar screens, either in 1995 or in the second survey in 1999. And yet, the authors of the *Science* report comparing the surveys simply assumed that Americans were less fearful of genetically modified foods because they were more science literate than Europeans. This puzzled me, since I didn't know many Americans who were conversant with the promises and perils of genetically engineered (GE) crops. All I knew was that "better living through chemistry" had been sold to us by DuPont and its likes before, without any mention of the perils and pitfalls.

As I read through the last few pages of the report, I pondered its conclusions. How could most Americans understand even the most basic advances associated with genetic engineering when I can hardly keep up with them, even with my long-standing interest in agricultural sciences? How can most of us even shape ethical responses to all these technological advances, given that they are changing agriculture so rapidly? Do most consumers know or care whether the peaches they have eaten contain genes that were transferred from other plants, from microbes, or even from animals? Have they heard that Brazil nut genes inserted in soybeans can cause food allergies in infants who ingest them in their baby formula? Do they care whether "supergenes" to promote rapid plant growth in canola-oil-producing rapeseed have been found in fieldside weeds, as a result of inadvertent hybridization between the genetically modified crop and its weedy relatives? (A year later, I would learn that concern among Americans was rapidly approaching that of Europeans, and the Americans who were most concerned about the risks of genetically modified crops were among the most educated, science-literate individuals interviewed.) As I finished off the last page of *Science* that had been floating around the yard during the night, I vowed to learn more about how grave these potential risks might be, and whether they were associated with only a few biotechnologies, or many. If there were already genetically modified organisms in my kitchen cabinet and medicine kit, I wanted to know what perils they potentially posed to my health, or to the herbs and wildlife living around me.

As these weighty questions first crossed my mind, I had no idea that they would occupy much of my time over the coming summer and fall. They seemed remote, intellectually ponderous, but not much related to the task immediately before me: finding out which wild fruits might be ripening next. I was brought back into the lovely world before me by a voice rising up from under the white sheets on the patio: "Peach cobbler! Peach cobbler! Did you say that you had some homemade peach cobbler to share with me?"

II

Summer

The Fertile Months

Chapter Six

Saguaro Fruit
and Cactus Icons

I felt it on my skin, down to my bones, from the very first light of the morning: The world had heated up. It was not merely a matter of higher temperatures. With the shorter nights of summer, the sun had warmed the ground beneath us for many more hours and had barely cooled off by the time I awakened at five in the morning. Because the walls of the house reradiate heat most of the night, Laurie and I had opted to sleep outside ever since the evening of ripened peaches. We sometimes spread ourselves out on cots, sometimes hung in hammocks, or sometimes curled up in the half-opened sleeping bags on pads placed adjacent to my pollinator garden. Each morning carpenter bees, gourd bees, and hummingbirds stirred us from sleep, thrashing about in flowers for nectar while it was still twilight.

As I heated my morning tea, I watched the bees and hummers drink from the thick, cool nectar pools in the cups of flowers. Then, as brilliant beams of light hit the tops of trees above me, I went out to run through the desert grasslands surrounding our home, encountering king snakes and coral snakes and patch-nosed snakes heading back to their burrows. The sun had burned its way over the eastern horizon, and the snakes knew it was time to rest in their air-conditioned refuges dug deep below where its rays can penetrate.

When I ran, I noticed that the last few flowers found in full blossom the week before were now spent, and they were rapidly forming fruits. Each sequential blooming seemed shorter, or perhaps more accelerated. I had hardly found those first few yuccas in bloom, when it seemed that they were all on their way out. I rescued the very last one along my running route one morning, gleaned the last of its thick white petals off its stalk, and this time boiled them and drained them. Added in with *nopalitos*—despined strips of prickly pear pads—and the three kinds of oregano I'd grabbed from my dooryard garden, they gave my duck-and-turkey egg omelette a boost of photosynthetic freshness this morning. It tasted as though I were eating a meal just one step removed from sunlight. It was in this manner that many of my summer days began sunnyside up. In these early morning hours, I tried to regain a sense of the foragers' and farmers' lives, trying to connect with the land through the kind of pursuits that had been obliterated over the lifespans of Chuck and my mother. I wanted to do something more than merely chronicle the decline of foraging and farming traditions; I wanted to ensure their persistence and revitalization. And yet a goal such as this was impossibly enormous; I had to find a way to break it down into tangible tasks, or else it would overwhelm me.

By six in the morning, I had latched a cactus-collecting pole to the roof rack on my Blazer and driven down to a cactus-gathering camp in the valley. It was the one where I had been visiting O'odham friends for two decades running. I had first learned how to pick saguaro fruit off the towering arms of columnar cactus from a mischievous old lady named Juanita Ahill, who labored here with her *kuipoḍ* cactus pole for more than fifty years.

cutting saguaro

The old lady had left this sunny world behind, but I still checked in with one of her kin, Stella, who kept the seasonal camp alive in much the same spirit that Juanita did. Stella Tucker Wilson was closer to my own age but just as prone to joking as Juanita. A full-time cook at a nearby school for O'odham children, Stella moved out of her home to camp here among the cacti for several weeks each summer. Today I brought her barrel cactus candy and some mescal; she told me to help myself to her first pickings of fruit, for she had already been making the rounds among the cacti this morning.

"You should have been here yesterday, there were so many ripe ones," Stella sighed as she dropped off one load of fruit and headed back out into the desert. As I watched her walk through all the stickers and thorns, it was clear that Stella had been comfortable meandering her way through the desert scrub since she was a little girl. Now fully grown, large framed, and beautiful, Stella talked aloud as she wandered around looking for ripe fruit, speaking as if she were talking to the cacti themselves.

"Oh, you're ripening so fast, some of you are fermenting right up there on top of the cactus. Why are you trying to make wine on your own?"

It seemed that whenever I went out to the cactus camp, I encountered someone who had heard of eating cactus fruit but had never tried doing it. They came to ask about the flavor, perhaps too shy at first to ask for a taste. But trying to explain what saguaro fruit tastes like was a little like explaining lovemaking to a virgin: I groped for decent analogies but none of them seemed adequate:

Yes, I said, they are as juicy as watermelon or peaches, but the texture is nothing like either. Yes, they have seeds embedded in them like figs and kiwis, but they are black and shiny, somewhat crunchy.

I found myself pausing, sighing, knowing that what I had just said was altogether inadequate. As the tourists sensed that there was more to hear, I stopped trying to explain away cactus fruit, and Stella flashed a knowing look at me, as if she too had tried and decided that it was hopeless. Even comparisons to prickly pear fruit or tunas didn't do justice to the columnar cactus fruit known in Spanish collectively as pitahayas; they have more of a winelike flavor and less of a mucilaginous texture than their pad-forming kin do. The slightly fermented ones had an after-taste all their own. Their juices sizzled and bubbled on my tongue in a manner that reminded me of champagne. I thought of what my friend Carlos Martínez del Río said about the white-winged doves that we found roosting and drinking around the tops of saguaros on mornings like this: "To say in scientific terms that the doves are utilizing the water and energy of saguaro nectar and fruit for most of their own metabolic needs does not explain what is occurring. The doves, isotropically at least, are literally *becoming* saguaros."

I watched the doves dipping their grayish heads into cactus blossoms, or plucking away at the seeds in the blood-red cactus fruit. There is a little patch of red on their facial feathers, as if they'd been stained with the crimsons of saguaro fruit for so long that a red patch had been engraved onto their genes. The desert's doves had indeed become shaped from saguaros, and by saguaros; their beak length was different than that of any other white-winged doves, probably because of their need to poke a certain depth into cactus flowers and fruit for their sustenance. As I thought about the doves, I caught sight of Stella again, humming under her breath an O'odham song about saguaro wine bringing summer rains. Her connection with these cacti was orally rather than genetically transmitted, but it seemed just as strong. Her culture had shaped itself around these cacti, in story, song, ceremony, and sustenance.

Stella had gone wandering out among the cacti once more, intent on picking enough fruit for syrup making before the sun got so high in the sky that looking up at twenty-foot-tall cacti was no longer enjoyable. I chose a different route so as not to edge in on her harvesting area, and walked across the road, crossing a fallen-down barbed-wire fence that marked the boundary between two federal agencies' domains.

Picking up an old footpath on the other side of the fence, I found an old harvesting pole of spliced-together cactus ribs, wrapped tightly with rusty bailing wire. The pole was fifteen feet long with a wire loop on its end, which allowed me to encircle a ripe fruit and deftly knock it off its attachment to a cactus arm ten feet above my head. I temporarily swapped it for the pole I had brought along from home atop my Blazer. As I caught the falling fruit with the bowl in my other hand, I was amazed at how well designed this old pole was compared to the one I lashed together in my own workshop. I realized that it was just the kind of ergonomic design that Juanita had been using, ten years before, around the last time I saw her out at camp.

I had stumbled upon the archaeology of an old friendship, still well preserved in the dry heat of the desert. A decade had gone by, but the rust had not weakened the bailing wire, and the termites had not decomposed the poles. The desert's very dryness had protected Juanita's legacy, her tool kit for reaching up into cactus heaven and sending its heavenly fruit down to earth.

I remembered then how Juanita had demonstrated the use of the most local of all technologies for opening up the leathery skin of the cactus fruit. When the recently withered flower of the saguaro was still attached to the ripened fruit, you could snap it off the bottom of a fruit just like you could a stem off a pumpkin. The breakage at the brittle base of the dried-up flower was razor sharp and stiff enough to slice into the side of the blushing fruit with the precision of a jackknife.

Making an incision along the side of the fruit, I splayed it open with my thumbs, and plucked an egg-shaped mass of juicy pulp onto my palm. I popped the whole thing into my mouth, closed my eyes, and savored its succulence.

As I sampled this first fruit of the season, I placed the opened skin on the ground, faceup to the sky, as Juanita had shown me years before. Do that, she told me, and the rains will come good and strong. Forget to offer sustenance to the sky, she warned me, and you will suffer through a miserable summer of drought. And so I did that in memory of her.

Later, after I had harvested enough for the morning, I walked back to find Stella. I noticed that there were many fruit skins opened up to the sky scattered around the camp. Stella too had remembered to bring the rains along. Without mentioning it to each other, we had participated in the same cycle, propelled by its wheel of hope.

We believed that the cacti were something akin to lightning rods, cloud seeders, and swamp coolers. After a rainless spring the clouds began to build up only when the blushing cactus fruits appeared. Shadows came over them, and the cactus fruit began to ripen more rapidly so as not to get soggy and spoiled by an early downpour. The red fruit cascaded down from the tops of the cacti on their own, or we would pluck them down.

Either way a mess of seeds inevitably found its way under nearby bushes, ready to germinate just as the monsoons came on strong. These torrential downpours came just in time to save the sprouted seeds from withering heat. If the rains were sustained and the rabbits didn't find them, these sprouts would grow into giant cacti, producing fruit our great-great-grandchildren could eat 120 years from now.

Rehearsing this cycle in my mind as I approached the camp, I worried that I had become a little too anthropocentric, a little too teleological for the science geek I was supposed to be. And so I turned the metaphor inside out: Perhaps I had become just one more way a saguaro seed got to the right place to germinate, to make more cacti. My worldview instead became "cactocentric": saguaros produced delicious fruits merely to attract a number of us in the local faunal community to disperse their seeds, to ensure their regeneration. And speaking of seeds, I might as well have conceded that I was merely a means for sperm to generate more sperm.

I arrived in camp with a big bowl full of fruit pulp ready to give to Stella. Her sidekick, Ely, an African American from Virginia, was brewing a pot of coffee on the wood fire. I offered him most of the fruit for their syrup making, taking just enough with me to satisfy me for a lunch.

"Ely, you mind giving these to Stella for me? I'll come back around this evening to see her."

"No trouble at all. We'll be having our happy hour here just before sunset."

I took a circuitous route home after a morning of picking cactus fruit, past Saguaro National Park and the movie studio called Old Tucson, on toward the local post office near the Yaqui Indian village of New Pascua. When I got beyond the park, I began to notice sign after sign with the saguaro cactus used as part of a logo, as part of a billboard-size image of the Wild West, or as an icon of the desert itself. That big cartoon cactus with outstretched arms was beckoning folks to come to the desert, to buy real estate here, and to live a Sun Belt–style life of leisure. Was it the same cactus that I had just walked among, whose fruit I had eaten?

When I came indoors and opened the fridge to get something cold to drink, I realized that there were all kinds of cactus in my food supply already, or at least their labels suggested so. Laurie and I had unconsciously purchased the locally brewed Palo Verde Pale Ale with a cactus and a desert mountain on its label, Saguaro brand potato chips, and "Ass-Kickin' Black Bean Dip," which featured the hind end of a mule and a two-armed cactus as its logo. Another, multiarmed saguaro stands tall next to the bar code and ingredients inventory for the salsa, which include black beans (probably grown in Michigan or New York), water (from fossil groundwater below Glendale, Arizona), tomato paste (probably grown in Sonora or Arizona hothouses), honey, salt, habanero pepper (originally from the Caribbean), red chili (from New Mexico), garlic, and spices. But no cactus juice, from saguaros or any of their kin.

Saguaro cacti seemed ubiquitous in the advertising of food, fiber, and frolic in the American West; they were even embossed into the leather cover of the special edition of James Michener's historic novel *Texas,* even though no saguaros grew there naturally. But who besides biogeographic sticklers cared about such details? What matters (at least to the ad man and the real estate broker) was that the sight of cacti made us feel as though we were in the Wild West. The West, of course, was big business, as I saw when I passed twenty cars turning into the cowboy movie set of Old Tucson on my way home. The human population of southern Arizona's cities has grown a hundredfold since World War II, thanks to the lure of the cactus.

What struck me odd was the way Westerners treated real saguaros. Our most notorious exemplar was David Grunman, a gun-toting drunk who stood under a huge saguaro, and shot up at its arms, only to have one of the two-ton appendages break loose and fall on his head. Fortunately for Grunman, he was instantly killed; it would have been hard for him to explain how he received the tattoolike markings left on his face by the thousands of cactus spines that pierced his skin.

In addition to shooting them and dressing them up in Santa's caps for Christmas, my neighbors in Tucson have another peculiar ritual they engage in with saguaros. They uproot, transport, and reroot thousands of saguaros each year as they try to accommodate the many folks who fall in love with the sunsets and stickers of cactus country. The greatest human migration of any fifty-year period in human history was the post–World War II emigration of Yankees and Mexicans to the Sun Belt of southern Arizona, California, and adjacent states. Cacti have become both their icon and their curse.

Developers still clear about forty acres of saguaros off Sonoran Desert lands each day to make room for retirement homes, golf courses, and shopping malls. They salvage as many of the "transplantable" cacti as they can, and resell them for as much as twenty dollars per linear foot of trunk height; more if the specimen has many curvilinear arms or weird fanlike mutations. Then they plant them back into the rocky ground in front of "senior living" subdivisions, where most of them die within a matter of a few years. The transplants seldom bear fruit or leave behind progeny. They are a perfect symbol for Arizona's "retirement communities"—senior living—that is, those gated developments that do not allow any children to live within them. Although Arizona's Sun City, Anthem, and Green Valley call themselves "communities," they are not by any moral definition. Their elderly immigrants to the Sun Belt refuse to pay school taxes in this state because they have already done so elsewhere. The barren, dying saguaros transplanted to a seedling-free spot outside their gates will not survive much longer than they will.

And yet saguaros are no more than a symbol, and certainly not sustenance, to most of my neighbors. Does it matter how long transplanted saguaros live? Does it really matter much how many of us eat fresh saguaro fruit pulp, or dry and grind their seeds into a nutritious baby food? Does it matter that Stella's grandparents made a sacred fermented wine from saguaro fruit juice in clay pots to celebrate the desert's new year, when the summer rains began? Does it matter that they too—Stella's ancestors, the Tohono O'odham—have also become little more than icons in most Arizonans' minds, hardy folk who once walked with pots and baskets full of cactus fruit balanced on their heads?

I kept the refrigerator open a little longer and purged it of all its products that carried saguaros on their labels without having saguaro juices in their ingredients. I emptied their contents into the bin going to the food bank, or into the compost, and soaked their glass jars in hot sudsy water until their labels slipped off. I went to the pantry and did the same there. I never again wanted to eat anything that commodified cactus as an image without contributing to the conservation of cactus as a living thing.

I returned to the cactus camp eight hours later, and sure enough, Stella and Ely were sitting around a picnic table, nursing cold beers. Now that the day's work was done, Stella had untied her long black hair. It cascaded down around her shoulders, shining in the late afternoon light. She sat leaning her elbows on the table across from Ely. She was barefoot, wearing a loose-fitting dress, and obviously exhausted after hours of work in the heat. Ely, lean and somewhat more tightly strung, was in jeans and an oversize T-shirt, one hand scratching the black and gray curls on his head. He then began tapping the table with his fingers, tapping them right next to a little cardboard box.

After chatting with them a few minutes, I noticed why Ely was so preoccupied by the box: There was a baby pack rat inside it. The O'od-ham call this desert wood rat *koson,* but it is more like a little rabbit to them than a rat. It has probably been decades since O'odham folks have caught and eaten them, but *koson* roasts were once a big deal in these parts. This one, I soon learned, had been rescued while Ely was trying to evict an entire clan from a tumbledown ramada just forty feet from the camp.

"Those pack rats were just making us too much trouble, stealing our spoons and salt shakers and even our car keys and other such things," Ely explained, shaking his head sadly. "So I went over there to roust them out, which I did. The papas and mamas was running every which ways, but then I saw this little one, and I couldn't let it just suffer there all alone. You think it will make it?"

"Well, it has gotta get back under the care of the older ones sooner or later. You know where they went?"

Stella nodded her chin toward another, more distant heap of fallen-down camp debris. Ely pointed in the same direction.

"Does it seem like it's okay?"

"Oh, I suppose so. We've been feeding it cactus seeds and giving it cactus juice to drink. It's not acting weak or nothing like it's dying."

"Well, look, let's just take him over there and make a little shelter, then check him every so often, maybe see if the others have come for him."

After fretting over the baby pack rat all afternoon, they seemed relieved to have someone else come up with a plan. I took it out to the pile of boards, tar paper, and wire, and constructed a low-walled corral for it, one that mature pack rats could enter but babies couldn't escape from on their own. I placed some fruit pulp in with the furry ball of life, then let it be.

When I came back to the table, they had already opened a beer for me as if in payment. I laughed. "You know, Ely, I'm raising a few turkeys now, but I've always wanted to manage a pack rat ranch. Stella's ances-tors used to grill those little suckers just like they were bunnies, or just like those people in South America who roast up guinea pigs. You wanna become a rat boy with me and herd pack rats from horseback when I get my ranch?"

"I'll pass on that one," he chuckled, "but then if you ever want a partner in the turkey-raising business, you can count on me. I not only reared a bunch of them back in Virginia, I had a business smoking them for restaurants before I became a chef myself."

"Well, I got a smoker in my backyard, but only seven poults at this time. I'd sure like to know how to smoke them right when the time comes."

"That's it—most people don't know how. You gotta prepare them for smoking, changing their feed from grains to more greens the last few weeks before you butcher them. Then you baste and inject them to get the meat as moist as it can get, or else they ain't worth anything at all. Most folks have never tasted a turkey smoked right. They think that dry, flaky, crumbly meat is all you can get from a turkey."

"I've tried smoking a few store-bought ones, which I baste with olive oil and garlic, but they still get dry."

"Of course they're dry. Most of those store-bought turkeys have been finished off with that dry mash full of chemical additives. Don't you go near that stuff. The meat ends up tasting like a drugstore. You give them fresh greens—pusley and goosefoot and such—and then you got to give a lot of time to basting them and filling them with juices for at least twelve hours before you smoke them."

"What do you use as your baste?" I asked.

Stella laughed. "You think he's gonna tell you that? He won't even tell me that! I've been a cafeteria cook for more than ten years, but this man's a real chef. And that means he don't tell any of his secrets."

"Now, come on, I'm not that tight lipped." He grinned. "But since you've been a cook so long, what do you think is the essential ingredient for a baste for smoking turkey, or for that matter, any other slow-cooking meat?"

Stella sipped on her beer, and then quipped, "I ain't guessing, cause

I'm gonna be wrong. Whatever I say you're gonna say that's not what chefs do. Gary, you go 'head and guess. You'll be wrong too."

"Garlic juice?"

He shook his head, laughing.

"Chili? Lemon and vinegar? Olive oil?"

"Wrong again! Dry mustard!"

"Dry mustard?" Stella and I looked at each other as if Ely had come from another planet. We use dry mustard now and then, but neither of us would ever call it an essential.

"All right, that's not my only ingredient, but I don't like to up and tell my trade secrets to everyone. . . . Well, I'll do it for you as long as you invite me over for some of that turkey. After you've butchered it but before you cook it, you let it set inside your 'frigerator for a day, its cavities filled to the brim with beer and mustard. Some may add salt and pepper, chili powder, or olive oil, but the main thing is giving that dead bird enough beer to keep him moist, and enough mustard to bring out his own natural flavor. Once you taste it done this way, you ain't never gonna go back to something else."

As I finished the beer, I realized that I hadn't been home to feed those turkeys for hours. In this heat they could have roasted on their own.

"It's turkey-herding time back on the ranch," I said, putting on my cowboy hat. "Gotta get them fed and watered. Thanks for the beer and the smoking lesson."

"Thanks for the fruit this morning and for the help with our little pack rat problem. Look, here's a little jar of saguaro syrup to take home with you. Why don't you check on the little rascal over there before you go home."

"Okay," I said, picking up the jar full of smoky-flavored, blood red cactus syrup. I dipped my index finger into the jar. "Ooh, that would be goood for making a barbecue sauce."

"He's already bugging me to start a little business with him doing just that," Stella moaned. "Don't encourage him. I'd have to stir that kettle of fruit for days to get enough for him to mix into big batches of barbecue sauce."

Ely and I burst out laughing at her righteous anger, then walked over together to check on the baby pack rat.

"He's gone! And I don't see any snake tracks or evidence of other predators."

"Hallelu-jah!" Ely laughed. "His mamma's probably found him and is licking all that cactus juice off his lips!"

Later in the evening I sat on my back porch under a yellow bug light, reading. I read the kind of article that I doubt Ely had ever seen—one in an obscure mailing called the *American Livestock Breeds Conservancy News*—but I am sure that it would interest him as much as it did me. It was entitled "The Perilous State of Turkey Varieties" and was written by livestock scientist Dr. Robert Hawes, who had recently retired from the University of Maine. Hawes conducted a survey of the domesticated turkey varieties remaining in the United States, cognizant of the fact that the U.S. Department of Agriculture and all land-grant universities in this country had abandoned their conservation and breeding programs for turkeys several years before. He found that only twenty-three small hatcheries produce 90 percent of all turkey poults and eggs distributed to backyard poultry keepers in the United States, and that these hatcheries now produce only ten breeds, eight of them extremely rare. Each of the seven rarest breeds are maintained by fewer than a dozen hatcheries, which annually produce no more than six thousand individuals of all these breeds combined. Howe concluded that the genetic richness of domesticated turkeys—the only livestock species North America gave to the world—is in grave danger of extinction:

> The non-commercial, colored varieties of the domesticated turkey are not used in the industry, and many of them have become rare. . . . Today, Large White Turkeys reportedly account for more than

90% of the commercial market. In fact, there are three international mega-companies who own over 90% of the breeding stock in the world . . . Nicholas Turkeys, British United Turkeys, and Hybrid Turkeys. These companies have their major farms in the United States, Canada, England and Scotland.

I went from the porch into the backyard, where my bronze turkeys were already up on their perch, resting beneath the downturned branches of the pepper tree. Just five hatcheries in the United States kept naturally mating birds of this feather in the hands of hobbyists like me. The birds stirred as I approached them, chirped a little, then settled down again after they heard my voice. As I fed them each evening, they gathered around me, nuzzling me with an apparent affection I hardly deserved. And yet I was among only three dozen members of the American Livestock Breeds Conservancy still interested in being involved in the breeding of minor varieties of turkeys. The next summer I hoped to start in earnest with two separate populations of rare breeds. This summer I had simply taken a step in competently raising turkeys; they would serve only as a source of meat this year, not of genes. These turkeys will become my Phoenix birds: smoke and ash this year, new life the next. Ely had fueled my interest in smoking turkey meat, and I hoped that the diligence to be an accomplished turkey breeder would rise out of the smoke. But I began to see through his eyes that keeping birds was not enough if at the same time we lost the old knowledge, the old ways of smoking meat. It didn't matter what breed of bird was being eaten if it was poorly raised, poorly prepared, or poorly presented to hungry stomachs and minds. The savory secrets kept by men like Ely will keep the rest of us from being satisfied with what large meatpackers offer. They will remind us that the quality of a food is derived not merely from its genes and the greens that fed it, but from how it is prepared and cared for all the way until it reaches our mouths.

Chapter Seven

Mesquite Tortillas and Duck Eggs

Stella and Ely had given me hope, hope that there were many others within my neighborhood and county who were happily engaged in the pursuits of native food production and processing. But as the summer went on, I became less and less sure that I had very many neighbors who were also out there foraging and farming. Most of them must have been hidden from sight, or there simply weren't many folks nearby who were as preoccupied with these pursuits as I was. I'd drive around with my daughter, putting up fliers in all the country stores, suggesting the swap of hand-harvested goods. Laurie placed an ad for me in La Abra's local weekly, seeking eggs, wild game, homemade cactus jam, and the like. As June rolled on, those ads helped us encounter just a few kindred souls: one neighbor who bootlegged prickly pear wine and beer, another who raised turkeys, and a third who kept a covey of domesticated quail. Fortunately we now had our eyes and ears open to the undercurrents running through my community like invisible tides. We began to find other foragers, farmers, and food producers by "accident," or better, serendipity.

When I first met him, Javier was parked on the roadside eight miles below our home. He had a table set up in front of the local clinic, and he sat under a parasol attached to the back of his lawn chair. I had stopped because of the hand-lettered FRESH TORTILLAS FOR SALE sign he had set up right next to the pavement.

"*Me gustaría comprar dos docenas.*" I said to him, putting down three dollar bills. He passed one back to me, then handed me two bags full of tortillas the size of dinner plates. The bags felt warm to my touch. I opened one bag, pulled out a soft, floury wheat tortilla, folded it in half, and sampled it right then and there. It nearly melted in my mouth.

"*Que milagro!*" I blurted out.

"*Gracias, mi amigo.*" And then he added in perfect English, "Thank you, my friend."

"Thank *you,* they're very fresh."

"No, I will thank for you my wife and my daughter, Esperanza. They don't let me sell their tortillas unless they are fresh and warm like this. As soon as they get them done, they send me out of the house with them."

"Do you live nearby?"

"Well, we have a place off Sandario on Calle Lucido, but we are from a little ranch down by Agua Prieta, Sonora."

"I thought so. They seem like the kind of tortillas I've eaten in the *zona serrana* of eastern Sonora."

"Yes, that's right. We don't make those *gorditas* they do elsewhere."

"Well, I hope I can buy some more from you."

"Well, if you don't find me here, look for me down on Sandario about five in the evening. You know, by the mailboxes there where you turn off Ajo Way."

"That's on my way home from work. We'll look for each other. *Nos vemos pronto.*"

I did look for that man and his pickup truck for days on end, without any luck. And then, the following Saturday, I saw a lovely dark-haired woman parked in a car at the same place Javier had parked. She was also selling tortillas, under his parasol.

"Are you Esperanza?" I asked.

"How do you know my name?"

"Is that man who sells tortillas here your father?"

"His name is Javier. Yes he is. Would you like to buy some more?"

"Yes, I would . . . I think they're the best tortillas I ever had. Do you only make wheat tortillas?"

"We don't make corn. Is that what you mean?"

"No, I'm not interested in corn tortillas. Let me show you what I mean." I went over to my car and brought out a twelve-pound bag of mesquite flour and a two-pound box of grain amaranth flour. I did not mention that the early Catholic priests in Mexico banned the traditional use of amaranth grain as a ceremonial tithing by the Aztecs. Until the ban families under Aztec rule would provide bushels of grain that the emperor's workers would mix with wild honey and the blood of humans ritually sacrificed on feast days. They would shape this sticky mix into statues of the gods, and called them candies of happiness, or *alegrias*.

"I know your mother probably doesn't make tortillas with these, but if anyone could make good tortillas with them, I bet she could. This is flour from the *péchita*, you know, the *mesquite*, and this is from the *alegria* seeds that they pop and make into candies. It's called *amaranto*, like the greens of one of the *quelites*."

"Sure, I know *péchita* and those *quelites*. They are all over our ranch. I know my mother used to eat both when she was a child, so she might be willing to try making tortillas with them. Why do you want them?"

I said nothing for a moment, not knowing how to explain myself. "I'm kinda on a special diet."

"Like for diabetes or something?"

"Like that. I am trying to eat the native foods that lower blood sugars and cholesterol, but also because I'm trying to eat only what grows around here."

"Well, I can't guarantee you that we can do it, but if you want me to take this home, we'll try."

"Thank you. If it works, I'd love to buy three or four dozen a week. Here's my phone number."

"We'll see. I just don't know. We'll see."

I received a call from Esperanza a week later. Her voice burst across the wire with excitement.

"We have some mesquite tortillas for you! We kept trying to make them different ways, but we finally got something I think you will like. The first ones were too brittle. Finally my father, who likes to join in experiments, he had us change to olive oil and to mix the masa differently. Where can I meet you to give them to you?"

"How about at the mailboxes on Sandario."

"Fine. We'll meet you there in fifteen minutes."

Javier and Esperanza were both there waiting for me when I arrived.

"We used up a lot of your flour in the trials, but I think we can make them on a regular basis without too much trouble," Javier explained in hesitant English. "They taste just like the foods my grandmother used to make with the *péchita,* the mesquite beans. Tell me, where do you get that flour?"

"For now I get it from a friend, Carlos Nagel, who has been working to market mesquite for years. But I have a special grinding mill that can break the seeds free from the flour in the *vainas,* the pods. I'll show it to you when it comes."

"That would be good, because I want to try to make my own. I am somewhat of a machinist. I mean, I design small machines to help me with my work."

"How much do I owe you?"

"You decide! We used up most of your flour," Esperanza said, gesturing her inability to even guess anything appropriate.

I gave them fifteen dollars and promised to bring them more flour. We decided when and where to rendezvous next, as if we had become partners in some crime against the commercial food lords. The clandestine transfer of hot tortillas outside the reach of the global economy. No checks, no receipts, no taxes, no food handler's permits.

I got back into the old Blazer, and opened up one of the bags. The unmistakable aroma of mesquite wafted into the air, filling the entire cab with its bouquet. I took out one tortilla and ate it. It was sweet and smoky, not as soft as a flour tortilla, but not as brittle as a wafer. It was like a Grandma Moses painting, a homemade masterpiece. I tenderly cradled these first warm bags of mesquite tortillas in my lap, the first evidence that an ancient desert food had been revived in my neighborhood.

If a native food tasted this good, why did it ever fall out of favor? When the Spaniards and Moors first encountered foods made from mesquite in their early explorations of American deserts, they thought its pods tasted like those of another legume tree found on the arid edges of the Mediterranean: the carob tree, also known as Saint John's bread. And so, they first referred to the mesquite tree in print by the name *algarroba,* derived from the more ancient Arabic term, *al-jarruba.* They initially recognized its food value and prized its richly hued heartwood for making church beams, furniture, and crosses. Today, however, most Americans think of mesquite only as something that imparts a smoky flavor to grilled steak and fish. What had happened in the interim?

It was hard to say why mesquite went into decline as a foodstuff in the nineteenth century, after ten thousand years of dominating desert diets in the New World. Over the last twenty years I have asked dozens of food historians, anthropologists, and ecologists why mesquite's popularity slipped away, but none of them have offered an airtight answer explaining away the winds of change. However, they all agree that somehow our ancient connection with mesquite as a food was off course by the nineteenth century, blown off the superhighway along which modern American society had chosen to drive.

Perhaps the simplest reason for mesquite's demise had nothing to do with the intrinsic taste, yield, or nutritional value of mesquite as a food. It simply became less and less in vogue for the *gente de razón,* the "civilized residents" of the desert Southwest, to eat wild foods. Both mesquite and amaranths became hardly more than fodder for their farm animals. As some farmers and ranchers grew wealthy, they used as a sign of their sophistication the fact that their own diets were based on something other than what sustained their livestock.

We were weird creatures, ones who habitually assert our otherness by distancing our tastes from those of other creatures. If hogs like mud baths, we must proclaim that taking mud baths is a piggish pursuit, even if the feel of mud on our bare skin was delicious. When Spanish missionaries observed Indians celebrating the emergence of amaranth greens by getting down on all fours and grazing on them while they were still attached to the earth, they themselves would not stoop to this same ecstatic pursuit. Instead, the priests condemned their brethren as "little more than wild animals." It did not matter that their own predecessors—the earliest monastics in the Middle East—also foraged on their hands and knees, delighted by the delicious wild greens their Lord blessed them with. Those monks believed that they were literally following Christ's instruction to imitate the birds of the air and herds of the field, and they took refuge in caves and trees to experience fully the sacredness all around them.

Amaranths and mesquite were once the most abundant, widely eaten wild foods during the summer months, but modern Christian sensibilities had suppressed their inclusion in the diets of desert dwellers over the last few centuries. I recalled the root meaning of *amaranth,* "the flower that does not fade," and only wished it had meant "the flour that did not fade away from use."

Nevertheless, the thrill of my encounter with Javier and Esperanza redoubled my drive to find other local food producers hidden in the fabric of my neighborhood. I soon became a devoted customer of "the Egg Lady," an attractive blond woman in her late thirties who always seemed to have a bunch of muscular men and boys resting on her couches when

I knocked at her door. There were always a couple of her sons or her husband's coworkers around, and they all seemed exceedingly comfortable in the nest she had made. And yet most of these guys seemed bewildered whenever I came to ask for eggs, as if they didn't know what I was talking about. Sometimes I wondered if I was the only man in the valley who responded to the EGGS FOR SALE signs at either end of Ms. Soto's circular driveway; the rest of the males around here seemed so smitten by her warmth and beauty that they had not even noticed her deep devotion to raising turkeys, ducks, chickens, and geese.

Each time I knocked Ms. Soto would soon appear from a back room and take me to a fridge filled with distinctive duck eggs, sizable turkey eggs, oversize goose eggs, colored Aracauna eggs, and little bantam eggs. The prices always seemed to change from one visit to the next, perhaps because each breed of poultry had its particular season. As I placed in her smooth, delicate hands a pile of quarters or a few crumpled dollar bills, Ms. Soto always told me to come more often, expressing disappointment that so many eggs were piling up in her fridge. She didn't know anyone else in the valley raising birds for eggs, and was glad to hear that I had picked up turkey keeping as an avocation. She offered me tips about how to deal with the peculiarities of my poults, still months away from being able to produce any eggs of their own.

There were other weekly contacts besides Javier, Esperanza, and the Egg Lady. They were a scattered, motley crew: the folks at the National Fruit Market at Twelfth and Ajo Way, whose vegetables and fruit came from a dozen farm towns within two hours' drive of South Tucson. The old Chinese grocery that sold venison from Globe, Arizona, one hundred miles northeast, and shrimp from—of all places, Gila Bend, Arizona—down the dry river from me another one hundred miles. The Rodriguez fish market, which featured Gulf of California catches brought in daily from Rocky Point, Sonora, which is Arizona's adopted seaport, since it lies within an hour of the international border. All this reminded me of simple fact: While I was busy obtaining four out of five of my meals within a half day's drive or a ten-day walk of my home, most of my fellow citizens in Arizona were sourcing four out of every five of their meals from distant lands. By 1980 Arizonans were already gaining less than a third of their food supplies from Arizona crops, livestock, poultry, and eggs. Since then the balance has shifted even further. The restaurant offerings planned for New Year's Eve 1999 in Phoenix, Arizona, were more like what my brothers shared with me at the Club Du Lubnan in the ancient Phoenician port of Juniye than they were like what Arizonans ate a century ago.

Nevertheless, I no longer doubted that there were others in my neighborhood, county, state, or country who preferred informal food exchange networks to purchasing groceries at supermarket chains. As Laurie and I spoke on the telephone with family neighbors and friends living in other regions of the continent, they would tell us of their delight in finding similar networks where they lived: a small harbor on the Atlantic seaboard where you could purchase fish directly from the boat on which it was caught; flea markets, swap meets, and garage sales where berries, jerked meat, and sour mash whiskey could be purchased out of the trunks of cars, amid used exercise equipment, paintings on velvet, and eight-track tapes of Elvis live in Las Vegas. Church bazaars where old farmers would auction off their home-cured hams, or a couple of spinsters would offer the sassafras root beer they had brewed. Without involving any advertising agencies, shipping firms, fancy packaging, or middleman markups, millions of pounds of American foods have been bought with cash in hand, bartered for, or given away as gifts every summer of our lives. It is the true commerce of the continent, the kind that Walt Whitman would have loved: these cactus pickers, turkey smokers, and egg gatherers, and all the fishmongers, ham curers, bootleggers, and mushroomers, all the root beer brewers, persimmon pluckers, ginseng diggers, clammers, nocturnal crawfish prowlers, and crab potters still out and about in the shallows, woods, and little fields, happily working the "land of ten million virgin farms—to the eye at present wild and unproductive . . . [but able to] last longer, fill the esthetic sense fuller, precede all the rest, and make North America's characteristic landscape."

And yet even Whitman himself worried what might happen to these little farms, orchards, woods, and wildlands if experts had their way. While in Washington, D.C., he had heard of those who wanted to clear away this characteristic landscape of small producers, to irrigate large swaths of the great American desert, in order to "grow enough wheat to feed the world." Somehow, a century after Whitman expressed his wariness about such schemes, a few little farms were still hanging on as they had since his own era, and others were being revitalized.

An hour before the summer sun burned off all the remaining moisture in their little fields and orchards, I arrived at Sehe-Ya Farms to walk around with Andrew and Nina Hipps, a young couple living on the edge of the Elfrida Valley, an hour and a half west of us. The valley was once the dry-farming hub of southern Arizona, prosperous and productive. When a decade of lower-than-average rain came to Elfrida in the fifties, that hub broke down, dried up, and blew away. It had become a scatter of a few working farms amid mostly foreclosed ones, retirement homes, and marginally profitable ranches. Many of the former "communities" in the area were now featured on maps as "ghost towns," the ghosts I guess being the spirits of farmers whose lives were foreclosed.

The Hippses lived and grew crops out near Cochise, a town named for the Apache warrior and not much more populated now than it had been during his own lifetime. Somewhere between the tenure of Cochise and that of the Hippses, its dryland farms boomed and then busted. I was grateful that a few farmers could somehow hang on to some of the land out there. It was the first time I had a chance to see the Hippses, although I would sometimes catch Nina and her kids as they delivered a box of homegrown vegetables to Laurie and me once a week. Because they grew crops at a slightly higher elevation than we did, the Hippses offered us vegetables, fruits, and nuts that we would have a hard time growing ourselves.

As I came through the gate at Sehe-Ya Farms, where they leased their land, I was surprised to find that they were only cultivating four acres of gardens and another of berries in the middle of a commercial pistachio orchard. Andrew was tending and harvesting the pistachios in exchange for the chance to try their hand at the gambling game called "CSA."

CSA stands for Community-Supported Agriculture, a farmer-to-consumer scheme that formally began in the United States in 1985, but one with a much longer track record in Japan, where *teikei* partnerships between farmers and consumer clubs began around 1965. In essence CSA consumers either pay growers a "futures" fee for fruits and vegetables or offer to work on the farm during planning, planting, and harvest in exchange for a weekly delivery of fresh produce during the seasons of their availability. In a little over a decade after the first CSA was launched in the northeastern United States, the concept had spread across the continent to more than a thousand farms in seven hundred communities. By their very structure CSAs offer more than just a direct supply-and-delivery system. The late Robyn Van En, who launched the American CSA movement at Indian Line Farm more than fifteen years ago, once highlighted their loftier goals in this manner:

> CSA members are supporting a regional food system, securing the agricultural integrity of their region, and participating in the community-building experience by getting to know their neighbors and who grows their food. . . . [But] CSA also helps bridge socio-economic gaps. . . . Knowing you like good, fresh food has nothing to do with money, status or where you live. Members range from people who use food stamps to those who pay extra to have their vegetables delivered. Together they guarantee that local farmers survive.

Given that philosophy, I was recently surprised to learn that the CSAs had come under attack from social critics who condemned CSAs as being unworkable for the poor. They argue that few low-income families have the slack to pay the preseason payments necessary to help spread the risks farmers would otherwise have to shoulder themselves. Families qualifying for welfare have indeed been prohibited from using their food stamps to participate in CSAs. This is because the government regards such preseason payments as "investment futures" on the upcoming season's crops rather than direct food purchases.

Regardless of this bureaucratic interpretation, some CSAs have not given up on the food stamp option, but in the meantime donate their surpluses to food banks in New York City and provide internships, sliding-scale share prices, and deferred payment to low-income members. Other CSAs quickly developed work-a-share options for neighbors with little or no cash income, or sponsored community gardens in vacant lots where the homeless congregate. Notwithstanding, critic Patricia Allen has continued to rail against CSA philosophy because it "tends to fetishize farming and elevate it over other forms of labor," as if fresh food appeals only to upper-income urban professionals and not to low-income families who, in addition to being consumers, may be farmworkers, packers, or processors of food themselves.

Unfortunately, in making such academic arguments such critics gloss over the fact that the government has categorized some of the managers and wage workers on small farms—including Andrew and Nina—as being among the "poor" in "low income brackets." As such, I doubt whether the Hippses and other CSA farmers are uncaring in their stance toward other low-income families. A lot of informal exchanges, handouts, and gleaning arrangements occur on CSA farms that never gets recorded in the formal ledgers of contracts and deliveries. And as the many new CSAs have gained some stability and slack to have time to collaborate with other folks interested in changing the food system, they have rapidly responded in more formal ways to the needs of the poor who live nearby them. Today numerous CSAs deliver fresh vegetables to inner-city residents associated with Just Food in New York City, the Hartford Food System in Connecticut, and similar projects in California's Bay Area. Within fifteen years of their emergence across the country, CSA memberships are actively discussing and dealing with such issues. Is the same level of compassion for the disenfranchised found at the National Corn Growers' Annual Convention or at board meetings of SYSCO, the largest institutional food supplier in the United States? Wherever Laurie and I traveled, we ran into folks involved with CSAs who were also involved in social and environmental justice issues. Health food was not their only concern; a healthy society was just as much an issue for them.

As Andrew escorted me around the garden and we gathered some tomatoes together, he spoke frankly about how hard it has been to jump-start his own dream of self-sufficiency. Sun-burned and athletic looking, Andrew was a recent transplant from Davis, California, where soils were richer and marketing easier, but he decided to move here with Nina for she had lived in southern Arizona for most of her life. Andrew farms simultaneously for his family and for the pistachio orchard owner, while Nina tends their little kids and drives baskets of fresh groceries into Tucson one day each week, and on another day, delivers them around the Elfrida Valley.

"At this point we're only sending out ten CSA baskets a week, getting twenty dollars for each of them," Andrew admitted, a bit disappointed that he had no time to market his goods on top of six to nine hours of farmwork a day. "So we're only clearing a hundred fifty dollars a week from the shares, if you only take into account our out-of-pocket expenses like gas for Nina's runs into town. Of course, we grow most of our own food and sell other vegetables and nuts and honey here at the house. But I don't think we can afford to do this next year . . . well, for a number of reasons."

One of those reasons was that Andrew and Nina could not afford to purchase the land they were farming, and developers were interested in purchasing it from the current owner so they could build retirement homes there. The same dilemma faced young people interested in farming wherever they sought land in America: Could they ever afford to pay what housing developers could pay for the same land? As a result we have witnessed as much as a million acres of arable land fall out of cultivation in a given year, and much of it will be built on rather than reclaimed by future farmers.

While Andrew continued talking about their meager income, the tough bargains with his landlord, the long hours, the high transportation costs, and the poorly defined markets, my mind drifted away from his accounting. I admitted to myself: I had never been much good at agricultural economics. I could never tally in my head all the loan values, expenditures, and income figures that most farmers must constantly keep in theirs. My eyes have glazed over every time I have had to study statistical summaries from the USDA's agricultural economists, a cadre of government workers who almost outnumber the small farmers remaining in this country. But Andrew's words did echo some bare economic facts that I had recently read in a USDA report (from 2000): The last year had been among the worst farmers had experienced for a century, and their anticipated income over the coming year was expected to be only 88 percent of their average annual earnings over the last decade.

Andrew's words reminded me of an obituarylike article I had recently seen in the newspaper. It listed the number of states that would be losing more than a thousand of their small farms this year. Arizona was not on that list; it did not have even a thousand small farms left by 1978, when I left the state's college of agriculture with my master's degree in growing beans.

I glanced at the bushel baskets in the back room of the Hipps household. The whole place was wonderfully cluttered with cabbages and king-size cucumbers, chilies and zucchini, melons and corn, snap beans and eggplants, tomatoes, pistachios, and berries. Laurie was partial to their melons, tomatoes, and eggplants; I devoured their zucchini, chili peppers, beans, and berries. Each basket was a different mix, each week a new surprise.

I paid Andrew and Nina for an extra batch of peppers and tender zucchini, and started home. As I drove, I turned Andrew's words over and over in my head: what he had said about the time investment needed to do it right, sobered by the many trials and errors he and Nina had suffered, just as Javier and Esperanza had. There were like-minded folks all around me who were interested in locally produced foods, but few of us knew how to support one another very well. Certainly the USDA did not sponsor, subsidize, or otherwise support this kind of local experimentation, so those who attempted it seemed to live pretty close to the bone. They worked to solve little puzzles about living from the land, persevering at their tasks even when the rest of us hardly even noticed their ingenuity.

With the first of the summer storm clouds rising above me, I drove home, thinking about just how few times in my life I had seen the fields where my purchased vegetables have come from. I seldom knew whether they had been grown on lands where wind and water erosion took their toll, or if their farmers had labored long to control such losses. And yet I had heard that most technologically driven American farmers were letting inches of fertile soil erode away from every field they plowed—whether they noticed it or not—and that each of those inches took microbes and earthworms five hundred years to form. Even when we find farmers willing to grow a portion of our food by taking care of the land the way we have always wished it to be taken care of, we seldom make time to understand the shadow history of past abuse of that very same land. It seemed to me essential that each of us somehow begin to volunteer time in the fields and orchards that produce our food, and to grasp how they change from season to season, year to year, and decade to decade.

Thunder and lightning reached my neighborhood about the time that I did, and fortunately Laurie was home, offering to help me bring the fresh groceries in before the torrent hit. As the first raindrops hit our roof, I sprinkled some olive oil and sunflower and squash seeds into the frying pan while she pared long, thin slices of peppers, tomatillos, and squashes on top of them. The vegetables sizzled and sighed. They made a simple meal, nothing fancy. Some morsels held the minerals washing out of the Dragoon Mountain limestones above the Hippses' garden into the Elfrida Valley soils they occupy, while others came from the Sierrita's decomposed granites that had washed downslope for centuries into what is now our own backyard. Laurie and I were barely beginning to learn where our own skin, bones, grit, and juices come from.

Chapter Eight

Tomato Hornworms and Summer Storms

Following the first few torrential summer monsoons, weeds had sprung up everywhere around my garden. I would no longer have to irrigate my garden plots as much as I had been doing, and could replant the recently fallowed beds with quick-growing summer crops, just as my O'odham neighbors had done for centuries. But as I compared my modest garden with those I had seen at Sehe-Ya Farms, I recognized that the difference between them was not merely one of size; my vegetables had recently taken it in the shorts. The leaves of my tomato plants had been gnawed down to nubbins, and there were caterpillar droppings all over the stems. It was hornworm time again in the desert, meaning no tomato time for me.

Tomato hornworms were the usual culprit for such pruning, but their emergence was often simultaneous with that of the smaller caterpillars of the white-lined sphinx moth. I had gained affection for these moths over the last few years because they were the pollinators of my favorite cactus, the night-blooming cereus. I had come to realize that no caterpillars means no moths, which means no cereus pollination, which means no delicious red cactus fruit for me to eat. And so I had grown tolerant of the caterpillars, even though the little buggers were brutal pruners of my garden crops.

The caterpillars had another value, according to my friend Marci Torre, who realized that larvae had historically served as critically important wild food before the summer crops matured to the point that desert dwellers could subsist on them. When she read of my accounts of O'odham friends collecting them, eviscerating, roasting, and eating them, Marci decided to run them through some nutritional analyses. She found these two-inch long larvae to be comprised of about thirty percent fat, thirty percent protein and ten percent carbohydrate. If we could ever become as accustomed to eating caterpillars as we were to eating shrimp, mussels, and snails, sphinx moth larvae might be featured on the menus of many regional restaurants. Today, however, they are being hit and killed as they cross the pavement of desert highways.

Marci and I decided to go caterpillar hunting together, so that we could ask my O'odham friends more about their preparation techniques for this traditional food. We had decided to meet at an intersection near my house, and when I arrived there, I spotted her lovely black hair before I noticed what she was holding in her hands. She shyly presented me with a necklace of dry-roasted larvae—a traditional preparation she had read about in one of my articles—to nibble on while we hunted. We rode out into the desert with our mutual friend Brad, who probably knows more about desert-adapted gardening than anyone else alive. The three of us talked up a storm about native crops, edible insects, and other such desert culinary esoterica. But as we passed onto the Papago Indian Reservation, larvae began to appear by the hundreds, crossing the highway in droves.

We pulled over below Kitt Peak, where some of the world's most sophisticated telescopes were located, and began our Neolithic hunter-gatherer routine: Find their spiderling host plant, glean the largest larvae from its leaves, squeeze the green innards out of them, lop off their heads, and toss them into our bags. As we chased a few onto the highway, a few of the O'odham drivers passing us saw what we were doing, and swerved wildly to give us wide berth.

"Gary, do you know if it's *legal* for outsiders to harvest worms on the reservation?" Brad asked me as he squeezed a plume of green goo onto the ground.

"I don't think folks will mind, really. . . . I mean, it's not like we're limiting resource availability for local residents. . . . Hardly anyone will even admit that their grandparents ate *ma:kkum* larvae for decades."

"But what if the tribal police stop us?"

"We'll tell them we're looking for the hallucinogenic mucus of desert toads to lick so that we can get high. . . . Just kidding. Look, if they interrogate us, we'll just say we're gathering a gift to take out to friends near Big Fields village. Of course, they might jail us for our bad taste in gifts."

We visited several groups of friends who were all willing to try Marci's preroasted larvae but were a bit dismayed by the caterpillars still wriggling in the bag. As I sampled a few roasted ones myself, I conceded that they had a pleasant crunchiness but that their taste was muted, perhaps because Marci had prepared them several days ago.

Our friends who worked for the Tohono O'odham Community Action's traditional foods project took Marci, Brad, and me to see some of the traditional floodwater-fed fields they had begun to revitalize. Usually dry washes had been channeled over to a nearly flat alluvial plain, where floodwaters spread out and sank into unusually fertile soil for this desert valley. There rows of untasseled corn, bean sprouts, and shoots of squash vines were emerging from the moist, dark soil. The crops in these small desert fields were also loaded with hornworms. Should I think of them as part of the harvest or as a pest? I realized that most statistics defined agriculture's productivity far too narrowly, merely measuring the yield of intentionally sown crops in a field, ignoring or even discouraging the rest of life that clusters there.

Over the last half century the productive volunteers historically associated with farmlands have been all but eliminated: edible greens, larvae, small mammals and birds that had shown up on their own, momentarily enjoying prosperity with intentionally cultivated crops. The use of fungicides, herbicides, and pesticides on American farms increased fiftyfold over five decades, and the average pesticide toxicity to wild organisms increased tenfold. How many millions of nontarget caterpillars have gone down along with the two pests that were targeted, the European and Southwestern corn borers? We too often forget the simple fact that while some invertebrates are pests, others can legitimately be considered food, *authentic* food. Because they can hardly crawl more than a half mile an hour, hornworm larvae as well as snails are the epitomes of *slow food*; they couldn't make it two thousand miles from host plant to dinner table if they tried. Of course, other spineless (invertebrate) creatures contribute to agricultural productivity in more obscure but no less direct ways: they pollinate our crops, rebuild our soils, and reward us with their beauty and intricate stories of adaptation and survival. Invertebrates, along with microbes, are the little lives that run the farm, and the world as a whole.

Sometimes I wished that we could undergo a moral metamorphosis, one that would enable us ethically to embrace them, offering gratitude for the way that their own metamorphosis delights and humbles us. Brad and Marci discussed this dilemma all the way back home, where I pondered it a while longer as I fed the turkeys a bunch of grasshoppers I had caught. The turkeys deftly leaped after them, snagging them with their beaks.

After the turkeys were watered and fed, I prepared a smaller dinner for myself, for Laurie was away with other work for a few days. I eviscerated a few more worms, rinsed them, then stir-fried them in oil. When they cooled off a little, I sampled the outcome.

I quickly came to the conclusion that their taste was too subtle for them to be served by themselves. I looked in the fridge for sauces, and found that Laurie had made some pesto from the basil in our garden just before she took off out of town.

As I added a couple of tablespoonfuls of pesto to the stir-fry, I realized the visual joke I was playing on myself: I had just spent a half hour squeezing green goo out of caterpillars only to dress them up in a pesto sauce of exactly the same hue and consistency. No matter. The caterpillars *al dente* tasted much better than they looked, and I was grateful to Marci for reviving my curiosity about foods prepared from insects and other terrestrial invertebrates.

When I went out to my garden the next morning, I was given another reminder that invertebrates rule what we can or can't cultivate in our worlds. I had decided to check on the two squash varieties that I had planted in the satellite dish atop the Minstrel Hut. While climbing up the stepladder I kept next to the hut, I brushed up against the long cascading vines of squash plants, with dark green luxurious growth. But as I climbed above the lip of the dish, I discovered that there were also yellow dried-up leaves on withered plants. Until I clearly saw where the squash plants were rooted in the dish, I didn't understand why some stems were fruitless and dying.

The withering stems all emanated from bushy zucchini plants, the ones that I had grown from the seed I had brought back from Lebanon. They were infested with squash-vine borers. Their thin, brittle stems offered no resistance to the caterpillars, which sucked the remaining life out of them. In contrast the thick, hairy stems of the O'odham squash had dealt with caterpillar invasions for centuries by enclosing each developing larva in a gall-like growth, while the vines continued to spread, root, and fruit. Even if the caterpillars did serious damage to one stretch of a vine, the O'odham squash had the capacity to send down roots at several nodes, and their entire mandala of vines seldom succumbed to the assault.

Less than three months after my experiment began, vine borers completed my comparison of squashes native to the Sonoran Desert with those recently emigrated from my grandparents' distant homeland.

The natives won out. I would have to learn to make stuffed *koosa* with the baby-girl squashes my O'odham neighbors call *ha:l mamad*. My love of the steamed and stuffed squashes of my childhood had not diminished, but if it was to flourish in this Sonoran Desert setting, it would have to embrace the kinds of squash best adapted to this peculiar land.

Such adaptations to prevailing pests do not come easily. Either they evolve through natural selection over centuries, providing plants with multiple genes for resisting the pests in the agricultural habitats, or we speed up the process by intentionally breeding a gene or two into a vulnerable crop. However, many of those hybrid crops are grown on such large acreages that the pest mutates and overcomes, or "breaks down," the crop's resistance in a decade or less. The prevailing alternative to breeding for pest resistance is the use of toxic pesticides, but some evolve so rapidly that they can also overcome the toxicity of the chemicals sprayed onto the crops they prefer. In the meantime there is collateral damage: Nontarget organisms killed by the millions by toxic sprays. Whatever risk these pesticides pose to vegetable consumers is nothing compared with what they pose to farmworkers. And the risk posed to human farmworkers is nothing again compared with the risks posed to nature's farmworkers: pollinators, soil fertility makers, and the like. It did not much matter to me whether hornworms or squash-vine borers made for exceptionally good eating; they were good at what they did in other ways, reminding us that we no more often see the field for the crop plants than we do the forest for the trees.

Chapter Nine

Scouting for Wild Greens and Chiles

After a weekend of wild rains I had become perhaps too overly optimistic that my local food gathering and gardening would take care of itself. When I began to look around in the garden and out on the range, it was clear that plants were rapidly growing, but I could see that most of their fruits were not yet ripe. It was still touch-and-go: I was nowhere near food self-sufficiency simply because the rainy season had *begun*. The storm patterns could collapse any day, and trigger several weeks of drought. It was too soon to predict what harvest might be next, or how large it might be.

"Admit it," I muttered under my breath one cloudless scorching day: "You can try as hard as you may, but you're not in control of how much food will come this season." I decided to spend the rainless days catching up on office work, dealing with the pile of unopened mail on my desk.

At least the first letter I opened brought some good, long-overdue news: From the U.S. Forest Service, it formally announced that it had at last granted a wish I had made twenty-two years before and had worked for off and on ever since: to set aside a four-square-mile reserve north of the Mexican border for the conservation of twelve wild relatives of food crops. The newly designated botanical area was not even twenty miles as the crow flies from my home. It was a place where I had done fieldwork and wild foraging since 1978, and that my colleagues at Native Seeds/SEARCH had struggled for long after I had lost my patience with the slow pace of Forest Service bureaucracy. I was relieved by the news that the area would at last receive some real protection, since it harbored the wild kin of so many food crops: native tepary beans, gourds, grapes, cotton, walnuts, prickly pears, mescal, onions, and amaranths among them. What I could not accomplish alone, the next generation of Native Seeds staff had accomplished winningly. I decided to drive down that way after work, to check out chiles and another wild food crop, the acorn

acorns

of the Emory oak; it would be an afternoon for reflection as much as for celebration.

Ever since I harvested wild chilies and acorns with O'odham friends in the 1980s, I had wanted to go down toward Nogales to harvest a heap of acorns on my own. But when I got down into the land of oaks and *chiltepines,* neither wild crop was ready for me to harvest. The *chiltepines* were still green—edible though not fiery enough for me— but the acorns were nowhere to be seen. I traversed a rocky slope, moving from oak to oak without finding a single ripe acorn. Finally I took a close look at one venerable old oak and noticed that a few miniature acorns were developing on it. There was a botanical generation gap before me, one that I had never imagined possible.

Apparently the snows that forced the abortion of cholla buds on Easter Sunday had also stunted the growth and development of the region's acorns. There would be a total crop failure this season. Not just here, as I later learned, but all over northern Sonora as well, where hundreds of campesinos usually depended on this seasonal harvest for their summer's cash income.

I took heed of this sober reminder: If I had to be fully dependent on wild foods this year, I would have suffered from the loss of two major harvests, cholla buds and acorns. But, unlike my Sonoran neighbors, I was financially and socially buffered from such natural disasters, such generation gaps. I could go and get "all the food in the world I ever wanted" as long as I could pay the costs that my neighbors to the south could not.

I looped back from the Nogales highway toward Arivaca and then went up the "back way" to my home on the Sasabe highway. The paucity of acorns and *chiltepines* did not keep me from bringing at least something edible home. I discovered that there were plenty of wild greens growing along the roadside: amaranths, lamb's-quarters, and purslane, known locally as *verdolagas.* Collectively, Sonorans called these greens *quelites de los aguas,* the wild spinaches of the summer rainy season. I harvested several garbage bags full of their tender growth tips, avoiding the older, more fibrous leaves and stems.

Tonight I entered *quelite* heaven, enjoying the freshest greens I could imagine. I grilled some scallions and poblano chiles, then added a mound of hand-washed greens to the saucepan. They wilted as the moisture on their leaves sizzled on the bottom of the pan. I served them immediately. Their flavors were so fresh, so buzzed with their recent photosynthetic surge that my meal sizzled with sunshine. Within minutes of devouring them, I felt greener, as if I were on some folic acid high. I dreamed that night of having chlorophyll in my skin, as if I had become green as the Green Giant himself.

An hour or so after having savored the meal of wild greens, I was struck by the notion that they were, in a sense, "road food," or "fast food." After all, they had been collected at the side of the road. The gathering required less than a couple of minutes for each herb, and it took no more than five additional minutes to wash them, cook them, and deliver them to a platter on my table. If everyone simply stopped to take advantage of the most obvious and abundant wild foods growing a hundred yards back from the roadside on his or her way home from work, I'm sure that radical changes in our society's entire perception of foods and their costs would follow.

As it is, there are already more fast-food outlets in the United States than there are sit-down (table service) establishments. In fact, a quarter of all fast-food outlets do not even provide seating; they assume that you have no time to be seated or you would have gone to Mom's Café across the street. By 1997, the sales of fast foods had topped 100 billion dollars a year in the United States, and most of that was eaten on the road. Both McDonald's and Burger King reporting more drive-through sales than indoor sales. To paraphrase the poet Galway Kinnell: Surpassing the porcupine, we have become the species most adept at eating and shitting on the run.

"You always said the highway was your home," sang Stevie Earle in "Fort Worth Blues," "but we both know that ain't true." If the truth be known, we eat on the highway almost as much as we eat at home. By 2007, the USDA predicted, more than half of what Americans spend on food will be spent on meals we will eat away from home, up from 30 percent spent in 1965, the year I gained my first job for regular wages away from home. The old spiritual bonds that linked healthy foods with family life in the home have been ruptured to be sure, regardless of whether you want to call carry-out foods and home deliveries the causes or the symptoms.

Is it that we can't stand to be at home, with ourselves or anyone else? If so, there is little reason to garden, pickle, or thoughtfully prepare vegetables for dinner at home with one another. There is little reason to be surprised that Pizza Hut needs 3.2 billion pounds of milk each year to put cheese on our carry-out pizzas, or that McDonald's annually orders more than 650 million pounds of beef, 250 million pounds of chicken, and 1.3 million pounds of potatoes just to keep us fed while we run away from home. And the foods run faster and farther than we do. In just twenty years, the cost of moving our food around increased 82 percent, from $182 billion in 1972 to $332 billion in 1992. In the United Kingdom the same trend is evident: Before being eaten, food items travel 50 percent farther than they did two decades ago.

As we run, and our food runs, so do the salmonella run, as do the *E. coli*. In 1997, 25 million pounds of ground beef were recalled by Hudson Foods from all over the country, due to microbial contamination. Microbes will always run circles around us; they mutate faster than we can control them with new antibiotics, and they sneak into places before we realize that they are in our presence once more. The only way we can beat them is by slowing down and keeping our food in place. If we choose not to spread a single batch of contaminated meat from coast to coast, if we contain microbes in places close to where they are produced, the feedback loops to detecting them are tightened and human suffering minimized.

Of course, this means that we must change *our* behavior rather than that of microbes. While they are fast mutators, we are presumably faster learners.

Or are we? Are our food habits among the last behaviors likely to change, or the first? Is multigenerational continuity in food tradition something easy to retain, or the toughest task of all for those of us living in this new millennium? As I took the road back home, these questions rose up before me like wild animals suddenly running across the asphalt.

Even with a brief, midsummer drought, the summer's overwhelming abundance finally began to come on strong. Fortunately (for me at least), it still came in discrete pulses. Even before the wild *chiltepines* kicked in, my backyard's buckets filled up with cultivated chile peppers, their domesticated kin.

I had read all the statistics about peppers: By the early 1990s hot sauce had surpassed ketchup as the number one condiment in the United States, and more herbs were being sold in U.S. supermarkets than ever before. But when the summer rains poured it on again so hard that I couldn't keep up with my own backyard production of jalapeños, *guajillas,* serranos, and *pasilla* chiles, I wondered why so many people with yards, balconies, and windowsills still purchased herbs and spices. My garden beds were burgeoning with Mexican oregano, *epazote,* basil, chives, and mints. Even if you were a lousy gardener in the borderlands, you could always find nearby a wide range of wild oreganos and chiles, lavenders and mustards. If you lived within walking distance of a spring or seep, there were usually watercresses and mints coming out the wazoo. And yet we tended to purchase high-priced dried herbs and spices, even when we live within reach of ones that taste wilder, fresher, and more flavorful than anything a store can offer.

For most of my adult life I have been as guilty and gluttonous in the unfettered pursuit and purchase of herbs and chili products as anyone I know. From the time of my very first job, when I used to go to the only

Mexican restaurant in town to flirt with the *gitana* daughter of the proprietor, I have been addicted to spicy food. At age sixteen I started on tacos, tamales, and enchiladas, but within two years I was competing in jalapeño-eating contests against a pepper-addicted bunny rabbit, at a Mexican café darkly named the International Wetbacks of America Club, in the historic red-light district of Gary, Indiana. By the age of twenty-six I was the wild-chile-eating champion of Tucson, Arizona, masticating and swallowing more than sixty of those hot little suckers in one night to win the prize. Nevertheless, most of the chiles, salsas, and other spices that fed my addiction were purchased on the street and were not homegrown.

This summer, however, a tragic event occurred not long after my return from Washington, one that sent me on another trajectory.

serrano peppers

When I arrived at home one night, it looked as though a gangland-style murder had just been executed in my kitchen. At first glance there was blood sprayed everywhere—across the floor, against the dining room mirror, and onto the little Navajo rug stationed at the sliding door between the kitchen and the screened-in porch. As I turned into the kitchen, I saw what had actually gone down. The custom-made shelf had fallen, the very shelf that had formerly displayed sixty salsa bottles I had collected from four continents over the last twenty years. As neighbors later told me, a sonic boom had hit the neighborhood. The bottles of hot sauce fell off the shelf, bounced to the floor, and broke wide open, releasing a blood-red slurry that sprayed itself all over every other human artifact within reach.

After I put on gloves, picked up the glass, and mopped up the chili sludge, I vowed never again to become so dependent on store-bought herbs and spices. I had become like the Saudi princes who trade barrels of crude oil for jets full of bottles of Tabasco. Adios to Global Warming, adios to Ass-in-a-Bucket, adios to *La Viuda Sanchez* and to the McIlhenney's. I was back in control of what burned me for the first time in three decades.

I immediately went outside and gathered up some mesquite chips from under my stack of locally cut firewood. Placing these in a bucket, I soaked them in water while I moved a dozen mesquite logs over to the stuccoed adobe oven I had built several summers ago. The oven was round, with the opening to the cooking chamber a foot off the ground on one side, and two fuelwood chambers on the other side, one above and one below the cooking chamber. After getting a good fire going in the bottom chamber and moving a couple of the logs to the upper chamber, I left the oven and went into the garden with a big platelike basket, ready to select jalapeño chiles for smoking into chipotles.

I had been taught how to select chilies worthy of the chipotle ritual by the resident drunk in the cantina at the Hotel Arizpe-Sainz in Saltillo, Coahuila. Years ago I used to frequent that old hotel while collaborating with Mexican scientists on pilot projects to bring wild oreganos and *chiltepines* into cultivation. I had learned of this Master of the Smoke one afternoon when I had asked my collaborators how to make the wonderfully smoky chipotle barbecue sauce that we had been eating with our *barbacoa del chivo.* Overhearing my question, Francisco "Paco" de la Garza put down the goat leg bone he had been nibbling on and announced: "I swear by the grace of the Virgin Mary I have at last found someone who can apprentice with my uncle Fernando to become the next Master of the Smoke! He has wanted me to be his intern since the time of my First Communion, but now I have found a worthy surrogate who can be trusted to keep our ancient chipotle tradition alive!"

At the end of Paco's speech, everyone stopped eating their barbecued goat meat, drank their last bit of beer and loaded into the car to look for Don Fernando over at the Arispe-Sainz. There he was, nursing some Herradura tequila, studying a colonial-era painting on the barroom wall. When his nephew Paco explained to him what I wanted to learn, he eyed me carefully. He drank another slug of Herradura and sneered.

"A gringo? From the Sonoran Desert? This is an eastern Mexican tradition, my way of making chipotles. I doubt whether you can even find suitable jalapeños over there in Sonora and Arizona. The climate is not right for the slow maturation of chiles there."

"But I live at an elevation slightly higher than the Sonoran Desert. They grow grapes for white wine at my elevation . . . ," I stammered.

Paco bought his uncle another Herradura and took him aside, whispering quietly in his ear while wildly gesturing at the same time. Don Fernando, his silvery hair slicked straight back, his guayabera shirt a third unbuttoned, listened intently. Finally he slowly began to shake his head up and down, as if a deal had been struck, but one with some restrictions built into it. He spun his bar stool around and embraced me.

"Look," he said, staring me straight in the eyes and speaking to me slowly from six inches away from my face, "I'll explain the process to you today, step by step, and you can write the whole thing down in your little notebook there. But tomorrow you have to come by my house and see how it is actually done, then do it yourself under my supervision.

And I must have you promise three things: you will never divulge to others all the steps in my process of smoking chipotles; you will never pick a chile for smoking that is not completely streaked with white striations; and you will never try to use any of those worthless jalapeño hybrids. Stick to the *razas criollas* (native races of crops)!"

"Oh, poor deceased Uncle Fernando," I moaned to myself, as I picked the white-streaked jalapeños in my backyard. "If Don Fernando were alive today, he'd be rolling in his grave."

While I have not violated Don Fernando's mandate to keep his special smoking process secret, and I have not succumbed to using unstreaked, immature chiles, I have been hard pressed to find jalapeños that have not hybridized with the so-called improved varieties. The reason is simple: The old-time bonafide jalapeño has nearly disappeared from Mexico and the southwestern United States over the last decade, as hybrid vegetable seeds have become ubiquitous and the packagers insist that their commercial growers provide them only with varieties that the packagers themselves have selected. The genetic diversity of most other vegetables has gradually declined this last half century, but chile diversity has declined more precipitously, thanks to one man's recent monopolization of the North American vegetable seed industry. Today, more than 40 percent of all vegetables sold in the supermarket chains of the United States and Mexico were grown from seeds produced by one man's empire. That man, billionaire Alfonso Romo Garza, is the undisputed Global King of Vegetable Seeds, reaping twice as much revenue off vegetable seeds than his nearest competitor. (He is also one of nearly five hundred billionaires in the world who, together, control as much wealth as one-half of the world's human population collectively have available to them.) In the mid-nineties Romo quietly began to purchase the vegetable seed divisions of companies such as Asgrow, Petoseed, and Royal Sluis, until his Seminis corporation offered eight thousand varieties of sixty fruit and vegetable species, including many chiles. During one spurt of growth for Seminis, his empire spread to 120 countries and gained control of a fifth of all fruit and vegetable seed sales worldwide.

Aggregating the largest private vegetable seed bank in the world, Romo bragged on the front page of the *Wall Street Journal,* "Seeds are software. And we have the seeds."

But seeds and their diseases are not software; they are living, mutating organisms. Regardless of whether or not genetic engineering techniques are used to improve them, hybrid seeds take several years to develop, multiply, and release. While Romo's breeders have been breeding chiles for resistance to one strain of virus, a new, unanticipated strain may wreak havoc in the chile breeders' fields, requiring that additional sources of resistance be found before the improved variety is released. Even if the breeding and marketing of Romo's new chiles had proceeded as planned, their ultimate profitability has been constrained by the economic and ecological problems that vegetable farmers are suffering wherever they live. If agriculture itself is not healthy and thriving, Romo is like the proverbial sower who scatters his seeds but sees their sprouts wither on thin eroded soil or get choked out by the weeds and their thorns.

By early 1999 profits from Seminis vegetable seeds started to decline precipitously, due to what *Market Guide* called "an unfavorable horticultural industry." That forced Romo to replace his chief operating officer and retire some of his vegetable breeders as part of a "global restructuring and optimization plan" for his ailing empire. His optimization team decided to drop one-fourth of the commercial varieties they had formerly marketed, which include both patented and standard varieties that are currently less profitable but historically more reliable. Some critics claim that more genetically diverse, open-pollinated varieties will be among the first two thousand varieties to disappear from seed catalogs.

Assuming that most of the old varieties will be cleared from the shelves, seed salesmen for Seminis will try to convince farmers to pay extra to grow the most recently released, genetically engineered hybrids that Romo has invested so much in. But look what we might find in our supermarket instead of the fiery distinctiveness of the traditional jalapeños that Don Fernando taught me to smoke: "Corno Verde F1, a totally reshaped, large sweet bell pepper. Some people refer to them as sweet chiles," the Seminis website tells us, "but Corno Verde has no detectable heat. It's a sweet pepper that looks like a chile."

As I picked the last of the jalapeños in my garden and grieved the recent death of Don Fernando, Master of the Smoke, I tried to imagine what he might think of living in a world where all chiles have had all their pungency bred out of them, cucumbers have been rendered burpless, and beans fartless. Yes, Fernando would be rolling in his grave, asking for another shot of tequila to kill the pain. There would be no place at all for him in a world without bite, burp, bark, and bliss.

After I had placed the last of the hand-selected chiles in the oven, I added the water-soaked mesquite chips to the coals above and below the cooking chamber. The smoke billowed up and wafted into every corner of the backyard enclosed by our stone walls and ocotillo fences. By the time Laurie came home that night, I could offer her some freshly made salsa. It had the smoky bite of chipotles to it, one that would have made Don Fernando semi-proud.

Chapter Ten

Seed Saving and Foraging in the Heartland

Laurie and I were flying over the heartland of North America, west to east, wondering what this American land is all about these days. Somehow we had ended up in Reno, Nevada, on the edge of ranches run by Shoshone cowboys and Basque sheepherders; then, somehow, we found ourselves heading across the Great Basin, the northern Rockies, the Great Plains, and the tall-grass prairies until we reached the temperate forests of the Midwest, or what's left of them. We would first fly to Minneapolis and St. Paul, Minnesota, in the headwaters reach of the Mississippi, where we would pick up an air shuttle to Rochester, Minnesota, then rent a car and drive down to Annual Campout of the Seed Savers Exchange. The Seed Savers Heritage Farm was nestled in the wooded rolling hills of northeastern Iowa, not far from where Grant Wood painted that whimsically stern farming couple as *American Gothic*.

But my thoughts would fly from Reno to Rochester without much regard for all the ailing farms that could be found below us, and their farmers, neo-Gothic or otherwise. Instead, I was not thinking, but dreaming with my eyes wide open, as I looked down on the lands below the fuel-guzzling jet that propelled us. As I watched the land change from west to east, I visualized all the strange and wonderful wild foods that have been eaten on this continent since long before the first farmers planted seeds in this American soil. I tried to recall the accounts I had read of the foods that Indians and white settlers had survived on far to the north of where I had been foraging desert foods. While Laurie sat beside me, praying as she often does, and looking out at the clouds, as an angel or a Georgia O'Keeffe would do, my eyes glanced downward, trying to ferret out which fish, fowl, or beast frequented each watershed; which tuber, fruit, or stalk still sat below us, ready for the picking. I studied this cross-section of American land as a hungry Walt Whitman would do, celebrating the ripened seedhead glistening above the leaves of grass, howling for the wild persimmon ready to pluck and savor in its juiciest state.

As we rose out of the Reno airport, I saw the Great Basin before us covered with big sage and crested wheat, and the Sierra Nevada's ranges off to the side, jacketed with piñon pine, juniper, and the occasional patch of oak. The pine nuts of the single-leaf piñon were what first came to mind when I tried to imagine the staple foods of the Northern Paiute in centuries gone by. Except around springs and streams on the basin floor, wild foods were seldom abundant there, but when a mast of piñon nuts appeared in the ranges above the summer camps, the Shoshone, Goshiute, and Northern Paiute would gather together. John Muir saw the Paiutes mobilize for a bumper crop of piñon nuts in 1870:

> When the crop is ripe, the Indians make ready the long beating-poles; bags, baskets, mats, and sacks are collected; the women . . . assemble at the family huts; the men leave the ranch work; old and young, all are mounted on ponies and start in great glee to the nut-

lands, forming curiously picturesque cavalcades; flaming scarfs and calico skirts stream loosely over the knotty ponies, two squaws usually astride of each, with baby midgets bandaged in baskets slung on their backs or balanced on the saddle-bow; while nut-baskets and water jars project from each side, and the long beating-poles make angles in every direction. . . . Then the beating begins right merrily, the burrs fly in every direction, rolling down the slopes, lodging here and there against rocks and sage-brushes, cached and gathered by the women and children with fine natural gladness.

The outlying ranges of the Sierra Nevada were falling out of sight behind us, and the tawniness of the Great Basin opened up wider to the east. I saw greenish patches of marsh plants occurring here and there along slow-flowing streams, and remembered how the swamp potato, or *wappatoo,* was once harvested from these wetland habitats. The northern Great Basin tribes would "wade into the water and loosen these tubers with their feet," and then, "when they float to the top, they are collected."

Lewis and Clark's expedition was protected from winter starvation by another, more circumscribed harvesting practice; when food supplies were low, a few elderly experts knew where to look for *wappatoo* in riverbank caches where beaver and muskrat had sequestered them for their own future use. It was an energetically odd way to gain carbohydrates, by short-circuiting the food chain through robbing meaty herbivores rather than eating the animals themselves. *Wappatoo* tubers were as large as turkey eggs, but their bitter milky juices had to be leached or boiled away before they became palatable. After traditional processing, they were no longer bitter but exceedingly sweet.

As our jet flew eastward over the northern Rockies, I remembered reading about one of the first recorded food exchanges between mountain-dwelling Crow and Shoshone and the plains-dwelling Mandan and Hidatsa. In the summer of 1805 French-Canadian fur trader Larocque accompanied the Rocky Mountain tribes on their way back to Yellowstone country from the farming villages along the Upper Missouri, in what are now the Dakotas. Larocque was amazed how well provisioned the tribes from the Rockies were, even though "they have never had any [European] traders with them," for they were flush with guns and ammunition they had received from the Mandan and "Big Belly" Hidatsa in exchange for mustangs, buffalo-skin robes, and deerhide leggings. While the Crow and Shoshone camped near the farmers, the Mandan and Hidatsa "went to the newly arrived camp carrying a quantity of Corn raw and cooked which they traded for Leggins, Robes and dried meat." The Crow and Shoshone were anxious to purchase all the corn, squashes, and tobacco they could because they did not practice any cultivation of their own. Mandan and Hidatsa corn varieties were so well adapted to conditions along the Upper Missouri that they later enabled the survival of Anglo settlers to the northern plains, just as they provided needed food supplies to the Crow and the Shoshone. Before white settlers in Montana began to rely on flint corns from the Mandan and Hidatsa, they could hardly succeed at growing any crops. They produced barely ten thousand acres of dent corn before 1910. But when they finally adopted the hardy flint corns which native farmers had carefully selected, Anglo farmers' corn production in Montana achieved a fifty-fold increase in just fifteen years' time.

When ethnobotanist Melvin Gilmore learned of the great gains in self-sufficiency white settlers achieved by embracing rather than ignoring the climatically adapted native foods of the Upper Missouri, he decided that other European Americans might do well to emulate that process:

> We shall make the best and most economical use of all our land when our population shall become adjusted in habit to the natural conditions. The country cannot be wholly made over and adjusted to a people of foreign habits and tastes. There are large tracts of land in America whose bounty is wasted because the plants which

can be grown on them are not acceptable to our people. This is not because these plants are not in themselves useful and desirable, but because their valuable properties are unknown [to newcomers]. . . . The adjustment of American consumption to American conditions of production will bring about greater improvement in conditions of life than any other material agency. The people of any country must finally subsist on those articles of food which their own soil is best fitted to produce.

Gilmore's 1919 call for a truly American food sensibility echoed what Emerson, Whitman, and Thoreau had proposed some six decades earlier in terms of a truly American literature, one that was not merely derivative of European traditions. Nevertheless, changes in literary sensibilities are perhaps easier to embrace than changes in dietary preferences. Anglo-American settlers were less willing to embrace Gilmore's wisdom and more likely to look down their noses at Native American cuisine, thanks to the crude descriptions of native food preparation techniques that were written by Gilmore's contemporaries. In 1926 all that ethnologist Alanson Skinner could say about the food traditions of the Iowa Indians was assembled into a few trite paragraphs of truisms. As Laurie and I flew out over the tall-grass prairies, I read her the pitiful secondhand summary Skinner wrote, dismissing any possible complexities in Iowa Indian preparations of wild game:

All varieties of wild game animals were used by the Ioway as food, and dogs were eaten, at least ceremonially. . . . Meat was both boiled and roasted, although, as among most North American tribes, boiling was much preferred to all other methods of cooking. . . . A much esteemed food . . . was composed of the entire body of a raccoon with the fur singed off, and not skinned, so that the fat and juices were retained when the animal was cooked. It was called a "Chief's dish."

In one short paragraph Skinner presumed that the Iowa would prepare all mammals for eating in one manner, by boiling the unskinned carcass, just as he presumed most other Native American tribes did, and that the chief (a figure not recognized by most cultural communities in North America) always received the choicest dish (inevitably the one that disgusted Euro-American sensibilities). Such stereotypes turned many newcomers to Native American diets away from giving them due attention and respect.

As Laurie and I left the skies over the prairies to descend into the northern forests of Minnesota, I felt a sadness that it had taken more than another half century after Skinner to dispel such simplified notions of Native American cuisine and the natural diversity from which it emerged. Thousands of plants and animals were historically esteemed as foods across the continent, and various cultures had their own distinctive ways of managing their food resources, of harvesting them, and of preparing them. Fortunately ethnohistorians and folklorists have recently rescued many of the earliest accounts that hint at this complexity and diversity. As we landed in Minneapolis–St. Paul, I shared with Laurie the richness of the wild-rice-foraging traditions at the nearby Ojibwa community of White Earth, recorded by Joseph Gillifan in 1876:

> The Indians look forward to rice-gathering as a very happy time, as they then not only have an abundance of rice, but by a happy combination of circumstances, the ducks go in great numbers to gather wild rice at the same time that they do. So *they meet,* around the smoking board and elsewhere. The ducks are old and very dear friends of the Indians, their families having been on intimate and visiting terms for I know not how many centuries past . . . and the pleasure of meeting, on one side at least, is rapturous. Often the ducks get so fat with eating rice that they cannot rise to fly, and are therefore obliged to receive their friends who come to call upon them.

As Ojibwa elder Paul Buffalo told our friend, folklorist Tom Vennum, the mallards at ricing time lived more off bugs than rice, which gave them a "muddy, boggy, musky flavor" all their own. And so the time of the year and seasonal diet of the animal shaped its flavor. Wild rice from different rivers and lakes also offered distinctive flavors that elders could place by sampling the cooked rice dishes.

As we walked through the airport and noticed the tourist stores selling artificial, paddy-grown "wild rice," some of it coming in from California rather than Minnesota, I wondered why we are seduced by such surrogates for authenticity. Why would anyone want to purchase California paddy-produced rice in Minnesota to take home as a souvenir? Why can so few people today identify by taste what was grown in their own valley versus what was produced one valley, state, or continent away? How many of us have sampled even fifty different wild foods native to our homeland, or grown even five crop varieties in our gardens that had been grown prehistorically in the same soil type? What have we lost? What are we losing?

Laurie and I landed in the Upper Midwest weary and a bit disheartened. Our plane touched down three hours too late for us to partake of the dinner the Seed Savers Exchange had prepared for us. Worse yet, our bags were sent on to Rochester, New York, instead of accompanying us to Rochester, Minnesota. I was left without the bag of fried grasshoppers, tortillas, muffins, and cactus jam I had brought to survive on while in airports and on the road for the next few days.

Beyond that, seeing all the extensive cornfields of southern Minnesota and northern Iowa made me melancholy. Undoubtedly many of the fields we saw were loaded with genetically engineered corn, but you would never know it, because no labeling of fields and foods was required here even though a letter with a half million signatures was sent to the White House this last month requesting that such labeling be mandatory. We passed huge farms near the Minnesota-Iowa border nearly devoid of any life forms other than the stiff rows of corn. The land was broken by the demands placed on it by cornstalks and corn roots; its breath was corn's breath; it respired and expired with the rhythm of the corn-growing season. Corn dwarfed even the forest fragments clutching to the edge of the river bottoms.

Since 1850 more than five million square miles of North American forests, woodlands, savannas, and grasslands have come under the plow, and much of it has been planted to corn. This has resulted in a loss of natural vegetation and soil regeneration four times higher than in any previous 150-year era in the history of this continent. The verdant wildlands were first replaced by small farms where families found their lives intertwined with those of their livestock, poultry, pasture, and croplands. But for the last fifty years or so, our country has seen about a half million people a year move away from the farm. By 1993 less than 4.5 million people lived *and* worked on American farms, so the Census Bureau stopped keeping track of them. More than 85 percent of the farm laborers and 32 percent of the farm managers no longer lived on the lands that generated their incomes. Farmhouses were replaced by larger cornfields, more extensive hog yards, and highly mechanized dairies. Here in southern Minnesota such unpeopled farms stretched westward as far as our eyes could see. At dusk they took on a sickly greenish cast, the color of moldy Spam. We drove along state and county highways, listening to Patsy Cline moan with the rural sorrow we felt all around us.

When at last we reached Kent and Diane Whealy's Heritage Farm of the Seed Savers Exchange, everything changed scale, shade, and context: the smaller size of fields and orchards, their heterogeneity of colors and textures, their intimacy with surrounding forests and prairie-grass pastures. Kent and Diane hugged and humored us into their kitchen. I can't remember how many times I have slept in their home over the years, or how many times I have hosted them at mine. That night, however, they knew we were dirt tired, and so they had arranged for us to sleep elsewhere, in solitude. Diane winked at me and informed us that they had fixed up something special for us. We would await the morning for the swapping of stories and dreams to begin once more.

Their son, Aaron, escorted us over to an old log cabin, two miles away on an isolated knoll above a babbling brook. In it the Whealys had placed a bowl of freshly picked black cap blackberries; a loaf of bread from an heirloom wheat sown and ground by hand; a bottle of wine from a vineyard in an adjacent Minnesota county; local cheese and cottage cheese, and hickory nuts that Diane's father picked and shelled on his own.

However weary and grimy and disoriented we were from our transcontinental travel, this gesture of generosity washed it all away. They had given us the perfect gift to revitalize us and make us feel at home. Each berry, each hickory nut was flavored with their friendship two decades strong.

We awakened the next morning much later than usual, unaccustomed to sleeping in a cabin loft where the air was as sweet and thick as it was. Compared with thin desert air, the Midwestern air seemed so humid and heavy that I felt as though I were wading through quicksand. Laurie and I had breakfast out on the cabin porch, overlooking the brook. We traced its flow through all the pastures, meadows, and forests surrounding us. We silently savored the berries, the bread, and the cheese, went skinny-dipping in the brook, then put on some loose-fitting summer clothes. By the time we returned to Kent and Diane's backyard, the Seed Savers Exchange Annual Campout was going full blast. Kent teased us about sleeping in four hours longer than any farmer would, then took us to see his latest garden projects.

Imagine coming over a hill and spotting a couple of hundred campers, gardeners, and farmers wandering through gorgeous gardens of heirloom crops. When I tried to count the number of crop varieties planted around the farmyard, it was easily double that of the people. It was not uncommon for Kent and his colleagues to grow 350 kinds of squash or beans in a single year, in addition to dozens of other crop species. Inch for inch, row for row, this was the single most diverse farm on the continent, and perhaps in the entire world. Between its gardens, orchards, seed banks, and White Park cattle pastures, the Heritage Farm saves and displays more living riches each year than most zoos do in a century. But Kent's reason for initiating all this wasn't to "outdo" zoos and government agencies with his conservation efforts, as if his ark was bigger and better than theirs. He simply believed in the glory and grace of gardening, and the beauty that it brings to the face of this planet.

"Why do I still garden?" I heard him ask himself in front of a small group of seed savers who drooled every time he showed them another variety of heirloom crops. "It's those incredibly rich flavors and the tenderness of hand-picked, vine-ripened vegetables that are the major factors. All of us garden because we enjoy it. There's still nothing more magical for me than seeing seedlings break up through the soil."

The Heritage Farm had, over the years, become some sort of Eden, Mecca, or living magnet for lovers of diversity. The folks who were milling around were not idle spectators. Most of them kept large, diverse gardens of their own, or tirelessly tended minor breeds of livestock. They were skilled at doing hand pollinations, at performing air layering of fruit trees, at reciting the stories and songs that have followed Jacob's Cattle Beans and Dominique Hens as they've been raised at various places across the continent. I practically purred when I once again heard their outright joyfulness and downright droll humor as they talked to one another in the barn, or out on the lawn. They exuded an elixir that seemed to fertilize and foster a lusciousness in plants, humans, and other creatures. When they spotted an old friend, they kidded and cajoled him into hearing one of their raggiest shaggy-dog stories, as if it were an antidote against a world hell-bent on running away too fast for anyone's actual liking. They came to the Seed Savers Exchange year after year to slow that world down, reminding it to whoa and take a whiff of the bean blossoms.

Not too far into the afternoon, a stainless-steel triangle was rung and we were all called to assemble in the loft of the barn. It was filled with well over a hundred folding chairs and folks of all sizes and shapes sitting in them. Kent walked up to the podium and looked around, silent for a moment, half terrified and half overjoyed as usual, his curly hair and beard a bit grayer than most of us remembered them. At last Kent welcomed us and offered us his annual "state of the seed savers" address, with his characteristic fire-and-brimstone flair:

> We are now witnessing unprecedented attempts to break the ancient chain of seed-saving, attempts not merely to patent seeds but to turn their reproductive abilities off after one growing. The so-called terminator technologies of Monsanto, Delta Pine, and the USDA have genetically-engineered plants to kill their own embryos. On top of that, the industry boasts that ninety percent of all crops grown in the U.S. will be transgenic within the next decade. Already an estimated 58 percent of Canada's fields are planted with such genetically modified organisms. Some of their genes are escaping into nearby crops and weeds. Such biological pollution will become the ecological nightmare of the twenty-first century.

I could see horror, anger, and sadness in the faces of the farmers sitting around me. Kent continued:

> But our efforts are at the completely opposite end of the spectrum from terminator technologies, transgenic crops and other efforts in the seed industry. And today, we have new allies. Up until five years ago, those of us who grew heirloom seeds had a limited market. All that changed with the flourishing of the rapidly growing Community-Supported Agriculture movement. We are providing at wholesale prices bulk quantities of seeds for eighty-five varieties to CSAs, which will then go into the mouths of thousands more people, who will then immediately get hooked on their richer, fresher flavors. What's more, we've now found some 30,000 nonhybrid seed varieties in this country, and are bringing them back into circulation. Over the years, we've sent out at least 750,000 samples of seeds passed on to us from heirloom collectors.

The crowd cheered.

As Wendell Berry told us here five years ago, the way to start turning things around is with strong local food economies. That, my friends, is truer today than ever before. We are in the process of changing the way gardeners grow vegetables in America.

The cheers were deafening. Kent went on to remind us that our individual efforts were not insignificant. Over the rest of the afternoon we listened to other talks confirming that such grassroots efforts were making a huge difference in saving the remaining biological riches of the world. Suzanne Nelson, my fellow Tucsonan and one of my dearest friends, chronicled our work at Native Seeds/SEARCH, where some nineteen hundred seed collections of ninety-nine species were being kept alive. We listened to the folks from Old Sturbridge Village in Massachusetts and other historic farms, from an heirloom gardener-writer from Australia, and from Kent's son, Aaron, who recently opened up a Seed Savers store in Madison, Wisconsin. After a break we came back into the barn, so that Kent could roast me with his characteristic humor. He recalled the time we first met, a time when I tried to feed him an ungodly concoction of purslane greens, onions, and a gravy as thick as glue. Although he couldn't stomach any of it, he said with a wink, he just loved the enthusiasm with which I prepared it.

Then I had my chance to follow Kent. I could joke with him only so long before I could feel other sorts of words rising up from my heart, words meant for a barn full of the most motley but dedicated gardeners and agrarian reform strategists in the United States. I paused and looked out at the faces of friends and the faces of my mentors. I spotted Laurie, relaxing among all those young mothers in dresses holding their children in their laps. I saw the weary, overworked activists who were hoping for a new resolve to continue gardening on top of everything else they had to do. I saw elders who were raised on farms in an era when what Kent just reported seemed unimaginable; every one of them prided themselves on saving their best seeds back then, as they do now. I recognized whole families I had met several years before, families as food-self-sufficient as anyone I knew. And so it was not hard to speak, for I was speaking to a special breed, the Seed People:

> What if each of us, day by day, fully fathomed where our food comes from, historically, ecologically, geographically, genetically? What would it be like if each of us recognized all the other lives connected to our own through the simple act of eating? What if we understood which other species were regenerated, and which were contaminated or destroyed by what we choose to eat, by our care or by our carelessness? The way we garden, gather, fish, or forage can be a communion, or it can become an ecological calamity. The more we understand where our food comes from, the greater the chance there is that we can save the living riches of the natural world.

For another half hour, as I rambled through a chain of causes, effects, preventive measures, and reasons for hope, you could have heard a pin drop in that old barn. But when I finally asked everyone present to remember that we all needed support from one another—that I was on the verge of crumbling from the stress of travel until I found the Whealy's black-cap berries and hickory nuts waiting here to renew me— the crowd jumped to its feet, clapping and cheering.

They were clapping because they, too, get discouraged, and we are apt to remain silent about that discouragement. Most of the year each of us worked alone in our attempts to eat knowingly and gratefully from the land. By merely conceding that such work was hard and because of that, that we simply needed one another's encouragement, I must have relieved many folks' doubts about themselves. Each of us tended to think that others accomplish such tasks effortlessly, with few conflicting demands impinging on them. We tended to idealize one another, not realizing that the individual gardeners we chose as role models often suffered as many difficulties as we did. By acknowledging that each of us came to a gathering like this seeking the blessing of others, the blessings began to flow among us.

At last I announced that the time for more discussion had passed: "Enough of words, it's now time to dance." An old-timey string band of banjo, mandolin, bass, and guitar began a brilliant set of reeling dance tunes. After a while Laurie brought up her hammered dulcimer to join the band for several songs. When she was through, we danced another song or two, whirling around like dust devils blown in from the West.

In contrast to my panicked impression of the state of Midwestern farm country as we flew into Rochester, I was now heartened that there was much to celebrate in Iowa and Minnesota, and much more diversity remaining there than initially met the eye. But that diversity had been maintained against some pretty stiff odds by folks as courageous as Diane and Kent.

As a storm front moved in to molest the entire Midwest, we bee-lined it for Rochester. The storm forced the cancellation of our flight from Rochester to Minneapolis, leaving us with hours to kill in the nowhere land of airports. Thanks to the berries, wine, and hickory nuts that Kent and Diane provided us, we survived the cancellations, talking into the wee hours of the dark and stormy night. But more important than nuts, berries, and fermented grapes was the recognition, the comfort, that Laurie and I were by no means alone in what we were attempting to do. There were like-minded folks in many communities all across the continent who were trying to grow more and more of the plants that enrich their lives, regardless of what corporate and government forces were doing. Most reassuring of all, we reconnected with elders the age of my mother and Chuck, who had never given up their rural Jeffersonian values and had passed them on to their children. It was only when generation after generation can string their homelands' seeds together in an unbroken chain—a necklace of living tradition—that the seeds themselves can be considered safe.

Chapter Eleven

The Frontera Grill and the Frontiers of Technology

After the Seed Savers Exchange Campout, I was curious to see what happened to food after it left the farm. There was no better place than the Midwest from which to reflect upon the entire chain from field to packer to restaurant or grocer to consumer. Did good food go bad along the way, or was it taken care of so that its value was saved, even enhanced? Laurie and I went on to Chicago, where her sister would be getting married in several days, just forty miles west of where I grew up.

Because I had only known the Chicago of the fifties and sixties, I had smugly regarded the Windy City more as a haven for global meatpackers than for local foods connoisseurs. I was skeptical that I would find anything decent to eat there at all. As we wandered out of O'Hare Airport, I got a sense that some things hadn't changed all that much in my twenty year absence from the area. In O'Hare's specialty gift shop that featured "Chicago's Favorite Foods," at least half of the gift items were grown or packaged elsewhere: spinach pizza, bratwurst, and Wisconsin cheeses. A fast-food counter in the airport advertised "real potatoes hand-cut into homemade french fries." I was glad I had brought along with me some of Esperanza's mesquite tortillas, our own spring harvest of cholla buds, and some baby squashes from the satellite dish.

While we waited for our baggage, I picked up one of the local papers, which was promoting Chicago's own contributions to the nutraceutical nightmare. I had not even thought about those dysfunctional foods since Laurie had rejected them all at the brunch I made for her a month before. But there they were again, in the papers and in the airport's only "Health Food" stall: packages, bottles, and jars full of memory-enhancing, cholesterol-lowering, ejaculation-erupting ingredients masquerading as food—rich in promises, low on taste. I remembered the commentary of my rowdy friend, that Prophet of Midwestern Hedonism, Jim Harrison. Jim has predicted that as the United States abandons the thighs of free-range chickens for extruded soybean substitutes, it will become more like a "media-fueled cultural blender, increasing in size and power until that is all that there is. A blender as big as Ohio [or Chicago], which spews the trash, junk food, chatter and clutter we're all familiar with."

Of course, I did not have to go to Chicago to see the industrialized food blender swirling and crushing, chopping and whipping ingredients from around the world into one huge tasteless slurry. The mixmasters of the food universe had already piped their fast-food slurries to the farthest reaches of the world. Just ten transnational food and beverage corporations capture $2,000 billion in the retail value of their global food sales. You might not know their names, but they were no doubt present in your pantry as they were in mine: Nestlé, Philip Morris, Unilever, ConAgra, Cargill, PepsiCo, Coca-Cola, Diageo/Guinness, Gran Metro, Mais, and Danone. In just eight years, these conglomerates and a few others of their ilk were involved in 4,100 food industry mergers and leveraged buyouts. Their billboards surrounded us as we dove toward The Loop, for many of them had their regional warehouses here in

Chicago. And yet, they were just as ubiquitous in the deepest canyons, most remote bays, and highest mountains of the Mexican borderlands where Laurie and I had been working the last few years.

I remembered the ironic story my friend and mentor Richard Felger told me more than two decades ago. He had just come home from backpacking in the Barranca del Cobre, the maze of canyons south of the border that are larger, deeper, and more unexplored than Arizona's own Grand Canyon. He was guided by a Tarahumara Indian who refused all food that Richard offered him, claiming that he had enough of his own food in a little cloth bag on his shoulder to sustain him. As they descended deeper and deeper into the canyon, Richard began to ask what different food plants were called in the Tarahumara language, and his companion responded with a firm grasp of the flora in his own mother tongue. Finally, in the late afternoon, Richard offered him water, not having seen the Indian guide drink anything for hours. Again the Tarahumara man declined Richard's offer, but proudly pulled a sixteen-ounce bottle of Coca-Cola from his bag, treating it the same as he had the many native food plants he had shown to Richard: "Here we call this drink Coca-Cola. It tastes very sweet and is full of power. Do you have this drink in your country?"

We had two days to kill before the wedding, so I invited Laurie to go with me to the Museum of Science and Industry, the very first museum that I visited when I was a child. I vaguely remember that the museum featured an exhibit on the development of American food technologies, and I was eager to see if it was still intact.

Alas, sections of the exhibit had been given nineties makeovers since my last visit, but it continued to reek with the toxic perfumes of industrial agriculture, as it had when I was a kid. The best, cheesiest parts were all there: the plastic models of processed foods of known caloric quantities slowly moving along a conveyor belt to you and me, the grateful consumers of anything convenient.

The exhibit recounted glorious history of preservatives, freeze-drying, microwaving, and foil packaging, all of which have ensured that foods produced several years ago and thousands of miles away from our kitchen tables will be "ready to eat" whenever we want them. In fact, we learn at FOOD AND CIVILIZATION OVERVIEW II that the entire history of Western society is a trajectory away from having to grow and prepare our own foods so that we can become civilized and cultured. At last, by the fourteenth century, "[n]ot everyone needs to grow food. . . . There is time for some to study the movements of stars . . . to write a novel or poem . . . to create a new science . . . civilization has become social. . . . Europe is the center of scientific and cultural studies."

Several centuries later, we learn, American food technologists pushed this dream one step further: "Beginning in the nineteenth century, scientists learned that some foods could be improved by the addition of other substances: starch, fiber, gums, carotenes, beet juice, food colors, BHA, BHT, acetic acid, sodium benzoate, sodium propionate, salt, calcium stearate, lecithin, monoglycerides, and diglycerides."

And what salubrious results these additives had on civilization! "Modern food processing permits lifestyles to change and enables man to eat while on the way to the moon. . . . Women are liberated. . . . There is freedom to pursue higher education, to advance science and the arts, and to participate in the world arena."

"To participate in the world arena." I love the naïveté of that fifties phrase, the heady hope for the globalized food economy that we are now caught in today. We can be proud of the freedom that our food technologists have brought upon the world: that transnational corporations now directly or indirectly control what is grown on 80 percent of the world's arable lands, using more than 100 million international migrant workers as their labor force, most of whom have been dispossessed of their own family farms over the last half century. Another 27 million people around the world are enslaved as bonded laborers and sharecroppers, most of them doing the remaining menial chores that machines cannot do in industrialized agriculture. There are now more people economically enslaved to the food industry than at any other moment in human history, and as British economist Kevin Bales has concluded, "the largest transnational corporations, acting through [300,000] subsidiaries in the developing world, take advantage of slave-labour to increase their bottom line and the dividends to their shareholders."

Despite the tawdry record modern food technology has in fostering true freedom—the choice to stay connected to the land, family, and community if one wishes to—the Museum of Science and Industry has given the food industry unqualified praise before our children for nearly fifty years. The museum glorifies E. Hirschberg's Freeze-Drying Company for giving us the first canned spinach, "dehydrated, cooked, compressed, and gas packed." It celebrates PRO-TEN, an early texturized vegetable protein, and idolizes meatpacker Gustavius F. Smith, the innovator of the refrigerated railroad car, which became the archvillain in John Steinbeck's *East of Eden*. We are greeted throughout the exhibit with little plastic replicas of food everywhere we walk; and in fifty years our food has become more like the replicas than we care to admit.

Fortunately there was an antidote to all this toxic food talk, just a couple of miles away from the museum. Laurie and I met her son, Jeremy, over on Clark Street, hoping to run into Rick Bayless at his Frontera Grill. He had just come in from a cooking demonstration at Chicago's first Organic Farmers Market, a venue he helped organize and support. Now in its fourth month, the market featured regional items ranging from organically grown blueberries to a leafy purslane. The latter "weed" was now bringing one Illinois farmer a nice income to supplement what he makes off his "real" (domesticated) crops. Rick took as much pride in bringing these products to Chicago families through the marketplace as he did in what he serves at his restaurant and the adjacent bar, Topolobampo.

After a half hour of wide-ranging conversation, Rick hurried away to help his staff, while we tried their corn masa crepes stuffed with squash blossoms, wood-roasted poblano chilies, and Cacciota cheese. They were served in pale green sauce conjured up from avocados and tomatillos. Then came the *tamales de cazuela,* another corn dish, with a crustiness and garlic-laden aftertaste that kept them in a class above the wimpy facsimiles of tamales served in most American restaurants.

Laurie shared with Jeremy and me her order of stuffed squashes, wilted purslane, and creamy roasted tomatillo salsa. We sat for a while in awed silence, wondering how the *campesino* character of rural Mexico had floated so freshly up to Chicago. If that were not enough to fuse our tastebuds with our imaginations, the waiter came to announce a surprise for us, one that Rick had prepared since his departure from our table: a dessert of *cajeta* caramel and fresh berries atop ice cream.

After offering thanks, good-byes, and blessings to Rick and his staff, we were suddenly back on the streets of Chicago's Loop, streets I had eaten along a hundred times while I was a teenager. Of course, there had always been havens in Chicago that offered foods so delicious that they stood apart from the Italian-American pizzas, German bratwurst, and Irish corned beef and cabbage of my youth. But La Frontera Grill had upped the ante in Chicago, and others nearby were already exploring additional connections with local growers in their own ways.

The day after the wedding that brought us to Chicago, I took Laurie on another outing, a detour to my childhood homeland, the Indiana dunes west of Gary, where my Lebanese-American clan had shaped my sense of taste. My niece from Lebanon, Michela, Shibley's daughter, was visiting her uncle George and his wife, Elaine. They had decided to host an open house for all our kin. We arrived late but just in time for some toasts with arak, some hugs and kisses from my octogenarian aunts, and a warm embrace from my younger brother, Douglas, who had been chaperoning Michela all summer long.

I felt at last as though I had truly come home to eat, as I had known family feasting during my childhood. There were stuffed zucchini grown, picked, and filled with walnuts, garlic, and salt by my tenacious aunt Emily. Aunt Emily had been told by Elaine "not to worry, everything is under control," but that did not stop her from spending several hours preparing the homegrown squash, stuffing grape leaves hand-picked from the dunes, and piling up layers upon layers of filo dough for baklava. Elaine had made her own Greek-style grape leaves, as well as kibbe and a meat stew with green beans, all of them drawing on a fresh-ly butchered lamb. The piles of pita on the table became our utensils, our dishes, our communion bread. The anise-inundated arak distilled by our cousins in Lebanon became our wine, the blood from our family's sacred homelands.

I sat on the floor, resting against the knees of my aunts, listening to their stories of my father, my grandfather, and the old country. Four gen-erations of Nabhans—those born in Lebanon as well as those born in the United States—their shared food and their heritage with one another. They also shared a sense of what kept the world flavorful, and free of tyrannical monotony.

Chapter Twelve

From Toxic Cornfields to Rattlesnake Roadkills

S pending a few summer days in the honey-colored heartland of North America allowed me to see firsthand the latest technological advance of the food industry. Leaving Chicago in nearly any direction you wished, you could survey field after field of genetically engineered corn, the latest laboratory-generated wonder of the DNA era. As *Consumer Reports* explained it, "Today, a mere three years after the first large-scale commercial harvest, genetically engineered crops cover one-fourth of U.S. crop land [and most of the Midwest] . . . genetically engineered foods are already on the shelves of American supermarkets in products ranging from baby formulas and tortilla chips to drink mixes, taco shells, veggie burgers and muffin mix. . . . American consumers are eating genetically engineered food without knowing it [despite] a number of serious environmental concerns [such as the threat] that Bt corn may imperil the monarch butterfly."

"Bt corn" was a nickname for a number of varieties of hybrid maize with genes inserted in them from *Bacillus thuringiensis,* a soil microbe known to be toxic to a number of corn pests. I had heard about that potential threat to monarchs only three months before, when national news covered a laboratory study published in *Nature* that found that pollen from this corn was highly toxic to monarch butterfly larvae. That was of concern because 80 percent of all monarch butterflies that eventually make their way to Mexico for the winter begin their lives in the Corn Belt. There were also fifty other species of butterfly listed as endangered by the U.S. government, but no one knew how many had been exposed to this corn's toxic pollen. Apparently the Environmental Protection Agency did not even test the effects of Bt corn on any butterflies before they approved permits to release it, nor did they ask the U.S. Fish and Wildlife Service to monitor its effects on any endangered butterflies. Scientists were unsure whether the laboratory experiment clearly demonstrated that monarch larvae would also be killed if they ventured into cornfields while the corn develops its tassels, and were even more in the dark about which other butterfly species might be affected. Since Jeremy had offered to drive us to St. Louis to catch a plane back home, I decided to take notes on butterflies as we migrated across the Corn Belt. While Laurie rested in the backseat, Jeremy looked for butterflies out of his side of the car, while I scanned the field edges on the other.

At first I thought I would enjoy this bit of field science after several days in the city, but it soon became clear that enjoyment was not in the cards. I was seeing cornfields filled with hybrid corn of unknown origin, cornfields with wild milkweeds growing right up to their edges. Milkweeds were what monarch caterpillars required as their larval host plants, and the biotech industry had claimed that milkweeds were seldom seen in or near cornfields where Bt corn was planted. Industry geneticists had ridiculed Cornell University professor John Losey—the senior author of the *Nature* study—for implying that milkweed leaves might ever be exposed to Bt corn's toxins when monarch caterpillars and butterflies were actively foraging in the Midwest. Siding with the industry, Cornell's agricultural administrators had denounced Losey for "prematurely" releasing his study to *Nature,* even though Losey himself had been careful not to read too much into his initial lab experiments. He had wanted to do field studies as well, the kind that—when they were finally done in Iowa—demonstrated monarch mortality on the edges of fields. Nevertheless, the USDA turned down Losey's own grant proposal to do such definitive field studies, preferring to rely on Monsanto-funded studies, just as the EPA opted to do.

So there I was, riding shotgun next to Jeremy, recording every mile between Chicago and St. Louis where I spotted milkweeds growing within five yards of corn. Of course, I didn't know which cornfields contained Bt corn, because the USDA did not require that the fields or their products be labeled. I realized that even if Bt corn was grown in these fields, the outer rows would probably contain another, nontoxic variety as a buffer to slow down the European corn borer's development of resistance to *Bacillus thuringiensis.*

For several years the Union of Concerned Scientists had been raising questions about what might happen if European and Southwestern corn borers and other pests overcome the toxins derived from the genes of *Bacillus thuringiensis.* Union scientist Jane Rissler had argued that the pests would respond differently to this microbe when it was embedded in the corn genome than they did in the thousands of gardens where Dipel and other commercial Bt products had been directly hand-applied to vegetables for decades. Bt's insertion into widely distributed crops increased the probability that its pest-control efficacy could soon be lost for good. When we plant Bt corn on millions of acres, Rissler and her colleagues predicted, rapidly evolving insects find a large homogeneous challenge, and develop resistance to the very toxin that farmers and gardeners had used as a pest-control tool for decades. In fact, a May 7, 1999, article in *Science* magazine confirmed Rissler's fears that the European corn borer had already developed dominant genes with resistance against Bt toxins, allowing them eventually to become even more virulent pests.

At the same time spokespersons for the biotechnology industry were claiming that no risks from planting Bt corn had been reported by the farmers who had thousands of acres of it in their fields. They contended that Losey's experiment, reported in *Nature,* was merely a contrived lab experiment that didn't have much relevance in "the real world." They were sidestepping the issue. Some of them undoubtedly knew that Iowa State University scientists had already presented data to the contrary at a regional meeting of entomologists. In a progress report from their field studies in the heart of the Corn Belt, Iowa scientists found that monarch caterpillars ranging within a few yards of Bt corn-rows were indeed exposed to toxic pollen. And well before any U.S. scientists had signaled such alarms, Swiss scientists reported that Bt corn damages beneficial insects that feed on corn pests. Other European researchers had disproved the industry's claim that Bt toxins break down rapidly under field conditions, raising new concerns about the effects of Bt corn on the thousands of invertebrates per inch of soil that are essential to the renewal of soil fertility.

And yet, in the midst of the release of these cautionary field and lab reports, National Public Radio featured biotech industry spokesman Val Giddings, who dismissed these scientists' concerns simply as "nonsense." He claimed that any speculation about environmental risks were "ridiculous" and that the industry had already done its own studies to ensure that humans and wildlife would not be affected by Bt corn or other GE crops. That disclaimer about GE food crops got up the dander of an old hero of mine, Phil Regal, a visionary ecologist at the University of Minnesota. As Phil put it:

> One of their misleading claims is, "Well, there's no evidence that anyone has ever died, gotten sick, or even gotten a rash from GE foods," and this is their idea of scientific proof. How can anyone make a claim like this when the food is not segregated or labeled? People die, get sick, and get rashes all the time. How can we know if some of these things were caused by GE foods or not? We can't.

That's not science or scientific evidence . . . if these foods are not
labeled, you have no control group, no experiment, and you have
no science.

As Jeremy, Laurie, and I drove across the Corn Belt, my mind kept
on coming back to the statements by biotech industry spokesmen that
milkweeds could hardly be found in the vicinity of cornfields, thereby
making it unlikely that Bt corn would harm monarchs. I started to tally
my own observations about whether milkweeds and monarchs were
cohabiting with corn.

It was near the Gardner exit off I-55, south of Chicago, that I first
spotted milkweeds and swallowtail butterflies within a yard of a cornfield's border. We exited to confirm that drive-by sighting, and sure
enough, the big cabbage-leaved plant next to the corn in tassel did
indeed belong to the milkweed genus, *Asclepias*. Near milepost 220,
outside of Morris, Illinois, I recorded a larger patch of milkweeds
between the corn and the highway, and five miles later, south of the
Mason River, another patch within three yards of the corn. Mileposts
213, 211, and 198, north of Pontiac, had hundreds of milkweeds growing near them, just beyond the plowmark of the cornfields there.

And so it went. Another ten sites of milkweeds adjacent to corn
north of Bloomington, another sixteen down to Elkhart, Illinois. Before
we reached the Mississippi River, I had counted another sixteen milk-
weed-infested cornfields out my car window, while Jeremy and Laurie
spotted still others across the highway.

As we entered St. Louis I took a moment to tally up my results.
Along a 150-mile stretch of I-55, I found milkweeds within fifteen feet
of cornfields along forty-five-mile-long segments of the transect. Most
of the transect comprised soybean fields, urban landscaping, and woodlots. That meant that milkweeds were associated with the majority of
cornfields I observed.

As we passed through St. Louis, I wondered whether Monsanto
publicists working on this issue from their headquarters just a few miles

away had ever taken a look for themselves, to see whether cornfields in their vicinity were milkweed-and-monarch-free or harbored these wild partners. It took little special training to become a student of corn, milkweeds, and monarchs, but if Monsanto's staff made such observations before they released their products onto millions of acres, they had not shared them in any scientific journals or reports to the government that I had seen.

I was certainly not the only scientist in America dismayed by Monsanto's responses to public concerns about its genetically modified (GM) crops. In June the Rockefeller Foundation's president, Gordon Conway, had admonished Monsanto's board of directors for overtouting the humanitarian value of their GM crops, and for not undertaking extensive greenhouse and field testing before releasing the transgenic corn and soybeans to farmers. As a crop ecologist with thirty years' experience on the front line of agricultural development projects all across Asia, Conway was clearly impatient with unsubstantiated hype about keeping the masses from starvation: "I've told the companies they shouldn't claim their biotech products will feed the world," he said bluntly, as if he didn't care that his message would be received like the proverbial fart in church.

It was a message Monsanto and other biotech firms had long ignored. They had earlier dismissed it when it came from the grassroots activists who first raised ethical issues regarding GM crops, but they could no longer ignore it when it came from someone as credible and as politically persuasive as the Rockefeller Foundation's headman. As *Fortune* magazine later reported:

> In an eloquent speech, the scientist all but charged Monsanto with hubris—in the rush to market GM cotton, soybeans, and corn, he said, it and other purveyors had given short shrift to legitimate concerns and generated a backlash. He urged the company to make major policy changes and to forego the use of "terminator" technology, GM plants that bear sterile seeds so that farmers are forced

to buy new ones each year. The next day Conway stunned Monsanto by going public with his recommendations.

To his credit, Monsanto's CEO Robert Shapiro responded to Conway's critique by promising to shelve the commercialization of its terminator genes, which signaled a hard-won victory for the farming activists who had worked so hard to bring the perils of sterile seeds under broader scrutiny. Perhaps even more telling was Shapiro's admission that "[t]oo often we forgot to listen."

And yet, while crops with terminator genes in them were shelved, those containing Bt toxins remained in the fields, with the farmers who sowed them taking heat from both consumers and their sometime-allies in agribusiness. As American Corn Growers Association director Gary Goldberg conceded, "farmers got caught in the middle," unintentionally inflicting damage on the local fauna, and then losing their market when consumers became outraged that Bt corn had been released without adequate testing.

A Kansas farmer I knew looked into purchasing Bt corn, but did some quick calculations before he did. Because it is sold at a higher price per pound than other corns, he figured that he would need to harvest four extra bushels of borer-free grain to offset his extra expenses. Unconvinced that he could kick his yields up to that level, he kept to a variety that had already offered him relatively stable yields. Other American corn growers have gone with the same strategy of reducing their probability of facing new risks.

"This is already such a hard time for us," Goldberg admitted, "and then you compound it with this Bt corn uncertainty."

I wondered how so many other farmers had talked themselves into this Faustian bargain: In exchange for the promise of fewer pests reducing the constancy of their food supply, they had risked damaging their farms and the surrounding wildlife as well. We all wanted food security, sure, but at what cost?

Right then and there I thought of weaning myself from *all* corn products until I could figure out which particular ones included Bt corn—chips, starch, taco shells, masa, grits, and syrups. But that task would not be simple: Corn was hidden in dozens of other food products, cosmetics, and beverages. And some allergy-causing genetically engineered corns such as Star Link were approved for use only as animal feed, but were no doubt being mixed with batches used in making cornmeal and baby foods. It was just not as straightforward as other (earlier) agricultural issues put before the American public, such as Cesar Chavez's logic for boycotting grapes. Corn was so embedded in the American diet that I might have to spend a good portion of my waking hours reading labels to live with a clear conscience.

I could see only one thing to do: write the U.S. Fish and Wildlife Service director, Jamie R. Clark, to ask her to issue a "jeopardy opinion." That is the legal means by which EPA permits for the corns to be challenged on the basis of noncompliance with the Endangered Species Act. Because monarch butterflies do not belong to an endangered species—even though their migration is internationally recognized as an endangered ecological phenomenon—I had to focus my letter on Bt corn's threat to the eighteen other moths and butterflies federally listed as endangered species, especially those occurring in the Corn Belt. But because the Fish and Wildlife Service had recently signed an agreement with Mexico to help protect monarchs throughout their range in North America, I mentioned that as well. The letter later became the basis for a lawsuit that Green Peace and the Center for Food Safety advanced against EPA for failing to consider the Endangered Species Act or adequately inform the Fish and Wildlife Service once it was known that Bt corn pollen could kill butterflies.

About the same time I sent this letter, I was asked by the Union of Concerned Scientists and the Environmental Defense Fund to sign on to a similar letter to the Environmental Protection Agency. They also invited me to a meeting with EPA and other officials a few weeks later. I recruited Lincoln Brower, the country's leading monarch expert, to join us.

Before I knew it I was on another plane, this time to Washington, D.C. I carried with me a little box of mesquite tortillas from Esperanza, and a dozen amaranth-and-apple muffins I had made myself, hoping to avoid airline food made in Nowhere, USA. When I got off the plane, I flagged down a taxi to take me to a coffee shop where I would meet Jane, Becky, and others to discuss strategies while waiting for Lincoln to join us. A graying Rastafarian picked me up and agreed to take me to the shopping center where the Environmental Protection Agency houses its bureaucrats. He knew the place well.

"What you doin' down here, mon? You not even look de part. Where you from, mon?"

I looked up from my papers, and realized he was right. I had on an Hawaiian shirt and cowboy boots. While we talked, I pulled a blue blazer, a button-down shirt, and tie out of my bag.

"Oh, I'll be going to a meeting with some EPA muckety-mucks to see if we can get a ban on this genetically engineered corn that—"

The taxi driver waved his hand to interrupt me.

"You mean you be here for *dead-butterfly corn*?"

"What? Yes. . . . You know about Bt corn?"

Mr. William Donahue, my taxi driver, had formerly worked as a patent officer in Jamaica. He told me that whenever food-patenting and -permitting issues were brought up on talk radio, he listened intently, then tried to learn more about them in the newspapers.

"Dis genetically engineering life, it be poison. Dese multinational cumpanies, mon, dey be gettin' mo' 'n' mo' of de power over our food, our medicine, you know what I'm sayin', mon? From when I was de patent agent back home, I know. In my country de patent was all by America nation, Europe nation, we got nothin' for our own. Afterward I come to this capitol city, I see how it's all comin' down. Dese people, dey all live on de power, not on de food, but dey try to control de food. It make no matter to dem dat de tofu is from de genetically engineering."

"What?"

"Dat tofu, you know, soy cake, bean cake, mon. It be from beans dey make from de genetically engineering. It be poison to something mon, maybe to us too. No good. Dey talk on de talk show like dis is soo-prise, but I know it's no soo-prise. Long time, I've been listening to de prophesy. Dead Sea Scroll. Haile Selassie. Bob Marley. All de prophesy people, dey knew it be comin' down dis way."

Mr. Donahue dropped me off at the right place at the right time, but his soliloquy on genetically engineered soybeans had me all disoriented. I had never met Jane and Becky in person, and I knew that Lincoln would be arriving a little later than the rest of us. Before Donahue had started talking with me, I had been carrying around in my mind a stereotypical image of what a genetic-engineering activist might look like, hoping to match faces in the mall with that stereotype in order to encounter Becky and Jane. Thanks to Donahue, the stereotype was blown to hell: Jane and Becky might have dreadlocks or look like soybean farmers from the Midwest, for all I knew. After a half hour of my fruitless searching, Jane noticed me, perhaps by the desperation in my eyes.

Later in the day we all convened in a meeting room in the Interior Building not far from the Capitol. Science adviser Bill Brown welcomed us and fondly recalled how a *Scientific American* cover story by Lincoln Brower had opened up the world of monarchs and milkweeds to him. Lincoln's work with the natural chemicals in milkweeds had dramatically underscored the complexity of chemically mediated interactions between plants and butterflies, interactions that could easily be disrupted. Brown recognized the importance of such work, for he had worked as a field biologist when he was younger. Although he had become one of the government's senior advisers on biotechnology and the environment, he maintained a certain affection for other field biologists.

But, after introducing the twenty-some government officials scattered around the room, Brown left his biological instincts behind and expressed a behavior undoubtedly forged over several years of working to make big industries like Waste Management, Inc., both greener and more profitable. He made it clear that he was not interested in any initiative that fostered public distrust of biotechnology, since some genetically engineered crops had the potential for reducing pesticide and herbicide use.

Becky, Jane, Lincoln, and I glanced at one another as if we had arrived in the wrong room. When we recovered Becky explained politely that we had not come to debate the benefits and risks of biotechnology in general. Instead we were there to remind Interior officials that they had a mandate to ban any particular genetically modified organism if it had a known impact on endangered species. Jane then corrected Brown's assumption that Bt corn itself was fundamentally different than other pesticides. Bt corn, she maintained, was simply a plant with a pesticide inserted within its genome. The government needed to evaluate Bt corn with the same rigor it was required to use in its evaluation of other pesticides.

Flustered, Brown shared with us an editorial that had recently been sent to him by two eminent scientists, Peter Raven and David Pimental. They admitted that "Bt anti-insect protein is obviously harmful to moths and butterflies," but argued that it was a lesser evil compared to the pesticides that poisoned the songbirds Rachel Carson eulogized in *Silent Spring*.

A bit miffed by the implication that Rachel Carson would have signed off on Bt corn as something benign, I reminded Brown that butterflies were also a form of wildlife that the public cared deeply about. His own boss, Secretary Bruce Babbitt, clearly sanctioned legal protection for threatened butterflies as much as for birds.

Jane then set the linchpin: Currently available pesticide use statistics did not show any significant decrease in pesticide applications in fields where Bt field corn was planted. Bt field corn had been planted on millions of acres by farmers who had continued to use other pesticides and herbicides, so the assumption that songbirds were being spared while butterflies were being decimated was altogether unfounded.

The meeting ended in a standoff. Brown left the room before any of Interior's biologists had a chance to offer what they would be willing to do to monitor the problem. As we left to get something to drink at an Interior refreshment bar, one of the attendees slipped me a piece of paper: "Brown didn't invite any of the Fish and Wildlife personnel assigned to working on a response to your letters—don't worry, some of us are just as angry about EPA leaving us out of the Bt corn permitting process as you are."

Our meeting with the Environmental Protection Agency had an altogether different tone. Fearing a lawsuit from us, its bureaucrats had requested that both its lawyers and its scientists be present in full force. We were warmly greeted by Susan Wayland, one of EPA's highest-ranking administrators, who assured us that the "EPA takes this monarch issue very seriously. We are totally open to pursuing the questions through an open, transparent and scientifically sound process."

Not one to be sedated by platitudes, Jane patiently tapped her pen against her pad until she gained Susan's attention. Then she said quietly but firmly, "This is a risk that the EPA should have identified more than five years ago. We are twenty million acres too late and the risk is probably growing. We don't want this to happen again."

At that point Susan deferred to her experts, claiming that they would outline the scientific process the EPA had launched since the *Nature* article drew international attention to monarchs and Bt corn. One of Susan's program directors took over, flashing a big smile: "You will be delighted to hear some good news. The biotechnology industry has generously offered to pay for eight hundred thousand dollars' worth of studies this summer to evaluate Bt corn's potential impacts. Since EPA simply does not have the kind of budget to underwrite our own studies at this level, we will be preparing to evaluate the industry's studies this fall."

This did *not* delight us. We already felt that the relationship between the EPA and the biotech industry was far too cozy. We knew of former EPA executives who now work for Monsanto and other biotech firms, who regularly call their former staff members to "maintain good working relationships."

This time Lincoln Brower grew impatient, reminding the EPA staffers of the metaphor about "foxes guarding the henhouse." They pretended to ignore his comment, but I noticed that at least a half dozen bureaucrats in the room shifted their weight from one buttock to the other as Lincoln returned to silence. Then it was my turn to talk.

"Why can't the industry's money be used for studies that the U.S. Fish and Wildlife Service and EPA design, solicit, and supervise?" I asked. " Is it routine for industry to run its own studies, which EPA then passively accepts as the only information available?"

"Well, yes," someone clarified. "Yes, we depend on the information submitted by the corporation that is asking for a permit for its new product. We couldn't possibly fund our own field evaluations of the thousands of new products proposed for release each year."

Evaluations? I thought. The EPA had simply rubber-stamped the biotech firms' contention in their provisional permit applications that Bt corns could have no substantive impact on wildlife. They pretended that the toxins would be restricted to cornfields that no endangered wildlife would ever enter.

One EPA biologist finally spoke up. He agreed that if the *Nature* study of monarch caterpillar mortality had been published prior to the granting of Bt corn's provisional permit, EPA could not have justified issuing the permit until independent studies were accomplished. But, he shrugged, the timing was wrong. The EPA had promised the industry that it would wait to evaluate the new studies before reevaluating Bt corn's permits. Unfortunately the new studies were just not at the point at which they could confirm or deny widespread impact on butterflies.

Near the end of the meeting one of the EPA officials turned to me and Lincoln to learn more about what monarch butterflies were like. She was curious: "So you two have actually seen these millions of monarchs where they winter in Mexico? That must be something, huh?"

For the first time since we came together at the same table, I realized that none of the EPA employees in the room had ever had the thrill of visiting a monarch roost. They read our impassioned pleas as some sort of zealotry. They could hardly understand the unbridled passion for monarchs Lincoln and I carried with us from our many visits to the Mexican monarch sanctuaries. And yet we shared that passion with tens of thousands of other North Americans who had the honor to witness millions of monarchs shingling trees at the winter roosts, creating their own microclimate to survive the cold together. Once any human is present for this living miracle, it is impossible to forget. Most of us would rather eliminate corn from our diet than face the worry that each time we ate cornflakes, chips, or tortillas, we were diminishing the probability that as many monarchs would arrive at their wintering grounds.

As we got up from the table, I offered a parting remark:

You know, hundreds of thousands of children learn about monarchs in school and cherish the sight of them. Their teachers have informed them that the U.S. signed an agreement with Mexico and Canada to protect these butterflies throughout their North American range. Imagine, then, what it must have been like for them to hear on the radio that the government has permitted farmers to grow a crop on a third of the country's cornfields that potentially kills monarchs. Imagine how contradictory that feels to them.

The EPA conference room was quiet for another moment, but then the paper shuffling began. We were thanked for our opinions, and were promised that they would keep us in touch.

A few hours later, while flying home with my last two muffins in hand, I fell apart at the seams. Was it even worth it to go to Washington, taking time away from my efforts to eat close to home, to take better care of the land and plants close at hand? Was I not just one more affluent American in flight, guzzling fossil fuels in the name of a cause that no one will care about five years from now, let alone fifty? Did I even deserve to share this airspace with migrating bats, birds, and butterflies?

I couldn't answer my own questions, but when I got home I went ahead and wrote some congressmen anyway. And I wrote about the perils of untested crop releases for the local paper, for a regional paper, for a regional radio network, and for an international conservation publication.

I had begun to feel that we were at some turning point in American agricultural history. It had to do with what we were willing to tolerate in order to obtain cheap food; whether we were willing passively to accept whatever the biotech industry threw at us, or whether we demanded that their products be scrutinized with the same scientific objectivity *and* ethical rigor that we would use to scrutinize a new antibiotic or a new pesticide. As Jane had said, Bt corn was merely a pesticide inserted into the genome of corn, and had become a producer of toxins placed on more than 25 million acres globally. We were no longer spraying toxins across America, we were moving them from one organism's genome to the next, without much oversight, and virtually no *foresight* about potential side effects. The *precautionary principle*—a fundamental element of medical and biological ethics that encourages society to assess the pitfalls of an unprecedented action or novel product *before* unleashing it on the world—had been thrown out the window.

Back in the desert from Washington, I was desperate to celebrate the bounty we had right there, to remind my friends and neighbors that all the delicious food we could ever desire was at our doorstep. And so, with our friend Alison Deming, we gathered friends together for a "local foods party," featuring a prickly pear Margarita made with Sonoran mescal to attract even the diehards. We prepared a dozen salsas made with locally grown chiles. We laid out pickled cholla buds and road-rescued venison, as well as freshly picked amaranth, purslane greens, and some grandmother's apple pie. Alison prepared beef grown and butchered just two miles away from where we feasted.

If that were not enough, the day of the party I rescued a dying rattlesnake that I saw hit by the car in front of me while I was on my way home. Two hours after its tail was run over, it stopped squirming. That was the attraction for having rattlesnakes on the platter at parties: Once you tell guests that rattlers can actually bite you and poison you even after they are dead, this becomes a great stimulant for conversation. I skinned out the snake, removed its sinewy entrails, and chipped all the meat away from its ribs. Then I combined the meat with blue corn meal given to me by a Hopi friend—an ancient heirloom clearly lacking in toxic pollen—and made rattlesnake fritters.

An hour before opening the doors for this local foods celebration, I caught sight of migratory monarchs moving through our valley, presumably on their way to the oyamel fir forests of Mexico. They wafted through my backyard, their orange-and-black patterns glistening in the sun, then drifted out of sight up the wash to the southeast of us. We would never know if these particular monarchs made it safely to their wintering grounds, but as we ate Bt-free foods that night, we could at least feel good that we were not placing further obstacles in their path. If we boycotted such foods, as hundreds of thousands of other Americans were doing, perhaps farmers would choose not to grow them. By early fall both Gerber and Heinz had chosen not to use Bt corns as ingredients in their baby foods. A change had begun, and it was rippling out over the cornfields of this continent, reshaping everything in its wake.

III

Autumn

The Feasting Months

Chapter Thirteen

The Headwaters
and the Foodshed

The more I learned about the ecological effects of industrializing and *globaliz*ing food, the more I had but one prevailing inclination: to ensure that my friends and family ate in a way that supported the conservation and not the degradation of the creatures in our foodshed and watershed. If nearly half of all the sunlight captured was now being funneled into fueling only our species, what was happening to the rest of the gang? Given that most of my food was coming from the greater Río Colorado watershed and the Gulf of California into which it flowed, how was the wildlife out there faring? Were the native plants that had supported humans for eight thousand years still regenerating themselves, or were they being crushed by our big ecological footprint? That footprint—the amount of productive land needed to support each of us—as size twelve acres for the average American, size nine-point-five acres for Europeans, and size one-point-two acres for most residents of developing countries. I wanted to go out and see how the watershed that nurtured me was faring, to provide all of us within its school a report card on its ecological health.

When I tried to picture where my blood and bones come from, I saw the Río Colorado flowing like arteries through layers of calcium, iron, and sodium, through limestone, sandstone, and shales. For more than twenty-five years it has given me most of my food and water. My food-shed ran down from the mountains, into my garden, and out to nearby ephemeral drainages, which eventually coalesced in the big red muddy river itself. Laurie and I had been invited to see the state of this watershed in its most remote reaches—its headwaters—amidst the buttes, canyons, and mesas of the San Juan tributary to the Colorado. We would follow that river trip in the hinterlands with an excursion to the fertile bottom-lands, and then with a month along the Gulf. But if we were to gain this broader sense of our foodshed over a six-week period, we had to complete a more immediate task back home: butchering the now-fattened turkeys, which could not survive on their own during our absence.

For some time Laurie and I had known that we had to "dress" the birds before departing on this adventure from the top to the bottom of our foodshed. But here it was the end of summer approaching, and we were already so tired from earlier travel that we were reluctant to get moving again. Our garden was as lush as it had ever been, and the turkeys were rapidly putting on weight. We had not been able to find a single friend or family member willing to take over their tending for a month and a half, so I began an all-out harvest of our herbs, vegetables, and turkeys. Just five months after we had received turkey hatchlings, they were large enough to be killed, plucked, gutted, and smoked for future use.

Laurie was content to help me harvest a bushel of tomatoes, tomatil-los, and chiles; she cut, hung, and dried many of our annual herbs and froze others. But when I asked her to help me butcher the turkeys, it was as if she had not registered that at some point in the life of most fowl, the birds stopped living if they were to become food. They could become coyote food or cat food, but my preference was for them to become human food. At this point I had little choice but to butcher them before we left for the river and the sea.

I decided to butcher the first one while she was away for a few days, when I was to host writers Simon Ortiz and Luci Tapahonso and other friends for dinner. It was tricky business doing this butchering by myself. I could not reach Ely, who had earlier volunteered to help me, but had nevertheless followed his advice by switching their diet to greens, then isolating one of the toms and giving him only water for his last twenty-four hours. When I caught and moved him into an isolation pen, he was as gentle and affectionate as ever. I realized that none of these turkeys had ever chased, pecked, or bullied anyone—child or adult.

As the personality profiles of all five turkeys were running through my head, I paused for a moment and gave myself an emotional way out. These turkeys were only a handful of the three million waddled and snooded birds that would be killed this year on American butchering blocks. I had two other neighbors within ten miles of me who would be killing their turkeys this season as well, and there were thirteen big-time brooders and butcherers of turkey flocks in Arizona. If they could do their work, why couldn't I? If they could ignore the personalities of the turkeys that they had to butcher, why shouldn't I? And what about all the turkeys Arizonans eat that come from out of state, already butchered, packaged, and frozen? Is their butchering any cleaner, any better? If Arizonans produced all the three million turkeys we ate each year, we'd have at least twenty thousand acres of birds jumping around whenever we raised a butcher knife. Isn't it better that I just deal with this whole issue bird by bird, rather than hold all three million feathered lives in my heart all at one time?

And so I began my work, grateful to have raised such beautiful birds, but determined to unflinchingly do the dirty work that someone else had always done for me. I hung the turkey upside down above a pail full of water, held its feet, and cut its throat.

That was when I found out I was two hands short of doing my task as quickly and effectively as I had wished. You simply cannot hold a knife, two feet, and two wings at the same time without a lot of practice. The turkey fluttered and spasmed as I inched it down into the water, where it relaxed and died. But after the first ten seconds of wing-beating spasms, I was covered with blood.

A little shook up, I forgot to clean out the entire crop before plucking and dressing the bird. This little oversight tainted the flavor of the meat somewhat when I smoked it the next morning.

That night, Simon, Bob, Luci, and Alison ate the turkey appreciatively, without commenting on the faint fermented grain-fed aftertaste. Simon confessed that when he was younger and married to Luci's sister, he had trouble butchering sheep in a manner that pleased his Navajo mother-in-law. It was later, when he was helping his uncles dress deer at Zuni, that he gained an understanding that butchering can be a sacred ritual.

"We never call it butchering in our own language," Simon reminded us. "We're dressing a beloved relative. It is an elaborate ritual with a metaphorical language all its own."

Luci concurred. "I was horrified when I was teaching in New Mexico, and a student asked me how the Navajo kill and butcher sheep and deer. We never think of it that way. They are giving their bodies up for us; they are our kin."

The next day, when Laurie came home in the afternoon, she decided to take the remaining turkeys for a walk through our neighborhood. Two by two, I later learned, she put leashes around their necks, and guided them around the block, talking to neighbors as they strolled along.

"What are your pets' names?" the neighbors asked.

Laurie named them on the spur of the moment, a christening that I came to regret the next day.

I still knew nothing of the walk or anything of the naming when I asked Laurie to help me with the butchering.

"I'm sorry," she said flatly. "I've come to know them. They're my friends. And besides, I can't stand to see any more blood. I've worked as a nurse too long—I know what suffering and death are all about."

I was stunned. "But how 'bout reducing their suffering? We can't just leave them here. And if I butcher them, I want to do it as carefully, as quickly as possible."

"That is a contradiction in my mind. I am afraid I can't help you."

"*What*?!" I could feel my ears turning red, my neck heating up. "You knew it was my intention all along to raise these turkeys for meat. We've talked all year about taking responsibility, you know, for where our food comes from, including our meat."

I was still sputtering and stuttering with disbelief. "Dammit, if you eat meat, don't you think you should be involved in this? . . . Look, this is our last night home. I *have* to butcher them today, and I need help!"

"Then call Kit or one of your other male friends. Maybe they can tolerate the blood, but I can't. I may *think* I should be more responsible in my eating meat, but my *heart* is not up to doing this. Now, please don't force me to do something I don't want to do." As she walked away from me, she added, "Raising and killing turkeys was your project, not mine."

I was crushed, probably because of my own facile assumption that Laurie felt exactly the same way about animal raising and butchering as I did. I had raised chickens, wrung their necks, and plucked them; I had milked goats and butchered them with stone tools; I had caught fish, gutted and decapitated them without flinching. Each of these tasks could be messy business. I did not always find them pleasant, but I never shirked from them. The master hunters and farmers I knew accomplished their butchering chores with a swiftness and precision that had a sanctity to it.

Because I knew of Laurie's strong religious inclinations, I had presumed that she too would find something sacramental and necessary, if not altogether sacred, in the blessing and dressing of our homegrown birds. Wrong again, guy. Laurie went into town to drop off a few items at friends' houses, while I sat down and wondered what to do with the rest of the birds.

When I finally got over my moping and called my friend Kit, he fortunately had the time to help me. In a matter of an hour, we had moved the last four turkeys one by one to the killing floor out by the garage. We turned them upside down, wings held close to their bodies, and bled their necks into a bucket. I removed their heads and feet, thoroughly cleaned their guts and their crops, while Kit dunked them in hot water. Then we sat down on the ground in my backyard, broke open two warm beers, and plucked the feathers off each bird.

We did what guys are best at: We got a grisly job done simply by offering deadpan companionship and telling bad jokes.

One turkey would go home with Kit; another went across the street to neighbors who had fed the turkeys whenever Laurie and I went away; while a third went into our freezer. The fourth went immediately into the adobe oven to smoke, along with two more trays full of jalapeño peppers. As we packed for our watershed adventure, the turkey smoked over mesquite coals, stuffed with a *chiltepin*-onion-and-berry dressing. When the roasted bird came out of the oven, Kit came back with his wife, Ann, to collect all the turkey feathers for a weaving she wanted to make. We picked greens from the garden, sliced the moist, smoky turkey meat, and laughed about the way Laurie and I had sparred over the turkeys' last rites.

It was not until the next day that Laurie admitted to me that she did not touch a piece of turkey meat that landed on her plate, even though none of the rest of us had noticed. By that time we were off to the hinterlands.

As Laurie drove with me out of the Sonoran Desert, into the headwaters of the Colorado, we watched the land get redder, rockier, and more rugged. Larger and larger clouds built beyond Monument Valley, above the peaks of the Rockies in the distance, as if the very source of all rain was hidden up in those mountains. She pointed out to me how various cumulonimbus clouds took the forms of buttes, canyons, and mesas. She was right: The shapes of the land reflected the shapes in the heavens, and a cycle of water ran through them both.

We rolled the Blazer to a stop at Sand Island, a patch of loose sediment down inside a stone-walled canyon, the put-in for most San Juan River runners. Those stone walls were filled with petroglyphs designed to bring on the rain, as well as to bring on the wildlife that thrive on rainy season herbs. We joined a motley crew of aging watershed scholars and their mostly teenage kin: Santa Fe's Jack Loeffler and his daughter; Albuquerque's Enrique La Madrid and his clan, and Nevada City's Pulitzer Prize–winning poet Gary Snyder, with his daughter and niece. We helped one another unpack, and set up tents, but it was still over a hundred degrees when we gathered for a dinner of green squash and corn, cholla buds, onions, and turkey chorizo. I offered roasted grasshoppers for dessert, but found no takers. It was almost too hot to eat comfortably; better to swim and to sing a few songs after dinner, then sleep and begin anew in the morning.

As Laurie and I slipped into our tent, I thought I heard singing and drumming. It sounded as if it was coming from across the river, on the edge of the Navajo reservation. It reminded me of the cadence of peyote songs from the Native American Church. I nudged Laurie, who had already, instantly, fallen asleep. "Do you hear that?" I whispered.

"Sound of the river." She yawned, out for the rest of the night.

Maybe she was right: Perhaps I was only hearing the viscous bed-load being dragged along the river bottom. The sound I was hearing could have been the fragmenting of bedrock cobbles into gravel, the crunching of gravel into coarse sand, and the pulverizing of coarse sand into all the mineralized nutrients farmers might need in the valleys below. The working river thrummed and thrummed as I too dropped off into dreams in which muddy rivers and Navajos chanting peyote songs blended together.

We shared a breakfast of mesquite-and-blue-corn pancakes, then began our collective work: We pumped up rafts, lashed down frames, ran a car shuttle down to our takeoff point. We spun yarns, visited near petroglyphs, and shared with one another the oral history of the river. The teenagers went fishing for a while but had no luck: We would be eating what we had brought along for at least our first day on the river. Our last afternoon as landlubbers disappeared before we knew it as we formed a provisional economic community, one to float down the river, and that alone took all our attention.

The night prior to the put-in, Enrique offered to fix us his elaborate camp-style adaptation of paella Valenciana. My heart sank a little, for I had been hoping that our shared meals would emphasize the locally available foods, which I was sure we would all enjoy once we found them. But we had not found any on Sand Island, and Enrique had begun to make some exotic magic. I suppressed my disappointment in not achieving my ideal, then watched and listened to Enrique as the paella took shape. He had recently taken his New Mexican Spanish students to the Iberian Peninsula, and fallen in love (once again) with the paellas of his ancestors. While we peeled vegetables, he lectured me on the place-names on the Colorado Plateau that were transplanted from Spain, just as many food traditions had been transplanted as well. As he talked, he burned a little olive oil on the bottom of a big cooking pot, then tossed in ten whole cloves of garlic. Lacking the fresh rabbit and snails characteristic of good Valencian cuisine, he browned an entire chicken, added canned shrimp and clams, all imports from distant lands and seas. When Gary offered him a bag of fat-grained rice grown by Snyder's in-laws, Enrique snapped it up, adding green peas, onions, and artichokes to it. As Enrique stirred together chicken stock, saffron, and turmeric into a golden sauce, pouring it onto the paella with flourish, I realized he was offering us his clan's traditional comfort food. It was clear: We were not yet on the San Juan; we were hovering between that river and the hills of Iberia.

Needless to say, when the first forkful of paella touched our lips, we were fully transported—the water of the San Juan was turned into the wine of Valencia. Not far from here in 1765, Juan Maria Antonio de Rivera became the first Spaniard to visit the "unknown corners" of the canyons and mesas edging the Río Colorado's headwaters. I doubted that he could have brought paella fixings with him at that time, but didn't doubt at all that he brought along whatever he could to remind him of his mother country.

Just before we pushed off the next morning, Loeffler, the veteran river runner among us, looked around at this random assembly of "watershedders," saluted Snyder, and announced, "This is a *very* ragtag crew, *Capitán.*"

"Thank you for your opinion, Admiral Kropotkin; I'll take it under advisement," Snyder retorted, saluting back.

"Hard to say whether we can fish, forage, and run rapids competently," I added. "But if we don't make it out, we'll make good stew meat for the ravens and coyotes," I added.

Loeffler burst into his notoriously manic laughter, which echoed off the cliffs and came back to us seconds later. It was a laughter that rivaled that of the coyotes and ravens themselves, one so boisterous that it momentarily dwarfed the cascading song of the canyon wren. Jack's laughter and the canyon wren's call note were the overture of our journey downstream. We would float and eat, wander and ponder where our water, food, and energy would come from. We were all well aware that none of us could eat, drink, or live well if these uplands were despoiled. We set ourselves afloat in the headwaters, knowing that the health of the watershed is tied to our own, just as much as Ishmael and Queequeg's lives were linked by a lone fragile cord as the *Pequod* pursued the whale Moby-Dick.

What a motley crew we were, one Antonio de Rivera would have left for the bears to devour. Our rafts drifted willy-nilly down the meanders as we ducked under trees, got stuck in the shallows, bumped into one another constantly, and teased each person at the oars. But at last I felt as though we were breaking away from the larger global economy, taking a few of its essentials along but hoping to find enough wild native foods to nourish us as we went. As we floated off, I hoped that our new economy would be restricted to foods derived from this watershed alone.

It was then that I realized how I had been anticipating a week in the wilderness with another false expectation: that we would be surrounded by native plants and animals, many of them fair game for foraging. Instead, to my dismay, most of what we passed were not natives, but exotics, and loads of them: tamarisks, tumbleweeds, giant cane reeds, Russian olives, clovers, and chukars. Yes, there were some cottonwoods, willows, Canada geese, and ferruginous hawks, but the sheer mass of exotics choking the banks made me wince. From the riverbanks to the highest cliffs above us, it was clear that the land's surface had been colonized by invasive species.

Here in the headwaters of the Río Colorado, we were encountering one invasive weed for every five native species. In less than fifty years the lands between Sand Island and the Grand Canyon had had a third of their plant cover usurped by invasive weeds. And in the quarter century since I first ran the rapids up this way, exotic fishes like catfish and carp have taken over the river, now outnumbering native species by five to one. The dams placed on the Colorado and the exotic fish that followed them had wiped out 90 percent of the watershed's fish during my lifetime. The exotics were outcompeting half of all the endangered species that remained in the river. The Río Colorado pike minnow, razorbacked suckers, and their ancient lineages no longer swam from pool to backwater pool in the river we were floating. If we caught any fish, it was unlikely that they would be the region's ancients; our fried catfish would be no more native to the watershed than paella from Iberia.

As I looked out at the tamarisks on the river's edge and the cheatgrass on the slopes, I guessed that weeds were reducing our capacity for wild-plant foraging by at least a third. Why? Because exotic shrubs like tamarisks, Russian olives, and cane reeds grow in precisely the streamside habitats where most native plant foods were formerly found. Some of these shrubs had been intentionally planted at first, but soon they spread on their own, crowding out other species. Knock out natives from the places where special moisture and nutrient conditions had once kept them productive, and native plant food supplies were sure to plummet.

We camped our first night by Eight Foot Rapids, up on a bench above a cliff face. Canada geese wandered around our camp while we drank sangria and mescal bacanora. Discouraged by my inability to forage, I dished up some of Enrique's leftover paella. I slowly overcame my ideological disappointments after Laurie picked up her miniature Martin guitar and encouraged the rest of us to sing with her. We relaxed and listened to their medley of laments and blues as the full moon rose over the cliffs.

Our camp was surrounded by petroglyphs left by the Fremont culture, a group of prehistoric canyon folk who adopted corn agriculture and then abandoned it in favor of wild foods. It seemed that I always found my role models in the most unlikely places. Throughout canyon country, there were more glyphs recording the harvesting of wild native grasses than there were glyphs of corn. There were more glyphs of bighorn sheep than there were of domestic turkeys, and historically, of horses and cows. Kept awake by the full moon dancing through a diffuse range of clouds, I imagined myself having to give up tending turkeys and gardens for another, wilder way of life. Perhaps my own unquenchable wanderlust was hard-wired, and ultimately more compatible with wild sheep and native grasses than with plows and cows.

The next morning the adults who ran the rapids were a little more ragged than usual, the bacanora and sangria no doubt having something to do with it. Jack cracked a paddle in half at Lodge Rapid, Enrique got himself stuck big-time on a boulder, while Laurie and I spun hopelessly for a couple minutes before we finally placed one oar against a boulder to lever a pushoff. The youngest among us then took over, performing perfect runs through several small rapids, unimpeded by boulders in their paths or alcohol by-products in their veins.

We arrived at Mexican Hat, the last place we'd have to contact civilization and the last marketplace at our disposal. We sealed our fate. When we put in again, the river became a roller coaster of sand waves. As it meandered through the first set of goosenecks, we knew that there would be no other place to pull our gear out of the canyon for several more days. Our floating economy would have to learn to work on its own from now on, for what we had already had with us and what we could forage were our only options.

Two hours later, as most of us sat on the beach, reading and resting at Muhlenberg Camp, the last Achilles raft came into camp without a trace of Laurie in sight.

"You guys forget someone? Where'd you hide my bride-to-be?" I asked.

"We lost sight of her a ways back where she was floating." Enrique's oldest son announced. "We got stuck on a rock at a pouroff, and took in a lot of water. Before we nearly capsized, she jumped out. She was floating right behind us most of the way. She should be coming around the bend any minute now."

Fortunately Laurie soon came drifting along, somewhat roughed up. But we soon found that her gear remaining in the raft was even worse for wear. Her guitar was cracked, her sheet music soaked, and her sleeping bag was as heavy as a bed-size sponge. We camped on a narrow beach, where Laurie and I tried to salvage her gear while the others prepared a modest dinner in the drizzle. As the rains lingered on, I finally realized that my livelihood and food supply down in the desert was truly dependent on the same rains and stream flows that can threaten us here in the headwaters. "River Lord," I prayed, "please let this drizzle rehydrate our souls and replenish the irrigation ditches that run to our farmlands."

We slept amid the tamarisks and cane choking the riverbank, hearing the river gush and gurgle in our ears all night long. I dreamed of fish feeding, nibbling on our toes. I was not only immersed in the headwaters of my foodshed, I was subconsciously becoming a link in the food chain that bound these hinterlands to the desert valleys and seas below: algae, water midge, flannel-mouthed sucker, and me. Little fish, big fish, all hooked up to the same chain.

"It's all downriver from here!" I yelled to Laurie the next day as we plunged through Ross Rapid, the last real obstacle that could flip or damage the rafts. I had been the last to set up and run Ross, and luckily avoided the big hole at the top of the rapids merely by having watched how the others ran it. My luck gave out at the bottom of the wave field, though, for I ended up on the wrong side of the river from where everyone else was beached. When I shot the raft across to the other bank, the rest of the gang had to leap for our rope. They formed a chain and walked our Achilles raft back against the current to help us land where there were no steep cliffs.

As she hopped out of the Achilles, I could see that Laurie was relaxing for the first time since yesterday's trauma. She went off to collect sage and Brigham tea (*Ephedra* twigs) up the canyon while the kids reeled in some catfish from the shallows.

The mix of natives and exotics was now shifting. Tamarisks had not invaded all the habitats below Ross, so we began to encounter more and more edible natives: hackberries, banana yucca, an oreganolike mint, prickly pear, and hedgehog cactus. After our brief bout of foraging, we leisurely floated the rest of the afternoon through a series of slow goosenecks, observing the food chain around us. We watched great blue herons hunting for suckers in the backwater shallows, and violet-green swallows swooping down to snatch up dragonflies from just above the water. We caught sight of a few mule deer coming down to the river's edge, browsing Indian rice and deer grass inches from the muddy water.

Everyone here was eating someone else with leisure and pleasure. Jack delighted in these sights, laughing uncontrollably, then catching his breath and murmuring his favorite incantation: "Life is good." He paused. "In fact, death is good, too—that is, death making more life is good."

The hackberries were tart, the mint bit our tongue, and the prickly pear fruit soothed it.

Soon we were down to Slickhorn Rapids, edged by the most glorious beach camp I had ever seen in my life. It was covered with my favorite wild tea, an aromatic composite herb the New Mexicans called *cota*. We picked a few bunches, leaving many more around our rafts and packs. In fact, there were so many edibles and medicinals that Gary suggested that we lead a "plant walk," an old tradition that he and I shared with our friends. We knew that each plant here had a story, and most had a moral lesson to teach us as well. Four-winged saltbush taught adaptability. It had grown in the same spots for thousands of years, adapting to whatever climate came along. As the vegetation around it shifted from piñon-juniper woodland to desert scrub, it stayed in place and welcomed its new neighbors. Hackberries reminded us of how seed disposal by birds could shape the geography, morphology, and even the chemistry of plants. Thousands of years of natural selection by the desert's frugivorous birds had created these tart, red-hued delicacies that we too could enjoy as food. Willows, a source of salicylic acid, the key ingredient of aspirin, reminded us that all floods were not headaches. Some had the capacity to renew the nutrients and moisture of beaches from which willows could resprout, providing habitats where the now-endangered willow flycatchers could eventually thrive. Plants, Gary sighed, were not only good to think about, they were good to eat and drink.

After I'd shaken my initial disappointment that exotics would keep us from becoming a one-watershed-only food economy, the natives had begun to reappear. We would never gather all the resources we needed here, but at least we knew what still grew.

After swimming under Slickhorn's waterfalls, we passed on to Grand Gulch, a place of cliff dwellings and granaries in caves filled with little prehistoric corncobs barely the size of cigarettes. I was amazed to find corn so far up into the headwaters, in such rugged land. Less than one in a thousand acres on the Colorado Plateau was arable. And yet southwestern canyons such as this cradled some of the earliest experiments with maize north of Mexico.

How odd it was to know that while this crop was now sown on more than 50 million acres around the planet, no modern cornfield occurred within thirty miles of here in any direction. Corn had become overbred, outgrowing its prehistoric cradle. The cradle was empty now, while an overgrown monster trampled much of the continent.

Our final day on the river, down past Ojeto toward the Clay Hills, we saw another kind of organism leaving its cradle for the larger world. A peregrine falcon soared above her nest in the cliffs above us, trying to teach her fledgling how to eat on his own. She soared high with a mouthful of food—duck leg, kangaroo rat, lizard—and her offspring followed her, eager for a free meal. But as he caught up to his mother, she dropped her load of food on purpose. It fell from the sky. They dived after it, beelining down toward the river, hoping to intercept it before it sank into the water.

Each time the mother sent another meal plunging toward earth, the fledgling became a bit more adept at catching it. We watched them for twenty minutes or more, humbled by the rigor of the peregrine's teachings. Where peregrines and willows occurred, we gave the river a clean bill of health; where tamarisks choked its bank, we prayed for cleansing floods and a speedy recovery.

My earlier, naive hope had been to form a food economy isolated from all others, a bubble in space and time, nested within the canyon. Yet many current forces and historic events would not allow us to achieve a sense of complete isolation. Perhaps that was for the best; for the work before us could not be done in isolation. As we pulled out of the river, ready to head back by van toward towns, cities, and villages, I conceded that I did not even wish to be part of any economy that excluded urban areas, immigrants, or other traditions: I simply wanted all of us to have some wedding with the land. Yes, all too soon we would be barraged by minimarts, McDonald's, Denny's, sure signs that we had never been too far removed from the global economy. But as Laurie and I headed home across the Navajo Reservation, we bypassed the Safeway to stop at the Kayenta Swap Meet, an informal exchange of various and sundry goods pulled out of hogans, pickups, and canyons. We wandered around hesitantly until we realized we were on safe ground. Here among the Navajo we could relax. We could purchase hand-picked purslane greens, roasted lamb, and local green chiles wrapped in handmade tortillas. A young woman in a long velvet dress sold us three bundles of Navajo tea and threw in a fourth bundle for good luck. They were carefully folded bundles of *Thelesperma subhudum,* which Laurie clutched to her breasts as if they were a gift of the river itself.

It was the tea most beloved among all the tribes who have lived in the headwaters of the Río Colorado, it was the continuity between prehistoric healers and modern-day herbalists. It had come to be a symbol to me, one which speaks of the wild hinterlands that provide the water and nutrients that feed me, one which reminds me of times when economies were more local, and truly community based. Nowadays, whether I eat squash and onions from the field around Yuma, or corvina and clams from the Gulf of California, I know they are nourished by the streams that braid themselves into the Río Colorado, but they are also dependent on economic decisions being made about their destiny in Washington, D.C., Mexico City, New York, Hong Kong, and Rome. Even in a remote tributary of the big red muddy river, our rafts were gifted with the canned foods, the transportable commodities, and the cushions for buffering us against hunger that the Fremont culture never knew. However isolated and self-sufficient we felt, we did not have as strong a need relentlessly to track the cascade of local foods as the peregrine fledgling had. He was still dependent on his mother, as we are on a larger community, but in order to become less a parasite and more a functional member of his family unit, he had to hone his skills. We, too, must remember our interdependencies while further developing our capacity to produce food at a local level. Like the peregrine, we need to cast a far-seeing eye across the landscape, while knowing how to tirelessly pursue the food most fitting for us close to home. It's a tricky balance: when to soar high for the wide view, and when to dive for our own nourishment.

Chapter Fourteen

The Fertile Valleys and Their Wild Varmints

he Río Colorado's bottomlands cover much of Southern California and Arizona, and where arable land, divertible water, and
plenty of sunshine converge, there is often wealth to be made in the
growing of food. This is not true merely today; prehistorically the Colorado and its tributaries hosted some of the first and the largest experiments with irrigated agriculture north of Mexico. As my friend Laura
Jackson once noticed, a map showing agriculture in the lower Río Colorado Valley looks like a scratchboard negative of one from the Midwest. While agriculture in the Midwest occupies virtually every square
yard of upland soils, agriculture in the desert is restricted to the bottomlands of river-carried sediments.

On the way back from our river running, Laurie and I drove down
from the Colorado Plateau headwaters and entered the valley bottoms
that prehistoric Hohokam had farmed with river diversions for more
than a millennium. When early Anglo settlers first farmed the Phoenix

Valley, they often renovated irrigation ditches the Hohokam had abandoned four centuries before. But local diversion of river waters was not enough for the newly immigrated farmers; by the 1870s they began building larger dams that cut off flows to Indian farmers still living downstream from them. By 1911 the Roosevelt Dam on the Salt River became the first federally-funded irrigation project in the country to divert all of a river's flow into irrigation canals, leaving little downstream for fish, fowl, or other farmers.

Yet even this enormous water supply was not enough to quench the thirst of entrepreneurial farmers and city planners. By the 1920s they began to pump the aquifers below their fields as well, using centrifugal pumps run by rural electrification projects, and cheap natural gas. Within fifteen years the farmers and city fathers were pumping the aquifer dry, using twice the annual recharge rate, dropping the water table down below the deepest roots of trees. They irrigated their crops so lavishly that the alkaline groundwater left salty crusts on the soil surface. Because of how severely they depleted the fossil groundwater beneath them and spoiled the once-fertile soils with salts, southern Arizona farmers had to abandon nearly half the acreage they had brought into cultivation after only a half century of use.

South of Phoenix we drove through the now-abandoned fields of tumbleweeds and salty dust, flat as a pancake and as empty as a future could be. Laurie and I spotted canals here and there, ones that brought the reddish Río Colorado water some two hundred miles to make up for the loss of the aquifer below the fields. But the water in those concrete-lined canals had become too salty and too costly per acre foot after traveling all those miles, and few farmers wanted anything to do with it. Billions had been spent to pull the water out of the river and move it half way across the state, and now some experts claimed that its only real use would be to put it back in the ground to restore the aquifers their grandfathers had sucked dry.

I was more and more disillusioned by what had happened to the reddish waters of the Colorado and the San Juan, but still had some hope for the tannish ones of the Río Santa Cruz, closest to my home. After several days of catching up on chores, I made some free time for fieldwork along the Santa Cruz, one of the last free streams still running across the bottomlands of our state. Its waters splashed high on either side of me as the old Blazer plunged down into the streambed, its dusty veneer being transformed to mud. For a moment, rainbows and brilliant green cottonwood boughs filled my view, until I crept up onto the fertile ground of the cultivated floodplain. I felt as though the waters were parting to allow me to pass through to the Promised Land, where wild creatures and nutritious crops lived together in some primordial harmony.

In fact, I had made the effort to fishtail through the mud and floods brought on by the summer rains to see, if indeed, such a harmony could still exist anywhere within my food shed.

I once again attempted to visualize my foodshed, beginning with trying to wrap my mind around the rugged headwaters of the Río Colorado drainage, such as those where we had just run rapids and riffles in our inflatable rafts. Next I tried to feel the smooth shapes of fertile river valleys, on whose floodplains crops have been grown intensively for millennia. Those crops had earlier been blessed by the water and nutrients streaming into them from the wildlands above, but most had been spoiled. At last I tried to push my mind out the river's mouth to merge with the sea's bounty along the coast of Sonora, where Laurie and I would be living in another few weeks. The freshwater and nutrient-rich sediments that formerly flowed out of the delta of the Río Colorado fueled both the farmlands of southern Arizona and the fisheries of the Gulf of California. And here I was midway between the highlands and the sea, along a gently flowing river whose health had recently been restored, at least on the one farm whose gate stood before me.

Tubac Farms was situated along one of the most fertile stretches of that southern Arizona river. The Santa Cruz floodplain may have been farmed for more than 2,400 years, yet it had remained fertile and productive. I had come there to complete work on a list of the birds and the bees that frequented the binational corridor for migratory wildlife that used Tubac Farms as one of their stopovers. Along with a team of other local scientists, I had been trying to get a sense of the diversity of wild pollinators that were capable of inhabiting and working farmlands with as much fervor as they do wildlands.

The reason for our inquiry was simple: Honeybees had recently been hit so hard by parasites and diseases that there were fewer of them pollinating crops in farmer's fields than any time since World War II. We wanted to figure out what could be done to recover from America's "pollination crisis," a crisis that affected farmers clear across the country, and one that the USDA predicted would be likely to worsen before the pollinators began to recover.

Three years earlier, I had begun to work with bee restoration wizards Steve Buchmann and Jim Donovan to answer three questions. First, if domesticated honeybees were dropping like flies, could their wild kin take up the slack and successfully pollinate the majority of vegetable crops sown in floodplain fields? The second question was much more elusive. Were wildlands habitats adjacent to croplands a "safe harbor" for populations of the many wild bees and other insects we found entering the fields to pollinate the blossoms of Tubac Farm's crops? And finally, was there any easy way to bolster these wild populations to ensure the full pollination of fruits and vegetables just in case honeybee populations never recovered?

These big questions took the backseat as soon as I drove onto the farm and spotted its coowner, Mark Larkin, careening down the dirt road toward me in his old, doorless pickup. When Mark hopped out of it, I noted that his shirt for the day—like all the rest I had ever seen—had no sleeves. He had ripped them off. This guy was one helluva stripped-down farmer, the rural equivalent of a rockabilly guitarist with a flair for minimalism.

Although Larkin was old enough to have been a long-haired hippie at one point in his life, he wore his crewcut as if it had been his only hairstyle since he was four years old. To hear him cuss, you'd think he had been raised up out of the Santa Cruz mud, but he was academically trained in agricultural engineering, and had worked overseas on farming projects before settling along the Santa Cruz. He swore with equal proficiency in Spanish and English. He was a bit threatening to the conventional farmers and ranchers in the valley not because of his cussing, but because he relied on so many methods associated with organic agriculture. Nevertheless, he declined to go for organic certification because he wanted to reserve the option of selectively treating his fieldside weeds with Roundup or controlling grasshoppers with toxic baits in the years that they became perilous plagues.

In short, Larkin dismissed any formula whenever it failed to work, and practiced farming as an improvisational comic practices his art. He would use a horse-drawn plow if he had to, or borrow an expensive tractor. Every week he and his wife juggled caring for the kids, plus tending to thirty floodplain acres of a dozen kinds of vegetables, an orchard with four varieties of fruit trees, patches of zinnias and cosmos for the cutflower market, and several irrigated pastures for cattle and horses.

Mark and I stood by his truck and bantered for a while about Mexican heirloom vegetables, a favorite topic of mine. Since so many of his customers were of Mexican ancestry, he had sown many of the vegetables most beloved in Mexican cuisine. Nevertheless, he was also reevaluating his "you-pick" vegetable-harvesting operation, wondering if it was the best way for him to break even while improving the land's condition. In the middle of our conversation, he remembered that he had to redirect the irrigation water running down his ditch. He suddenly jumped into the doorway of his beat-up truck, and drove off, bouncing down the dirt road to his upper ditch, where he let loose some water on his alfalfa and sweet clover.

Mark was among the third of Arizona farmers who no longer live full-time on the farms they operate. But, with regard to one particular factor, he was unlike the vast majority of Arizonans who have tried their hands at farming over the last sixty years: He was still making ends meet without accepting government subsidies. By 1980 Arizona farmers owed the FHA more than $500 million dollars of back payments on farm mortgage loans. Five years later an FHA bureaucrat bragged to me that if he wanted to, he could foreclose on four out of every five farms in southern Arizona's valleys, their owners were all in such bad debt. For each of the six thousand Arizona farmers who have survived foreclosures to remain in business today, three others have sold out to developers, gone bankrupt, or had their family farms merge into bigger agribusinesses.

Some of the reasons for the failure of southern Arizona's agriculture were counterintuitive. For instance, how could farmers blessed with so much solar energy at their disposal go bankrupt because of soaring energy bills? As Arizona is one of America's sunniest states, crops hardly ever suffer diminished growth due to cloudy weather, which occurs in the southern half of Arizona fewer than forty days a year. Most of the farming valleys in southern Arizona enjoy a frost-free season more than 250 days in length, and some of its farmers could effortlessly grow irrigated crops year-round, unconstrained by clouds and cold. And yet an acre of Arizona farmland typically requires five times as much fossil fuel to produce its yields than an acre of crops requires on the average American farm. Why? A full two-thirds of an Arizona farmer's monthly energy bill goes toward paying the price of running his pumps, enabling him to draw fossil groundwater up to his ditches and laterally transfer it to the field of his dreams.

Of course, folks other than farmers want that water and energy, as well as the lands on which they are used. Most Sun Belt developers view farms as potential sites for housing construction, and farmers as water-guzzling competitors. By 1990 three-quarters of the people living in Sonoran Desert borderlands had chosen to live in cities, up 50 percent since 1940. Those new urban converts to sun god worship inevitably attract other converts, and most of them despise the presence of nearby cotton gins, pigpens, chicken shacks, manure piles, and hives of Africanized bees. And so they have been annually converting about thirty thousand acres of Arizona's prime bottomlands from agriculture to retirement homes, condominiums, golf courses, and shopping malls.

The thousands of urban residents who can be packed into forty acres of apartments, condos, putting greens, and pools use far more water per acre than the crops once grown on the same land, but that is water under the bridge.

The richest bottomlands in southern Arizona have already been paved over for good; it is unlikely that their fertile soils will ever be farmed again. Mark Larkin has so far survived the foreclosures and other economic pressures on his neighbors, but large housing developments are being initiated both upstream and downstream of Tubac Farms. Each time I ford the waters of the Santa Cruz and see his fields and orchards, I wonder which is more of a modern-day miracle in southern Arizona: a running river or a family farm?

While Mark was irrigating, I began my routine of taking field notes on the birds and the bees. A huge black carpenter bee buzzed by me, en route from the wooded bottomlands to the large patch of vegetables now in bloom. There Mark's melons and squashes offered nectar cupped in dozens of blossoms to the little native squash-and-gourd bees. The bees also pollinated the wild buffalo gourds on the margins of Mark's fields. Over the last several years Steve and Jim had identified more than ninety species of insects that we had collected in the blossoms of this thirty-acre vegetable garden. Most of these insects actually nested within the floodplain's riparian forest, or in adjacent hedgerows and woodlots, but pollinated crops in both cultivated and wild habitats. I tracked some of them moving along their daily nectar trail, from cottonwood and mesquite forest to field and back again.

But bees were not my main concern this season. I had been assigned the task of completing our inventory of birds known to visit flowers along the Santa Cruz. I stood between the orchard and the fields and used my binoculars to focus in on the birds moving around between various habitats. A hooded oriole came out of the woods, exposing its brilliant yellows and blacks as it moved among the limbs of the fruit trees. A hummingbird appeared for a moment in the same orchard, stopping to rest, then zooming off again to gather nectar god-knows-where.

Of the thirty-some migratory birds I have spotted visiting flowers along the riparian corridor of the Santa Cruz and in the uplands nearby, I tally ten that come out into the fields and orchards to feed. We have glassed and identified Anna's hummingbirds, white-winged doves, several warblers, northern mockingbirds, pyrrhuloxias, lesser goldfinches, lazuli buntings, and hooded orioles in and around these fields. While not all these birds may be diligent pollinators, they are at least occasional nectar feeders, and they inevitably do some of the matchmaking between pollen and pistil.

Regardless of how many species of bees and birds we recorded on his farm, the bottom line for Mark was whether his crops and orchards were being pollinated sufficiently. From periodic surveys of blossoms in his squash patch, we've confirmed that he is indeed recruiting for free all the pollination services he needs from the native fauna here, and thus he need never pay the rent on a single honeybee hive again, as he had been doing for the years before parasitic mites devastated them. As long as Mark's farming practices are "mostly organic," and as long as he can afford to keep a good portion of his farmland in riparian forest, scrublands, and hedgerows, he won't have to put up any more money to ensure that his vegetables get serviced by pollinators.

After my survey was done, I tracked Mark down to thank him for the access to the place. He tossed me some apples and peaches, and I ate his fat, juicy fruits while he explained his problems with running the "you-pick" operation. While he talked I realized that the very reason the fruits were so well developed and juicy was because they had been fully pollinated; an underpollinated fruit is often dry and shriveled by comparison, for it is unable to mature all of its ovules. The juices of Tubac Farms' fruits kept dripping down my chin, cooling me off. After we swapped a couple of bilingual jokes about the border, I left Mark to his work while I drove toward Nogales to purchase insurance at the border for next week's departure for the Gulf of California. I had witnessed the ways in which the land had produced nutritious, delicious food within my watershed; it was time to see how the fruits of the sea were faring.

Chapter Fifteen

Sea Turtle Soup and By-Catch Stew

Regardless of the season, it was always hotter in coastal Sonora than along the rivers of Arizona. Approaching the sea, we would bake and bake under the desert sun, hopeful that when we got to the ocean, everything would be cooler and more benign. Laurie and I were traveling with three sea turtle biologists in tow, Scott from San Diego, Hugh from Costa Rica, and Jeff, who splits his time between Tucson and Bahia de Los Angeles in Baja California. We had driven two hundred miles southward into Mexico, down to the Gulf of California. There we would offer the Seri Indian community a workshop about the effects of industrial trawling and drift netting on sea turtles. For centuries the Seri relied on sea turtle meat as their most significant animal food, but when sea turtles began to decline dramatically two decades ago, they began collaborations with conservationists in the hope that these sacred animals would not go extinct during their lifetimes. We shared their hope and agreed to help when they invited us to cohost a turtle workshop with them, but we forgot to take into account how taxing the rising humidity and temperatures of the coastal desert might be. I didn't dare venture to the shore until long after the sun had gone down. At first the sea looked calm at the surface, but as I stayed beside it in the dark, I sensed that it was in turmoil, that its guts were being churned up just as my own had been by the heat and road noise.

As I sat on the sand hugging my knees, I saw the cause—or the symptom?—of that churning. The only lights in sight were those of shrimp trawlers, twenty of them at work in the seas to the north of me, a low count compared with those I've recorded my last dozen visits here. Every time I have slept in Kino Bay in recent years, I have scribbled down in my journal the number of trawlers I saw: thirty-four, forty-two, sixty-four, and forty-eight the previous fall; then twenty-one, nineteen, and eight during the winter. They came from Guaymas to the south and Rocky Point to the north, but most of them were controlled by Korean, Japanese, and American investors, many of whom had never even seen the Gulf of California. They bought them up after the shrimp industry here collapsed around 1990. That was when more than five hundred trawlers were dry-docked because their Mexican owners could no longer harvest enough shrimp to keep from defaulting on their loans. And so some opportunistic foreign investors quietly moved in and paid off the debts, purchasing up to 49 percent interest in the trawlers—all the Mexican government would legally allow.

At least that is the little we know about how venture capitalists "rescued" the failing shrimp industry of the Gulf of California. Who knows what kind of bargains they signed under the table with their "business partner" *prestanombres* and government officials charged with watchdogging Mexico's fisheries.

To call these crafts shrimp trawlers, however, was now a misnomer—they had been retrofitted to process anything they could land—shrimp, specialty fish for sushi, smaller fish for canning, and all the rest to be ground into meal for coastal fish farms and livestock feed. Despite the fact that most trawlers are processing and selling a larger and larger percentage of their by-catch, they still dump anywhere from five to twenty pounds of dead and damaged fish for every pound they commercially process and sell. In doing so, trawlers that work their way around the Pacific and Gulf of California contribute as much as 9 million tons to the 27 million tons of nontarget marine animals killed globally as the fishing industry tries to capture 100 million tons of fish, invertebrates, and turtles to sell each year.

Yet trawling, drift netting and longlines have wrought so much havoc in Planet Ocean that it is doubtful that the industry will ever be able to reach its goal again during our lifetimes. Trawlers alone plow up more sea bottom each year than all the farm tillage of arable lands, wreaking havoc on bottom-feeding fish and turtles, sea-grass beds, and the myriad sessile invertebrates that otherwise "stay put" on the ocean floor. Twenty-two percent of all commercial seafood species show signs of decline in their natural habitats, while another 44 percent have been found to be in serious trouble.

Humans now capture and consume 35 percent of the primary productivity of continental shelves, and 8 percent of the ocean's productivity overall, which results in substantial collateral losses of other forms of marine life. The most painful loss the Seri have suffered is that of their sea turtle neighbors. Despite the promise that the Mexican government would ensure that turtle-exclusion devices (TEDs) would be permanently mounted on all trawlers, the Seri have documented trawler after trawler illegally entering their waters with their TEDs deactivated. The trawlers claim that the TEDs impede them from catching the fish they are legally allowed to take. Globally 150,000 sea turtles are still killed each year by the illegal activities of trawlers and drift nets and longline fishermen.

To make up for the dramatic declines of wild shrimp populations brought about by such practices, aquaculture has come to provide one-fourth of the shrimp consumed in the world today. These cultivated harvests were considered inconsequential just twenty years ago. Nevertheless, 30 percent of the diet of marine shrimp grown in farms comes from wild species pulled out of their ocean habitats; that is, the blood, meat, and oil of sea turtles, sharks, and dolphins still stain the shrimp produced by most commercial aquaculture enterprises. Along the Sonoran coast of the Gulf of California, more than two hundred shellfish farms have sprung up within the last decade, and perhaps as many as 70 percent of them have illegally excluded local people and wildlife from using the once-rich coastal wetlands they have usurped.

The next day our group went out on the water with Seri fishermen to see the damage done to sea-grass beds by trawling and crab pots. Two Seri elders, José-Juan Moreno and Guadalupe Lopéz, dazzled our visiting marine scientists with their detailed knowledge of the food chain based on these eelgrass beds. At one point José-Juan asked the boatmen to cut the engines, while he chanted an ancient sea turtle song. Two hundred yards away two green sea turtles surfaced, and the younger Seri men along applauded, claiming that the old man lured them in with the cadence of his singing.

Back on the beach we invited the Seri elders to explain to us what they saw as the causes of sea turtle declines. The Seri had once depended on four species of sea turtles for nearly a third of the meat protein and fat they consumed each year; at the same time special turtles like the leatherbacks were never hunted because they were regarded as the most sacred and sentient animal in the world. However exact the Seri had become in their turtling skills, their annual harvest never approached the number of sea turtles inadvertently killed by being tangled in drift nets, hooked by longlines, or brought up by trawlers and irreparably injured.

Over the last quarter century the Seri themselves have had to abandon turtling as a way of life, knowing that fewer and fewer arrived in their territorial waters each year. Seri families had agreed with Mexican government conservationists to take only four green sea turtles a year, for ceremonial purposes only, and these typically came from those they rescued out of their neighbors' drift nets.

It was at such a ceremony that I ate some sea turtle meat, the only time I had done so in the thirty years I have frequented the Gulf of California. I was invited to the rite of passage for the fifteen-year-old granddaughter of one of my Seri traveling buddies. As I listened to his traditional songs and watched his grandsons dance on the girl's behalf, I was handed a bowl of soup cooked by the girl's mother and aunts. There was more broth and onions to it than meat, for the Seri men who were obligated to find a sea turtle had encountered only one they could rescue.

Just a month before our workshop, they spotted a young leatherback caught in a net, and rather than host the live turtle at a four-day ceremony on the beach, they let it go immediately. And as we prepared posters and handouts for our meeting, we were told that one of the would-be participants, Humberto, was in dutch with his cousins over a sea turtle hunting conflict. Fiercely protective of turtles, he had reported his own cousins to the authorities when they hauled in two green sea turtles to eat without having the mandate of a ceremony to do so.

In some ways the workshop was one sad scene: Twenty-five of us sat in the sand as the scorching sun descended behind the mountains of Tiburón Island, talking about the decline of marine life and its effect on cultural traditions. Antonio López, the handsome silver-haired elder of the Seri, spoke to his young people in their native tongue, then turned to us so he could repeat the same message in Spanish. As I translated for the English speakers in our group, a lump rose in my throat: "More than the damage done by any invasion of armed soldiers, we have been damaged by the competition for and depletion of our food resources, we have been broken by inadequate nutrition, we have been invaded by foods inappropriate for keeping our bodies strong and healthy."

And yet, when we brought up the topic of evicting all shrimp trawlers from the tribe's territorial waters, a few young men in the group could not yet embrace the idea. "They pay fees, sometimes as much as ten thousand dollars per season, just to enter the southern edge of our waters. And then, on top of that, they give us bushels of shrimp each catch to distribute to our families when we have nothing else to eat."

"But they don't stop where we tell them to," David Morales angrily replied. David had been jailed two years before for climbing onto a trawler, armed, and forcing the captain to get out of Seri territory. He was later acquitted when it became known that the trawler captain had paid the tribe no fee, only a bribe to a corrupt official. "They wreck the scallop harvest, they kill the little fish, they mess up the eelgrass beds that the crabs and turtles depend on."

"Still, it's one of our few sources of cash income," Guadalupe, one of the Seri schoolteachers argued. "Our own fisheries and crafts industries aren't bringing in what they used to."

We reviewed for them just how little they get of what is ultimately made from shrimp harvested in their waters. For every dollar that the trawler captain shares among his workers and the Seri, he and his investors gain eight dollars when they sell the shrimp in the international marketplace. Globally about one in every five tons of seafood leaves its country of origin to be sold in distant lands. The Guaymas shrimp that are flown across the border to Arizona are sold for fifteen times the value the local producers, packagers, and brokers shared among themselves back on the coast. By the time they reach a restaurant in New York or Beirut, their price will double again. The Seri gained less than one-fiftieth of the retail value of the shrimp taken from their waters, and yet they were the ones who had to absorb all the ecological and social consequences in the trawlers' wake. Their plight is much like that of the farmers and ranchers who hardly capture much of the consumer's dollar any more compared to what the middlemen gain, but shoulder all of the environmental stewardship costs of food production on their own.

Antonio and Guadalupe were shocked to hear all this. Guadalupe just walked away with nothing else to say, while Antonio ran his fingers through his silver hair, looking down at the dry sand. When he finally spoke he admitted that his predecessors on the Council of Traditional Elders had traded away the rights to shrimp and other resources for far less than they were worth. He said he would ask the navy for help in enforcing a trawling-free zone in their territorial waters, but then he was reminded that naval officers had recently harassed Seri fishermen for trying to capture two sea turtles for their sacred (midsummer) "New Year's" celebration.

"They don't respect our government-approved ceremonial needs, let alone recognize the fact that our cholesterol and diabetes are rising for lack of native foods in our diet."

Antonio unclenched his fist and sand dropped from his hand to the ground. He got up silently and left. All the remaining Seri men stayed silent for several minutes longer.

"We need to talk about this more among ourselves," David Morales finally said apologetically. "It isn't easy for us."

On the way back through Kino to take our friends to the airport, we were besieged by seafood vendors selling black-tipped shark meat, scallops, cabrilla, flounder, and halibut, clams, and shrimp. It appeared as though the entire innards of the sea were up for sale. Cheap. Too cheap. Our cooler remained empty, and our friends from other seacoasts took nothing home with them.

Not long after the sea turtle and trawling workshop, we listened as our friend, marine ecologist Luis Bourillón, offered a crab-harvesting workshop for the Seri. There we learned how they took into account the variable sizes and the sexes of the animal they called *xampt*. That was how they decided which blue eating crabs they should sell. Unlike their neighbors in Kino, the Seri threw back all females and immatures they found in their crab traps, harvesting only the more expendable adult males.

Luis explained to them why he sat on the beach one day each week when the harvest comes into Punta Chueca from the adjacent Canal del Infiernillo (Channel of Hell). They had all seen him measuring and sexing the crabs, comparing them with those he finds in Kino Bay, where non-Indian fishermen bring in the bulk of the harvest. By tallying up month after month of data, it had become clear to him that the Seri crab harvest did not deplete the crabs' regenerative capacity, while that of their neighbors did. He had recently invited conservation organizations to the Seri village to certify their crabmeat as sustainably harvested, so that the Seri could capture specialty markets where such a fact matters. But at the same time he warned the Seri that the local populations of crabs were still being overexploited by their competitors.

"Your neighbors still practice five kinds of overharvesting that affect the crab populations that move between your harvesting grounds and theirs. They remove too many crabs in smaller size classes. They wipe out the large females who produce the most eggs, sometimes a million eggs per individual. They kill crabs as well as everything else where they trawl the ocean bottom. They continue to harvest crabs even when the prices are poor, because the government subsidizes them to do so. And finally they respond to more and more human demand for crab-meat, even though the resource base cannot support it. In a Malthusian sense, there are too many consumers and too many crabbers for the crab industry's *own good.*"

The ghost of Malthus had swum half way around the world and was now hovering just above the surface of the hypersaline water in the Channel of Hell, ready to attack us with the viciousness of a sea monster.

We purchased fifty crabs from Seri friends and began to experiment with making crab cakes. We boiled them until they turned bright red, then shelled them and picked the stringy white meat from their claws and the buttery meat from their bodies. I mixed the meat with mesquite flour, onions, chipotles, and other fixings, panfrying them for a dinner feast we prepared for friends who came one night to our rented house in Kino.

Cleaning crabs seemed to make just as big a mess as plucking and eviscerating turkeys, but I decided not to mention the comparison aloud in Laurie's presence. She had been an enthusiastic participant in the crabbing, and I had no need to inquire about her ethical stance toward invertebrates. But I could see that blue crabs had one advantage over turkeys for the gentle hearted: they lacked the sort of crimson, coagulating blood that might remind us of how much we humans are like turkeys.

Chapter Sixteen

The Nomad's Movable Feast and the Taste of Island Chicken

While sharing crab cakes with us, one of our Seri colleagues asked us if we had ever been to a full-blown Seri feast. We weren't sure. We had been to puberty ceremonies and basketry ceremonies, but never to one of the traditional ones focused wholly on foods.

"Antonio, the elder, he wants to have a traditional feast to open up his traditional school," our friend informed us. He was Antonio's nephew. Then he added, "He wants you to sponsor it the way our own people used to take turns sponsoring feasts."

"We might be able to do that. When?"

"How soon is it before you have to go back to Arizona?"

"Five days more," Laurie replied.

"Good. We'll have it the night of the fourth day." Before we could catch him, he was gone, off to tell Antonio that it was a done deal.

Laurie and I had no idea what was involved in the Seri concept of a traditional feast, but decided that the only way to find out was to let the whole thing gain a momentum of its own. It would be a great way to end our stay along the coast, I guessed. Laurie expressed skepticism, but I forged ahead with the plans. I was becoming more and more convinced that individual eating patterns could not save the natural wealth of the land or the sea; we needed collectively to value and celebrate the food that came out of our own habitats in ways that safeguarded those habitats. This would be a chance to combine the riches of the desert watershed and the bounties of the sea into one meal, and to talk about conservation. Perhaps this would also be an opportunity for Laurie and me to see how another neighboring culture perceived what communal food celebrations should be. Perhaps.

A day later, when we were out on the water with old Antonio, leading his cronies on a food-gathering expedition, I realized that my idealism was once again leading us into a possible fiasco. Antonio had convinced me that we should build the feast around a communal harvesting and roasting of mescal, arguing that I may have seen non-Indian bootleggers roast agaves, but the Indian way was entirely different. When I asked him where we'd get the mescal from, he told me that we had to boat for six hours across treacherous waters, but that it would be worth it.

While I had anticipated that the Seri boat would be relieved and excited when we landed on Isla San Esteban, everyone was complaining. This was especially true of José-Juan Moreno, the eldest among us, who kept grumbling, "Who's got a good blade for cutting mescal? *No one,* it seems to me. No one brought a decent tool!"

I offered to show him the poor excuses for mescal knives that I'd brought along: a rusted machete, a dull ax, a GI camp trowel with a handle that won't collapse, and two fillet knives.

"That machete? No good."

So I showed him the ax. He tipped his cowboy hat back—in Mexico, old Indian fishermen always wear cowboy hats, just to confuse things—and then he grimaced.

"Too dull, won't cut a thing."

I showed him the others. He shook his head, disgusted.

"None of them will work. And we got out here too late. It's midday. September. Still hot! Even if we get our work done, the boats can't make it back to the village before dark. Well, let's get started with these miserable tools." José-Juan walked away into the bush.

For the preparation of a traditional feast, it seemed as though we had gotten off to a bad start. I tried to run through the morning in my head, wondering where we had gone astray.

Laurie and I had left the beach house in Kino at six, but the two pangas did not push off from the mainland until 8:45. José-Juan prayed hard and long as we left, as did his daughter, Maria Magdalena, and our friend and guide, Alfredo. They were all anxious to leave early with us, but the other boat full of younger men had a hard time getting their gear together. Three younger Seri men accompanied Antonio, the headman of the Council of Elders: Alfonso, Humberto, and Antonio's whacked-out son, Josüe. They pushed off at least twenty minutes after we did, but by hotdogging their *panga* (dory) all the way across the channel, they caught up to us by the time we reached Dog Bay, at the southern edge of Tiburón Island.

As we entered Dog Bay, I realized that we were fully in the thick of the marine food web. A magnificent frigate bird soared overhead, a silvery mackerel hanging out of its mouth. Alfredo pointed out a school of mullet that was running in front of us, and I asked him if the ospreys ate many of them.

"That's all they eat during a certain season," he replied, and I wondered how many "seasons" of the surging or waning of fish populations he recognized over a year's time.

Thousands of sardines began to jump above the water in large schools on either side of us, pushed along by larger predators chasing them. José-Juan and Alfredo spoke excitedly in Seri.

"Lots of sardines at this time signals us that there will be good fishing this year," Alfredo explained, "for schools this abundant will feed many larger fish."

Hundreds of white pelicans, some brown pelicans, cormarants, and frigate birds flocked around us, feeding on the sardines, then roosting on the rocky cliffs just above the high-tide mark. They had already garnered the benefits of the arrival of these sardines, demonstrating even more enthusiasm than the human fishermen did.

As we passed out of Dog Bay into the open seas south of Tiburón, we came upon hundreds of Mexican barracuda chasing the schools of sardines. Tossing my hook and line over, I immediately caught a four-teen-inch barracuda. We baited my hook again and tossed it into the barracuda feeding frenzy, as Alfredo talked to the fish: "*Mamale, chupele, no tiene huesos,*" he chanted. "Bite it, suck it, it doesn't have a single bone."

The other panga caught a couple more barracuda, and combined with mine we had enough for lunch. When we arrived at the cactus-stip-pled island of San Esteban at noon, Maria Magdalena and Laurie decid-ed to grill the fish on the beach while the rest of us went off to harvest mescal. We were hoping to bring back enough for the whole communi-ty to eat at the feast celebrating the inauguration of Antonio's traditional school.

But this was when José-Juan's grumbling began, and for good rea-son. He was among the few descendants of the lone survivor of a mas-sacre that occurred on San Esteban around 1900, one that wiped out the last of the Seri band that had lived on the island. Now, whenever he came here, he wanted to honor his ancestors by using the resources here only as they would use them. Our poor selection of tools made old José-Juan more intent on demonstrating to me how to select ripened heads from the clones of *Agave cerrulata,* subspecies *dentiens,* an endemic form of mescal that grew only on this island. It had a more compact head than the ones I had harvested with Beto and Chano in the Arizona uplands, but its heads were all loosely connected by a knotted network of sideshoots and roots just below the rocky surface of the island.

"See this one?" he asked me, pointing to a large agave as we sweat-ed up a slope of cobbles and cactus at high noon. The island harbored few species of plants, but most of them were thorny succulents, situated in dense populations on rocky slopes above the sea. The agaves formed unusually thick patches between towering cacti and stinking shrubs.

"It is big, it is easy to reach but it is not ready for harvesting. I will show you."

He pointed to the sheath of broad machetelike leaves in the middle of the plant, the terminal bud from which the flowering stalk emerges before the plant dies. "The leaves are not yet narrowing, not yet turning color."

The old man ambled higher up the slopes, wearing skimpy leather thongs on his feet. I was in boots with good heels, but cobbles kept tumbling out from under me as I climbed the hill behind him. He reached a smaller rosette of mescal, one with narrow terminal leaves that had a reddish cast to them.

"This. Pull it out," he gestured, as if yanking the ropelike rhizome that connected this rosette to six others around it.

"No knife?" I asked.

"Not yet. Pull."

So I pulled on the rhizome runner, as if in a tug-of-war with this clone of agaves. To my amazement—once a few cobbles were loosened around it—my tugging broke the ripened rosette off from the others, allowing the plant cluster to continue its growth while we harvested this one branch of the cluster. I rolled the rosette over to José-Juan, who then used his machete to trim all but two of its leaves away, shaping it into a pineapplelike ball. He slashed the lateral spines off the two leaves and tied them into a knot to create a loop for carrying the mescal. The next two plants he selected required an ax to loosen them from the others in their clones, but they were remarkably easy to unearth and remove from the hillside. In every case he selected just one rosette out of many in a large clone, so that the genetic individual continued to grow even after we pruned away the ripened head.

José-Juan's traditional harvesting technique stands in stark contrast to that used by the majority of Sonorans involved in bootlegging mescal on the mainland. Only the elders understand how to use this pruning technique so as not to deplete mescal populations. Sadly, the bulk of the younger Sonoran *jimadores* (mescal-harvesters) clear-cut entire clonal clusters, destroying as many as one million wild plants per year for the sole purpose of distilling bootleg alcohol. They also deprive bats and other pollinators of a rich nectar resource. In contrast José-Juan's harvest would have hardly any impact on the agaves of San Esteban, which have maintained healthy populations despite centuries of use.

We had been wandering for more than a half hour to obtain the fourth head of mescal when I heard José-Juan curse in front of me. I guessed that a cactus or agave thorn had finally penetrated his leathery feet, but I was wrong. He had spotted a spiny-tailed iguana, but when he lunged for it, it tried to bite him, then escaped. As he chased it under an elephant tree, he tripped on a piebald chuckwalla sleeping in his path. It was a chubby, wildly blotched lizard even larger than the iguana, and slower in its movements. He abandoned the chase for the iguana and grabbed the larger, meatier chuckwalla.

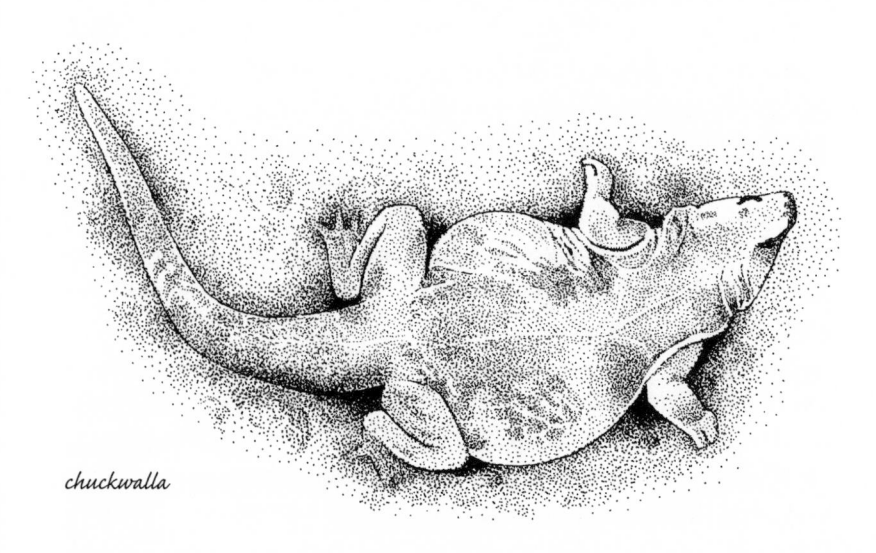

chuckwalla

I watched as he twisted and broke all four of its legs, a practice the Seri developed to carry live chuckwallas back to the mainland in boats without them running out of reach. He stuffed the chuckwalla beneath his belt, and carried one head of agave, while I carried two others and rolled the third down hill with my feet. When we were nearly on the verge of heat exhaustion, Humberto and Antonio appeared out of the thick brush in the wash to help us carry our harvest back to the beach.

Laurie and Maria had the fish nearly cooked. They had grilled them on the coals, and sliced open the biggest barracuda for us to eat. Using a tortilla to dip into the fish, I rescued a chunk of its meat, which was pleasantly greasy, salty, and saturated with smoky flavors. We sat back in the shadow of a beach cave exposed by low tides, happy to eat, drink, and have a few minutes out of the sun.

When we left, José-Juan, Alfredo, Laurie and I sang the Seri canticles of San Esteban, songs to protect us from being flounced upon by the giant whipsnake that guards the waters between San Esteban and Tiburón.

I thought that *Coimaj Caacol,* the giant whipsnake, was the only mythic sea monster in the Seri bestiary. But I heard about another mythic beast as we passed between two small islands and a jagged, partially submerged rock not far from Tiburón's southeastern corner. Beneath this perilous rock called *Hant Xnois,* there lived a gigantic octopus that ate anyone who shipwrecked there.

It seemed as though I had been paying attention to only one of the many marine food chains out here, the little fish–big fish–seabird chain of life. The Seri apparently kept in the backs of their minds other, more psychically unsettling food chains: taboo breakers and careless seafarers eaten by a huge octopus or snake.

On the way back to the Seri village, we passed three shrimp trawlers and one foreign yacht, all of them fishing in Seri tribal waters. Josüe could no longer stand it; he ordered Humberto to come up alongside the boats, and he boarded them, wearing his camouflage fatigues, a black hat with earflaps, and a bandana across his face. He recorded the captains' names, the boats' names, and their license numbers in his note-book, asking them not to fish in his people's waters anymore. Then he jumped back down into the little *panga,* reciting biblical predictions of doom and Zapatista slogans against the overexploitation of land and indigenous people, while all the rest of us waved politely to the crews. Pelicans scared up by our arrival circled around us, screeching, adding to the chaos. They were there to feed on all the bladders and guts and small fry thrown overboard by the fishermen.

Small fry. A politically loaded term, one used by big animals to describe anyone less powerful or voluminous than themselves. *By-catch.* A word used of the nine million tons of marine life discarded for every two million tons of shrimp landed. Like the destruction of other lives that enter the fields where we grow corn or soybeans, most of what enters the trawler's net is never eaten, just killed. *By-catch* is a euphemism for slaughter, one that implies that most marine life has less utility than our own, or than our target's. We load and unload the ocean with our biases, just as we empty our fields of pollinators and soil builders by lumping all insects together with the word *pest.*

Josüe's zeal made the other Seri chuckle uneasily. He was a bit too prone to polemics for the others' liking, but at the same time they agreed with his intentions. They knew that the seas were rapidly being ravaged by transnational corporations such as Spain's Pescanova, Japan's Taiyo, South Korea's Dong Won, and Tyson Foods/Arctic Alaska from the United States. None of them was any more tolerant of concessions to Mexican-owned fishing fleets, let alone foreign fishermen.

Within their lifetimes they had seen catches of fish like corvina decline from a boatful an hour to a bucketful a day. Josüe simply expressed in his theatrical manner what all the rest knew and felt every time they saw a trawler enter their waters.

When we neared Punta Chueca, the engines were opened full bore and the *pangas* were flung up onto the beach, where forty people awaited our arrival. They had congregated to see the *emme,* the legendary heads of mescal from the island. Then they all cheered and laughed when they saw that old José-Juan had also captured a chuckwalla for his supper.

After we emptied the boat, the old man asked me to get a large pit dug and a fire started while he trimmed the mescal and grilled his chuckwalla.

"Ironwood. You must make the fire with ironwood branches," he instructed me.

I groaned. "You know I can't cut ironwood myself here. It's against tribal law for outsiders to use ironwood from the reservation."

"It's for the community, so you're permitted by me and the other elders to do so," José-Juan replied, settling the issue, at least in his mind.

I couldn't get excited about cutting new ironwood, since I had worked with others, including the Seri, to protect this threatened tree species for nearly a decade. Instead I went into Kino and purchased scraps from the carvers there. Later Humberto and I went out together and pruned mesquite, throwing it in the pit and igniting it before José-Juan could see that we had mixed the two types of wood. But José-Juan came up to the roasting pit several hours later to throw in the heads of mescal. Just before he covered them up for a day of pit baking, he took a whiff of the smoke: "Ironwood *and* mesquite coals, huh? It might not bake as fast or taste as good . . . ," he grumbled as he walked off.

During the twenty-four hours that the mescal was roasting, I helped Antonio and his crew with several other tasks necessary to inaugurate the village's new traditional school, and to prepare for the feast. We painted the recently donated school building, swept it clean, mounted letters above its door, and painted traditional designs as murals on its outer walls. I purchased seven kilos of local fish—*lisa, cochito,* and *cazón*—for Raquel, José-Juan's daughter, to cook for the entire community.

The only trouble was that Raquel had never worked with an outsider on a traditional feast, and was unsure that I knew what we needed to obtain in addition to fish and mescal—she didn't have enough plates, cutlery, condiments, or firewood to host the entire village, nor did I.

I learned about these additional needs the hard way—in the last hour and a half before the inauguration feast—José-Juan angrily dispatched me to go get more firewood, cooking oil, salt, salsa, onions, and tomatillos. By the time I purchased these from the local markets, seventy people were congregated in front of the school. Adolfo Burgos and Jesús Rojo had begun to sing traditional *pascola* songs, and several young men were taking turns dancing in front of them. Meanwhile Humberto was helping José-Juan unearth the baked mescal, which had been cooked just long enough to make its flavor rich with smoke and sweetness.

Suddenly we had a traditional fiesta on our hands. Antonio Lopéz blessed the food on behalf of the elders, and explained the purposes of the school that he was initiating. It would teach the youth their traditions of the desert and sea, not inside the school building itself, but out in the field; the building would serve for planning meetings, for storage, and for preliminary instruction. He and the other elders wanted the community to think of the school as one more way of legitimizing traditional knowledge about desert medicines and foods, about sustainable foraging and fishing practices. Everyone applauded, tired of speeches and ready to eat.

Just as we guessed that it was finally time to eat, suddenly Antonio's son Josüe moved forward while his father introduced him as "a minister." Dressed up in a powwow costume, he sang a beautiful Seri prayer-song, gesturing wildly as he chanted. Everyone applauded once more, but at the same time inched further toward the food.

Then Josüe took a deep breath, bowed, and launched into one of the most eloquent fire-and-brimstone sermons I had ever heard in my twenty years of visiting indigenous communities:

"In the face of so many perils that threaten to annihilate us, threats emanating from both Mexican society and the global economy, we must revitalize the traditional strategies that have allowed us to survive as the original inhabitants of the Americas. The prognosis for continued survival appears bleak, but we must remember that our people have survived countless other perils over the centuries, and this has made us strong. We must remind others and ourselves that the very constitution of our oppressive government guarantees our right to survive as a sovereign people within our homeland. We must insist that our Mexican neighbors obey the constitutional privilege that has been bestowed upon us, so that we can ensure that future generations can proceed with our traditional livelihoods as an authentic indigenous nation. Now let us eat our native foods in a way that honors our ancestors!"

His rapid-fire delivery of the sermon was immediately followed by the serving of food—mescal, fish, mesquite pinole, and prickly pear fruit punch. Within minutes all seventy people were ravenously devouring the food of their ancestors. It was a feeding frenzy equal in intensity to that of the pelicans enjoying the arrival of the first large school of sardines in the spring.

It didn't take long for Raquel to notice that I was holding myself back from eating anything until I was sure that everyone else had been fed. She brought me a small plate she had sequestered for me.

I sampled what was on the plate. José-Juan's mescal was mouthwatering, but her own grilled fish was as rich and flaky as any I had ever had in the village. But there was also a small sandwich bag with some white meat in it.

"Chicken?" I asked. Cold fried chicken was what it tasted like. "I don't want chicken. This was supposed to be a feast of native foods."

Raquel saw my displeasure. "It's from the island," she whispered.

"There are no chickens on the island," I replied.

"*Coof,*" she replied, amused that I couldn't tell chuckwalla from chicken.

And so I ate a full meal of native foods after all, and the meal included an unlabeled reptilian delicacy I had never before anticipated eating.

Driving back to the beach house that night, I thought about why it even mattered to me whether the meat was chicken or chuckwalla. On the one hand I avoided factory-raised chicken in northern Mexico whenever I could because much of it was contaminated with salmonella, and my culinary interests lay with native foods. On the other hand chuck-wallas are considered endangered by many biologists and sacred to the Seri. I would not have sought them out on my own, and don't condone anyone other than the Seri eating the island species.

But did the meat taste different once I knew its source? Well, yes, subtly, subliminally. Memory, imagination, and taste are so tightly linked that water can become wine, and chicken chuckwalla.

Some O'odham friends of mine once told me about being offered bowls of turtle soup down on the Mexican border. They accepted, and while they were enjoying the savory stew, they assumed they were spooning up a broth made with the meat of desert tortoises, a tradition-al food familiar to them. But then the Mexican cook asked them if they'd like to see the other turtle, that was still alive behind the kitchen. He dragged out a small sea turtle to show the O'odham, who only knew of the animal by the stories of their elders who had made a sacred pilgrim-age to the sea. They knew that eating such an animal was showing disre-spect for the Ocean Power that generated the rains they needed to grow their crops. Even though it was unlikely that most O'odham would ever see such a sacred animal, eating sea turtle meat was strictly taboo. They pushed the bowls of soup to the middle of the table, paid the cook, and went on their way.

And they vomited continually for four days until a medicine man came to heal them. Knowing exactly what you are eating—and where it came from—is still a moral and spiritual necessity for many cultures in this world.

Recently the sanctity of religious food taboos became a political issue, thanks to Rabbi Yossi Serebryanski—an Orthodox Jew who supervises a kosher-certifying laboratory in Brooklyn. He recently became a coplain-tiff in litigation against the Food and Drug Administration because of its refusal to regulate and label thirty-six kinds of genetically engineered foods that have genes from viruses, insects, and hogs in them. The rabbi argued that rights granted him by the Religious Freedom Restoration Act were being violated by the FDA, in that he was being unknowingly exposed to foods he deemed to be religiously objectionable. In his view he was required by Hebrew scriptures and rabbinical teachings to follow a strictly kosher regimen that was free of certain food additives, ingredients, and genes from insects or swine.

Rabbi Serebryanski was joined by others, of the Eastern Orthodox and Roman Catholic faiths, who objected to consuming genes from viruses and pathogens inserted in traditional crops that they relied on during Lent. These folks are prominent leaders of their spiritual communities. A January 1999 *Time* magazine survey reported that 81 percent of American consumers believed that genetically engineered foods should be labeled. Furthermore, 58 percent claimed they would not purchase such foods if they were labeled. Former Secretary of Agriculture Dan Glickman recently declared that if the American public wanted them labeled, genetically engineered foods should indeed be labeled.

Nevertheless, there were powerful alliances between politicians and industry that would keep that from happening for a while. The congressional committees providing oversight to the FDA and USDA were stacked with politicians who received millions of dollars of campaign contributions from Dow Chemical, Monsanto, Novartis, ConAgra, and the American Crop Protection Association. Furthermore, Secretary Glickman formerly worked for a law firm that frequently represented Monsanto, and Michael Taylor, then FDA deputy commissioner for policy, had also done legal work for Monsanto in the past. The door was swinging the other way as well: Michael Friedman, a former FDA commissioner, became senior vice president for Monsanto & Searle pharmaceutical division, and Linda Fisher, a former EPA assistant administrator for pesticides, became Monsanto's vice president for government affairs. These alliances regarded labeling as an admission that some foods might not be safe for humans or for wildlife, and were not about to see the economy disrupted by consumer boycotts of genetically engineered foods.

It was as if the FDA, USDA, and EPA were saying, "What they don't know won't hurt them." But by mid-fall 1999, U.S. representatives no longer sided with the agencies. In October of that year, Michigan Democrat David Bonior sent a bipartisan letter signed by fifty members of Congress to FDA Commissioner Jane Henney asking for more safety testing and explicit labeling of foods derived from more than forty genetically engineered crops already loose on American farms. Within a month, Ohio Congressman Democrat Dennis Kucinich introduced Genetic Engineering Labeling Bill (HR 3377) into the House of Representatives. Legal protection against the potentially deleterious health and environmental effects of transgenic crops had suddenly become an issue for more than just seed savers and organic food enthusiasts. And it was *the* concerns that various faith communities had about the sacredness of food that brought this issue into the mainstream.

The mainstream. Laurie and I had completed our journey down another kind of mainstream—the Río Colorado and the Gulf of California. We had seen where fertile soils and native foods, wildlands and agricultural habitats, had been lost from the watershed, and we had located small pockets where they had persisted. Where old faith communities persisted intact—among the Mormons, Hopi, the Seri of the coast and even the mixed Anglos and Hispanics of the Santa Cruz—the food shed had not yet completely unraveled. It may have suffered some historic damage, but it could still be repaired and stitched together once more. Yet it seemed that such ecological restoration and agricultural revitalization could happen only if food continued to be treated as something sacred. Perhaps the traditional feast we celebrated was more significant than the mere number of calories it redistributed. Perhaps feasts were essential to keeping native foods *memorable*—in our dreams and in our prayers, in our daily lives and in our culture's plans for a rich and rewarding future.

Chapter Seventeen

Hunting Mushrooms and Grilling Salmon

When Laurie and I had completed our expeditions across our food shed, from headwaters to seas, I was encouraged to see how all that we had learned fit back into the larger picture of food moving across our continent. From the arid coast of northern Mexico, I flew to the humid coast of the Pacific Northwest on the invitation of Rick Bayless and other friends in the Chefs Collaborative. They were restaurant owners and chefs who sought the latest field reports on what was happening with regard to the sustainability of food production in various regions. When I caught up with them, they were in the midst of their annual gathering in Portland, milling around on the grounds of an insane-asylum-turned-resort and microbrewery. Their event that afternoon was called the Green Fair, a sort of bioregional marketplace of organic and native foods: Dungeness crab, black-cap berries, salmon, and mushrooms. I sampled a few of the foods but had more fun sampling the life histories of the people that such an event attracts, from the peculiar to the charismatic.

For starters there was John Kallas, a Midwesterner transplanted to the Northwest, who made his living guiding Wild Food Adventures. A sort of culinary Indiana Jones, Kallas takes folks on foraging trips, publishes a series of pamphlets on native and naturalized foods of the temperate rain forests, and lectures to every kind of interest group in the region, from survivalists to businessmen to tree huggers. He would be guiding a group of chefs on a foraging expedition for salad greens the next afternoon, and I promised I'd meet him for part of it.

Then there was Nora Pouillon, who runs the first two fully organic restaurants in the United States, Nora and Asia Nora. Since her childhood, Nora told me, she had been fascinated by the special foods various cultures regard as medicines. Whenever she caught a cold while she was growing up in Austria, her family lovingly prepared her garlic soup; for leg cramps, they always brought her fruit. She has carried this sensibility with her as she experimented with foods at her two world-famous restaurants in Washington, D.C., and with her recent venture, the online organic foods warehouse known as Walnut Acres. While she could talk business and food history with flair, I was struck by how many times Nora reminded me of the driving force behind all her activities: "The reason I've been eating organic foods all these years is the way they make me feel."

Perhaps the most curious character I met at the Green Fair was Lars, the homegrown guru of edible mushroom gatherers in the Pacific Northwest. Part self-trained botanist, part gambler, part grassroots entrepreneur, Lars has made most of his income from mushroom hunting since 1984. This fungal pursuit has consumed him full-time since 1987. On the most lucrative day of his wild-crafting career, Lars picked four thousand dollars' worth of chanterelles, those yellow fungi that carry a dense, apricotlike aroma. Lars too invited me to join him in the temperate rain forests of the coast range the next day, and I couldn't resist the offer. I would spend time with both John and Lars, whose foraging sites would be just a few miles away from one another.

I offered some words to the chefs early the next morning, but as soon as we hopped on a bus for the Oregon coast, I grabbed the seat next to Lars. While he sporadically chatted with those of us closest to him in the bus, it was almost as if he were talking to himself or, more likely, to mushrooms. He had put in years of working alone before joining forces with many of the four thousand-some Oregoners who picked mushrooms for profit. But when he could, Lars would still forage all day every day that the season was peaking. He was a man inclined to a singular focus and to solitary pursuits, who enjoyed searching intently under trees on muddy slopes, and the activity kept him conversant with beings other than humans.

Lars was so deeply immersed in the million-pound annual harvest of chanterelles from the Northwest that some of our questions didn't make sense to him. When one of the chefs asked him about the nutritional value of these mushrooms, he looked at her as if she were nuts.

"Look, an ounce of chanterelles only contains five calories, so it takes more energy to harvest the damn things than what you gain by eating them. Culinary value yes, nutritional value? Well . . ."

I had read that the harvest had become so intensive that Forest Service biologists had become worried that the harvesters' picking, raking, and trampling of mushrooms might reduce spore dispersal and, eventually, the yield of mushrooms. When I mentioned this to Lars, he scoffed, and asserted that harvesting impacts on mushroom populations were negligible: "And as far as the effects of commercial harvesting go, keep in mind that the wild mushroom industry is only twenty years old up here. In the only study I know—one that ran eight years—there was no long-term difference in abundance between areas of high and low harvesting pressure. In fact, one-hundred-percent removal of all chanterelles produced no long-term effect. There are still lots of spores hanging around on the forest floor."

It remained hard for me to imagine that the tens of thousands of commercial and avocational mushroom harvesters running around the Pacific Northwest each fall generated no ecological impacts while harvesting four million pounds of wild mushrooms from the forest floor. I come from the desert, where even a few hundred jojoba nut harvesters disrupted jojoba populations within a decade's time, trampling seedlings and disrupting germination in their rush to get rich on this miraculous shampoo plant. I was cautiously weighing Lars's words, recognizing that he knew these particular habitats far better than I did. While some of the twenty-five commercial species of mushrooms might be hyperabundant and widespread, I knew that others had more specific habitat requirements. And it was not merely local folks who came to those habitats to harvest these fungal gems. As long as a single collector could reap several hundred dollars' worth of mushrooms a day during the peak of the season, nomadic wildcrafters—including some five thousand Canadians—would find it worth their while to migrate in and out of various forest patches from Oregon through northern British Columbia. Because the choicest mushrooms are prized at fifty to one hundred dollars a pound, there had been recent outbreaks of violence between the locals and the nomads, including armed robberies of mushroom harvests. When that much mushroom money is at stake, there will inevitably be harvesters who will dig up hotspots to harvest all they can possibly obtain, disrupting the very relationships between the fungi and the firs and hemlocks above them.

I later learned how two field researchers, Rebecca McLain and Eric Jones, had documented that the unregulated mix of locals and nomads has already led to ecologically unsound mushroom harvesting at a few places in the Pacific Northwest. While Lars felt that harvesting impacts on habitats were being overdramatized, agencies in several states disagreed with him, and had recently set up Wild Edible Mushroom Task Groups, with regulations to ensure that harvesters' effects on forest health would be minimized.

We stopped along the coast where Lars had spotted some orange lobster mushrooms on a scouting trip a few days before our visit. The orange lobster was an edible fungus that grows well in North America's fog zones, but not in Europe or Japan. We climbed up a muddy slope loaded with Sitka spruce just above the coast, not more than three hundred yards inland from the ocean. After hunting in vain for more than a half hour, I finally found a solitary orange fungus rising up out of the moss and spruce duff.

Lars confirmed that I'd made an infield hit.

"Well, it's not that big a specimen, considering that most species of mushrooms grow way bigger in cool, foggy weather like this. But take it home, dry it down, and eat it. You have a mushroom there that's hard to overcook, so you really can't go wrong with it."

Barely an hour after putting our feet on the ground, we got back onto the bus, drenched, muddy, and happy. Several of us had gathered enough mushrooms that we could prepare a full meal back at home. I was pleased to know that there were still a good number of wild food gatherers who can make a decent living foraging out in the boonies. Of course, they were facing increasing competition from mushroom and car-producing multinationals like Mitsubishi, and there was always the risk of unexpected weather that would dampen the wild harvest at its peak. But the number of full-time chanterelle harvesters in the binational Northwest had climbed above fifteen thousand, and demand has remained high. The harvesting of wild native mushrooms in the Pacific Northwest already brought forty to fifty million dollars into the regional economy, and there was no indication that it had reached its peak.

Without a doubt, Lars had pioneered a trail that other mushroom wildcrafters have followed, and most observers had not yet seen any significant depletion of this wild resource in most localities. If the forests themselves could remain healthy, so would the foraging economy. It appeared that careers in hunting and gathering could not be dismissed as a thing of the past. As we parted, Lars reminded me that he and others were not merely in it for the income: "This mushroom business, it's really addictive. There are people in it who could easily make more money pursuing other options, but they can't tear themselves away from the forest, from the hunt."

That is the same way that wild ginseng harvesters in ten states speak of their annual pursuit of sixty tons of roots hidden in natural habitats around the Midwest—if it were only for the money, they wouldn't be in it, but there is magic as well. It is also true of the way other harvesters look at their work, whether they are out searching for wild chilies, piñon nuts, high-bush blueberries, acorns, echinacea, or pawpaws—there is something primordial about the pursuit of these foods and medicines in their natural habitats. It is an elixir for the soul, this drinking in of forest and marshland. It is a cure in and of itself, over and above the nutritional or pharmacological value of the plants.

When we returned at dusk to the Chefs Collaborative gathering, we were in time to witness a bunch of fancy dancers from the Warm Springs Reservation celebrate their own wild harvest. While the elders skewered chinook and coho salmon onto alder stakes to let them bake and smoke in a circle around red-hot coals, the kids danced wildly to powwow songs chanted over the bassy beat of a big leather drum. When the drumming subsided, one of the elders reminded us: "We couldn't do this for you if it was just a performance, just some form of entertainment. It would make us feel too bad, and in our culture, you shouldn't even cook if you're feeling bad about something. No, this food, these dances, they are sacred to our community, they are what we receive and give to the world. This salty, smoky salmon helps to round us out as a community, and that is why, before we eat, we form a circle of prayer around this circle of fish and fire. Join us!"

Chapter Eighteen

Feasting with the Dead

Our first Saturday back around the house, Laurie and I harvested squashes, then planted our winter greens, onions, and cold-hardy legumes in the morning. While we were working I suddenly remembered that we were invited out onto the Papago Indian Reservation to an honor dance for Danny Lopez. Danny, an old O'odham friend of mine, had recently completed his master's degree at the tender age of sixty-one, and his family decided to celebrate that accomplishment, among many others. I talked Laurie into taking a break from the gardening so that we could drive sixteen miles to San Pedro village on the eastern edge of the reservation.

Behind the village store, some hundred O'odham and Anglo friends of Danny's were parking their pickups and cars and assembling in a big field. They had come not so much to celebrate Danny's graduation but to honor his lifework in keeping O'odham farming, storytelling, and singing alive.

As we entered the crowd, I realized that we were witnessing part of the O'odham honor dance that was seldom done anymore. Each dancer shouldered a fifty-pound bag of tepary beans or wheat flour, enormous squashes or melons, then laid these goods down at the feet of Danny and his wife, Florence.

All the dancers were dressed to the hilt, but Danny and Florence outdid them, at least in sheer elegance. Danny had on his finest black Stetson-style hat, a richly colored snap-buttoned shirt, and shiny Western boots. Florence's hair shone with silvery ringlets, and her long dress had all the brilliance of a rainbow, all the hues of a field full of desert wildflowers, and all the subtleties of a desert sunset in it. They looked as though they had walked straight out of what they call the Flower World, the wilderness world, the ancient world of natural abundance.

When the dancers took a break, the feasting began. Like everyone else, we had been encouraged to bring a traditional O'odham food to the potluck, so we placed some of our cholla buds on the table. Joseph Enos, an O'odham spiritual leader who often doubles as a humorist, served as master of ceremonies. It seemed that I always saw him walking with a cane nowadays, the same one he had only occasionally used for his gout flareups when I first met him twenty years ago. He hobbled up to the podium, his gray braids dangling; he paused, straightened his glasses, then leaned over the mike: "Come on up, everybody, come on up. Come and sample all the traditional foods Danny's friends have brought to honor his work. We have cholla buds and cracked corn stew with chili, white tepary beans, and whole wheat tortillas," he announced like a county fair hawker. Then he repeated the same message in O'odham, holding up a bowl of each food as he spoke about it.

"We have wheat berry and pinto bean posole. And oh, yes, Muffin here has brought the muskmelon she calls *Ge:li Ba:so,* or old man's chest. That's what she says it looks like with all those veins in its skin. No—just a minute; Muffin is being corrected on the name. Well, that's not right exactly, some of the men are saying. They are reminding me that they call that very same melon *Oks Totoñ,* or old lady's knees. Whatever turns you on, come and get some. And don't anyone worry—these foods are all low cholesterol, so you won't get fat. Just eat and enjoy it!"

It was truly a feast of the desert, one that reminded us how the foods at our very doorstep offered flavor, nourishment, and healing. I had been among the men who had been joking with Joe about the names men and women gave to the same melon, so I decided to seek out Muffin and tease her some more. Muffin Burgess, the melon grower whom Joseph had mentioned, had begun her exploration of desert foods and farming about the same time I had, some twenty-five years ago, when each of us apprenticed with families in villages not far from each other. We hadn't seen each other for several years, so we hugged long and hard. She had lost her adopted O'odham grandmother a few years ago but had not heard that I had lost mine (Laura Kerman) within the last year. She was silent for a minute as she let that news sit in the air, and then she asked, "Will you be going out to Laura's to bring her food on the Day of the Dead?"

I had forgotten all about the ritual, but no doubt Laura's nieces had not. They were probably out in the cemetery as we spoke, cleaning up Laura's grave preparing to offer their recently deceased aunt her favorite foods.

"Thanks for that reminder, Muff. Got any more Old Man's Knees I can bring her?"

As we left Danny's honor dance, I realized that he and his family had been subtly reshaping the significance of feasts associated with funerals, with the Day of the Dead, and with other rites of passage. Historically the primary purpose of a traditional village feast on the Papago Indian Reservation was to redistribute food without making anyone feel bad about their poverty. Some O'odham families might have received rains sufficient enough for good crop yields, while others had lost their crops due to drought, grasshoppers, or floods. Such losses were hardly anyone's fault, so those who were lucky shared their momentary abundance with their neighbors.

But with the coming of government welfare programs, traditional farming had declined. Since World War II fewer O'odham families suffered from undernutrition because they were regularly provided with homogenized, fiber-poor foods from the federal surplus commodity programs. Ironically nearly all the foods the government issue to the tribes were less nutritious and more fattening than their native foods. Accordingly the average weight of Tohono O'odham men increased from 158 pounds in 1938 to 202 pounds in 1978. Feasts were no longer required to redistribute the food supply; in fact, fatty foods such as frybread and beef chili, once eaten only at feasts, became daily or weekly fare. The transition from feast and famine to stabilized food supplies since the Great Depression has had grave health consequences for most O'odham. Nearly every family on the rez now has three or more members suffering from adult-onset diabetes. Dietary change had done them in.

Today O'odham communities suffer from the highest incidence of adult-onset diabetes in the world, but Danny and Florence are not fatalistic about it. They have quietly improvised a way to let village feasting tradition express a message of hope. It is a message about diabetes prevention through the revitalization of native foods, ones rich in soluble fiber, fructose, tannins, and other blood sugar-lowering substances. Just as the honor dance raises the level of respect for all elders, serving native foods at feasts raises their cultural value among young members of the community. As one Pima friend of mine once said, "To be Indian, you gotta eat Indian."

As more and more kids on the rez take pride in their Native American heritage, the foods can be promoted as a fundamental part of the heritage. A similar transition took place once O'odham youth realized that their people had a remarkable tradition of long-distance running. Pride in that tradition encouraged many teenage boys to take up cross-country and marathon running. Now the O'odham are once again recognized for the fine performances in Indian Running events; their pride for their traditions has put them back on the road to health.

The following night, Laurie and I decided to drive out to Laura Kerman's grave, but we first stopped by our local pumpkin festival. We pulled up to the edge of the fields and got out of the car to scan the thousands of jack-o'-lanterns that our neighbor Nick Buckelew had grown. But the sight of all those uniformly orange pumpkins made me long to see a pile of O'odham squashes, their stripes, spots, bumps, necks, and stems all running every which way. So we got back in the car and drove another thirty minutes, out to the O'odham farming village of Topawa.

squash

That's where my adopted grandmother, 104-year-old Laura Kerman, was buried, after a dust storm and rainbow appeared during my eulogy for her. Like Danny is today, Laura had been a gifted teacher, a singer of traditional songs, a seed saver, and a gardener, one who shared her teachings and her seeds with people of many cultures in addition to her own. She was a devout Catholic, and at the age of 90 she had walked at dawn for a half mile down a desert trail to stand as a sponsor for my daughter, Laura, at her christening.

A few years later her relatives put her in a nursing home up near

Phoenix, but she broke loose after a while and had someone drive her back into the desert she loved. When her nieces hinted that they might send her back to the same nursing home if she kept asserting her independence, she locked herself into her old adobe house for a week and wouldn't let anyone in to check up on her. After her kin finally got her to open the door, they deemed her to be too old to live by herself, garden, or gather, so they forced her to move to another nursing home deep in the dark heart of urban Tucson.

She hated the gravy-laden cafeteria slop they tried to serve her there, hated being torn away from going outside and finding her own food. Every time I sneaked some native foods and medicines in to her, the nurses would find them and take them away. She began to wither, and lost her short-term memory. Every once in a while I would take her out to pick cactus fruit, or cook her wild greens and beans at my home, but she mistook me for an agricultural scientist she worked for in 1912. Soon she refused to speak English with me or anyone else, and we communicated only in O'odham. When at last her body failed her in the nursing home and was returned to the desert soil she loved, I was relieved.

As Laurie and I approached the graveyard, I wondered whether someone might have put some O'odham squashes out for her in the cemetery already, as a ritual offering of food to the deceased. The feeding of the dead is a long tradition in Mexican and U.S. Indian communities, particularly among those that were historically encouraged by Spanish-speaking priests to celebrate the *Dia de los Muertos*. But when we reached Laura's grave, we saw that, though it had been raked clean and beautified by her relatives, no one had yet left any food for the dead.

It was my turn to feed her. I had cleaned out all the stray canned goods from our cupboards once again, offering Laura the last of our Green Giant peas, Progresso lentil soup, and Herdez tomatillo sauce, items I had once seen her purchase for her brother. We placed them under a tree near her grave, hoping to return the next day to offer her fresher food.

When I came back alone the next afternoon, I felt ashamed: Someone had found all the cans and hurled them away from the graves. Canned foods had angered the spirits, I recognized. I walked back out of the cemetery to the Blazer, and this time brought out only fresh food. I returned just in time for the Catholic priest's blessing of the graves. As soon as his Day of the Dead mass was over, I placed mesquite tortillas, cholla buds, and tepary beans out for Laura, then hugged and talked with her old acquaintances who had come to celebrate the mass. They were curious to see what I had brought to feed Laura's spirit, and no one mentioned finding the cans.

They invited us to join their families for an all-night vigil and feast, but I was too weary. They returned to their homes for prayers, and for a ritual meal in honor of their deceased ancestors. I returned to the reservation highway and drove back home under a yellow moon, remembering how Laura used to limp around her garden, two dogs following her, as she talked to all her plants as if they were the human babies she never had, as if they were listening for her voice to guide and encourage their growth. Nearly an hour after I left her grave, I turned into my driveway, realizing that my lips were caked with salt. I had been weeping all the way home, regretting that I had not broken her out of the nursing home one last time, so that she could eat one last traditional meal of desert foods and die at peace in the desert.

To get over my regrets I turned my attention toward preparing for Thanksgiving. However hokey or truly it seems to some, Thanksgiving is what I love most about being American. The story of native foods being offered by Algonquian-speaking tribes to new European immigrants still touched me somehow, despite the tragic facts that the Indians had already been racked by European-introduced diseases, and that the Pilgrims subsequently usurped Indian lands and waters. It was a story filled with ironies, as most memorable stories are. My mother usually prepared a huge Thanksgiving dinner, but that year we decided to treat her to one that she did not have to direct. Laurie and I painstakingly planned and prepared each dish, while Laura served as archivist, recording each recipe.

I had thawed our last homegrown turkey the day before, and had filled its cavities with beer from a local microbrewery and chili mustard made by a family friend. I then proceeded just as Ely, my buddy at the cactus camp, had instructed me to. After injecting the turkey meat with garlic and juice from limes picked off our tree that morning, I set the bird out to smoke in the adobe oven out back. Laurie and Laura Rose conjured up a colorful cranberry chutney, while I pulled the bird from the oven and stuffed it with a blue-corn-and-piñon-nut dressing.

By midmorning on Thanksgiving Day, as the turkey meat was still absorbing mesquite smoke in the backyard, I went out running for several miles to work up an appetite. As I ran along the roadside, it began to register that I was jogging adjacent to an extensive windrow of trash and wrappers left behind by fast food aficionados: Miller Lite bottles, stating the obvious: "Ready to Drink." Gatorade Thirst Quencher. Sonic Burger's cardboard containers for french fries, proudly proclaiming "America's Drive-In." Dinosaur Fruit Snacks, "made with real fruit juice." Hundreds of windblown coupons for Schwan's Breaded Mozzarella Sticks, made with 100 percent real low-fat mozzarella cheese coated with Italian-seasoned breading, ready to bake or deep-fry in Personal Pouches.

While the homegrown bird smoked back home in the oven, I interrupted my jogging to pick up trash, not because I wanted to beautify America's highways but because I wanted to figure out what exactly my society is addicted to. I wanted relief from that addiction, not merely from its trash. Every day like this, I too could be seduced into shooting up such junk, to toss its wrappers out the window, and surge ahead on a chemical high. Or I could go cold turkey, and be humbled by the realities of gardening, hunting, or gathering in this wildly unpredictable land. It was not that I would never be lured again by the greasy smell of french fries or by the surge of sugar after downing a chocolate malt, but such addictions were slowly losing their control over my life. My pockets were filled with trash, so I turned around and jogged home.

In another hour the house was filled with friends and relatives. Some had prepared their families' favorite dishes, while others tried their hand at cooking wild foods or providing samples of Arizona wines. There were pies of cushaw squash, wild rice from friends who summer in Wisconsin, freshly picked salad greens, a tepary bean casserole, cholla bud pickles, and various dressings. When we all sat down to pray together, holding hands in one grand circle, we blessed not just the food but all the lives—human or other animal, plant, microbial—all the little unseen lives hidden in this feast. When we let go of one another's hands, we picked up forks, spoons, bowls, or glasses and sampled the cornucopia spread before us. We slowly sipped our wine and chewed every morsel that came to our lips. Each dish, each plate, each cup, each goblet contained a story; as we ate, each food's origins, harvests, and makers became revealed to us.

When someone asked about the turkey, I simply closed my eyes and remembered the day I brought the scruffy poults home, and how they later followed me around the pen, nudging my legs when I had forgot to feed them. As friends complimented Laurie on her squash pie, I could feel the coarse hairy stems of vines trailing down from the satellite dish in late summer. When someone asked where the white tepary beans came from, I could hear Terry Button tell me how he fell in love with Ramona, and moved back to the rez with her to become a part-time farmer.

Flavors and stories. Stories and flavors. They danced together into our mouths, pirouetting around our tastebuds, doing one last tango across our tongues before disappearing down our throats and into that darker, wild place below. We filled that place full of calories and memories, then Laurie and I took our guests for a walk across the desert grassland at sunset, where ripened seed heads glowed in the last light of day. If we were not already full enough, a primitive kind of patriotism swelled up inside us: a love of *patria,* fatherland, motherland, kindred earth. The foods and wine had blessed *us,* not the other way around.

IV

Winter

The Reflective Months

Chapter Nineteen

Of Vinegars Fermented and Memories Curdled

A day or two after Thanksgiving, Laurie and I sat with my mother on our sun porch, talking and taking in what little light the winter skies had to offer us. Of course, spending her first holiday as a widow had flooded my mother with images of Chuck, and other memories as well, from earlier days of her life. She was not wistful, though; she talked about her memories freely, without regret. Laurie and I were comfortable with letting my mother just tell her story to us, and did so as we sat there cranking a nonmotorized pasta machine.

I had probably eaten pasta every month of my life for the last four decades, but had never made any on my own. With the fall harvest in, and the winter vegetable beds barely producing, we had turned our attention from gardening to beginning our own efforts in food preservation and preparation. As my mother talked, we tried out hand processing of foods, which Stella, Ely, Javier, Esperanza, and Don Fernando had inspired us to engage in.

They were small steps, but worth walking. That seems all I can ever muster as the Winter Solstice approaches: I make little promises to myself to get my life wandering in the right direction, heeding all I've learned ethically, emotionally, or technically over the previous year. I did not want to change the world, I simply wanted to crank out pasta and try my hand at making cheeses and herbal vinegars. For the latter I would rescue dregs from a winery owned by a former agricultural professor of mine, and combine them with a vinegar mother that my friend Agnese Haury had given me for Christmas. She had sequestered that billowy mother in Ball jars since the late seventies.

While my mother shaped the pasta dough, I started on some *lubna* goat cheese, taking homemade yogurt which we produced from local goat milk, and straining it through a cheesecloth. And while I worked on the cheese, Laurie squeezed hundreds of limes that we rescued from the trees in our backyard orchard just before a frost, preparing to make a border lime pie, and juice to freeze for later use. We had become a veritable food factory on this cold wintry day, but we worked without a single trademark or patent to our names.

My mother kept up a pleasant banter with Laurie and me as we worked. Knowing how preoccupied I had recently been with food history, she had proudly brought with her from home all the recipes she used to make meals for us when I was a kid. They were written on prefab recipe cards distributed by *Woman's Day* magazine, by Quaker Oats, and by Betty Crocker. They promoted the use of those lovely stainless-steel appliances fashionable in the fifties, and were intended for wage-earning housewives who needed to produce a week's worth of meals in one fell swoop. Most of the recipes were suited to large families. My mother was one of twelve children in an Irish family that had so many mouths to feed that when her father's income plummeted during the depression, they farmed her out to some friends of theirs who lovingly served as foster parents for a while. But she had dark memories of those years that immediately preceded her time with her foster family: The food supply was stretched as far as it could go, and she was often sick because of it.

My mother still retained an uncanny capacity to recite the weekly cycle of meals that her mother had tried to feed the twelve children, making the most of starchy tubers, breads, soups, and stews to eke out the limited food budget. In addition to cooking for fourteen, my grandmother worked as head cook at a nearby cement plant cafeteria. There she fixed up enormous batches of industrial-strength food that still had an echo of home cooking as it sang itself into the bowls of blue-collar workers and the plates of her own litter. While I rolled the pasta through the machine, my mother recalled her only other memory of ever making noodles: "Now, I've never made *spaghetti* from scratch but I did help my mother make egg noodles and gravy loads of times. You know, I hated them, we ate them so often. Sometimes, instead of noodles, she'd make creamed chipped beef on toast. I hated that too."

"But then one day, after your father married me, he admits to me that he's curious about maintain American food because he had mostly eaten Lebanese food while growing up. He says, 'Honey, could you fix me this thing they used to make us eat in the army called Shit on a Shingle? You think you could find how to make it for me?' I told him I'd learn how to make it for him, if he wanted it once in a while. I didn't want to admit that I knew how to make it all along, because I hated the taste of it myself."

"But that's not all my mother would make. On Saturdays when we had enough money for fresh fruit and other groceries, she would cook and cook, bake twenty pies and cakes. Even though I suppose we were poor, she'd use those times to invite all our friends over after church on Sunday, and share what we had with them. We'd put out all those pies she made from scratch, and the best hot buns, with cinnamon, nuts, and sugar. The neighborhood kids would go wild."

"On Sunday we'd have chicken or a roast, the potatoes baked right in there with them in the pan, or she'd boil and mash them with their red skins mixed right in."

"On Monday, we'd go back to the basics: big steaming bowls of navy bean soup, with a little pork bone thrown in with them. She'd make two kinds of corn bread—a skillet bread and a high-rising sweet kind, same as she'd make over at Universal Atlas where she worked as head cook. Tuesday, egg noodles; Wednesday, spaghetti; then, Thursday, here'd she come with some Boston baked beans. No salads, no steaks, no pork chops, just beans. Friday there'd be fish, and Saturday she'd start to bake again. Because we were so poor, and what with a dozen mouths to feed, we didn't go to restaurants. I was already thirteen when my friend's parents took me to one. I got so confused there I didn't know what to do."

No wonder that some of those who survived the depression and Dust Bowl later indulged themselves in conspicuous consumption, in being proud of the fact that they had the leeway to "eat out" now and then. It is as cut and dried as an obituary column in a small town newspaper. For the three decades following the depression, Americans used their hard-won prosperity to purchase more and more of their food in ready-to-eat fashion, made by other folk's hands. To hell with fermenting vinegars, curdling milk, and cutting noodles.

But the generation of kids raised by survivors of those dark and dusty times accepted that luxury as the norm. From the seventies through the nineties, as the average American's disposable income increased by 40 percent, so did their consumption of processed foods. Even though they had the economic slack to immerse themselves in the pleasures of gardening and fishing, baking in wood-fired ovens and fermenting their own home brews, Americans spent less time preparing meals, and more time buying precooked packaged foods. When they weren't eating foil-wrapped TV dinners or microwavable pouches of designer cuisine at home, they were out on the town eating at restaurants, with franchises such as the Red Lobster and the Olive Garden getting their fair share of business.

Despite all the countercultural food movements, the average American today purchases 57 percent of his or her food as prepared meals and beverages—more than what is hand prepared and eaten at home. One USDA economist blandly put it this way: "Today, Americans count on the food industry to play a larger role in meal preparation."

As we carried the long strands of homemade pasta across our forearms from the sun porch into the kitchen, I asked my mother if she would be willing to cook a week's worth of her mother's meals for me. She was silent for a moment, then started to speak but cut herself off. Finally, she shook her head, her lips quivering slightly.

"That was too much work. It's not like what you're doing here, making pasta for pleasure. I'll talk about it all you want, Gary, but I don't want to go back there."

Her words sank down into me like a stone thrown into a pond, rippling out in every direction. However much I value elements of the old ways, neither my political fervor for them nor my intellectual curiosity about them would be enough to convince my mother or my aunts and uncles that there was anything more than drudgery in all that daily food preparation. The mere sight or smell of certain foods today fills them full of memories of a tougher, darker time. Whenever I tell them I'd like to learn some of our family's traditions in order to integrate them into my life, they hear but one thing: *He wants to go back.* And "going back" is not an option they will consider, for it is merely a romantic impulse of those who have never experienced the tedium and the pain of having no option except to eke a living out of what is available locally.

What is curious is that while my elders see "back" as someplace that progress has allowed them to escape from—the wrong end of a linear trajectory—I imagine my life as a looping and relooping, circling back to pick up something that we have forgotten, something that we desperately need for our health and our happiness, something precious we stoop down to cradle and carry along with us, as we curve out in a new direction. We do not ever escape our past, genetically, behaviorally, or ecologically speaking. Human bodies still need most of the same nutrients that they did when we emerged as a distinct species more than two million years ago. The very tastes we savored as children still seduce us as adults, those "comfort foods" that function for us more viscerally than what the abstraction—*nostalgia*—can capture. And socially we still feel the same deep sensory satisfaction whenever we feast with friends, sharing with them in whatever sacrament our culture has to offer: unleavened wheat bread and wine risen out of grape juices kept in oak barrels; corn tortillas patted out by hand and *pulqué* fermented from century-plant sap stored in deer or cow stomachs hung from the ceiling; bowls of purplish poi prepared from taro roots, followed by the drinking of kava, and the telling of stories sailed from one island to the next.

It *is* ironic that today many Americans are astonished to learn that folks of Italian descent gain health benefits from integrating elements of ancient Mediterranean cuisine into their contemporary diet; or that cholesterol and blood-pressure levels plummet when Mexican Americans cut the cheese and lard of Tex-Mex fame to return to the *nopalitos* and baked mescal of their Nahuatl ancestors; or that native Hawaiians lose weight and control their diabetes when poi and tropical fruits regain prominence on their dinner tables. Of course, some are hurt by the absence of traditional foods more than others are; although my mother's family suffered through famine and feast cycles much like those that my O'odham neighbors did before government food assistance arrived, only one of my cousins suffers from diabetes, while nearly all my Indian neighbors do.

It seems as though it is the poorest among us who most desperately need such traditional foods to regain their health, for they are otherwise treated as the dumping grounds for the worst of junk foods. And it is the poorest among us who are forced to work the poorest of land, who are driven to extract what little is left of its former fertility, and who are most frequently exposed to the pesticides and other poisons required to keep plagues and weeds in check when we have impoverished the biodiversity of rural landscapes. They are the ones who cannot typically afford to buy organic strawberries and tomatoes from Chile during the winter months when more affluent Americans regularly pay premium prices for such exotic prizes. And yet it is their compromised health that might benefit most from a pulse of vitamin-rich fruits and vegetables during a long and dreary winter, even though they seldom have the extra time to tend cold frames or build greenhouses to produce their own.

My mother and Laurie set the table while I went back out onto the porch alone to ponder a curious paradox. Whenever I think of my mother's dietary trajectory—her lifelong history of food choices—I realize that her choices have hardly ever been affected by heady arguments about how fresh, locally grown, sustainably produced foods might help her health or that of the farmworkers and the very land that surrounds her. What encourages her to engage in the time-consuming preparation of Lebanese phyllo dough and fresh spinach into the Arabic equivalents of *spanakopita* is the fond memories she has of my father's family and the pride she has gained from having learned their ethnic foodways when she was still in her twenties. What motivates her to dress a salad of our fresh greens is the alchemy she knows she can still bestow on us by using vinegar, olive oil, and fresh mint to ensure that a bowlful of wilted leaves will not be bland, but boldly transformed into something daring and delicious. As they called me in to dinner that night, and we sampled our first batch of homemade pasta, faintly tinted green by the addition of oreganos from our own backyard, she expressed her satisfaction in being part of a noodle-making family once again. If anything, it was the sensual delights—not the environmental costs we were spared or vitamins we gained by making our own pasta—that made my mother warble and chatter like an uncaged finch that evening. Her own hands had shaped their form, had woven into their very fabric a fleck of herbs.

Winter had come, and her mourning of Chuck's death continued, but there was something fresh and green inside her once more. She would be willing to make pasta again with us sometime, she said tentatively. It was not at all because she concurred with my various and sundry abstract motives, but because she felt as though she had been viscerally involved in something special, even priceless. She too had looped back, and had not lost anything by doing so.

Chapter Twenty

The WTO in Seattle, and the Spirit of St. Louis

The conversation with my mother had made me reconsider whether my preoccupation with growing and hand preparing more of my own food had become too rarefied, whether my concerns were shared only with an elite group of countercultural culinary aficionados. But hardly a week more had passed before I heard word that the first volleys had been fired in the battle at Seattle. As we all now know, the minor skirmishes there in no way determined the final outcome of the war, a global war that continues until this day. Nevertheless, the forced closure of the World Trade Organization's meetings in Seattle was something altogether unprecedented. For the first time, it became clear that millions of people were deeply worried about the ways in which globalization trends were wreaking havoc on family farms, migrant farmworkers, fishermen, and consumer food choices. Our future access to food is not an esoteric issue raised only by shrill Marxist scholars; the very survival of swordfish and sea turtle populations, of heirloom seeds and minor animal breeds, seemed to be at stake, and of interest to mainstream Americans, Europeans, Asians, and Africans.

Living without a television or a daily newspaper subscription, I was slow to hear the news that had already reached the eyes and ears of people watching and listening to CNN in some sixty countries. I stumbled on an E-mail message sent to me from a colleague in Berkeley who passed on journal excerpts from our mutual friend Paul Hawken. Hawken, entrepreneur, activist, and author of *The Ecology of Commerce,* had sent dozens of friends his field notes fresh off the streets of Seattle:

> Police pushed and truncheoned their way through and behind us, [spraying tear gas as they went]. We had covered our faces with rags and cloth, snatching glimpses of people being clubbed in the street before shutting our eyes. The gas was a fog through which people moved through in slow, strange dances of shock and pain and resistance. Tear gas is a misnomer. Think about feeling asphyxiated and blinded. Breathing becomes labored. Vision is blurred. The mind is disoriented. The nose and throat burn. It's not a gas, it's a drug. Gas-masked police hit, pushed, and speared us with the butt ends of their batons. We all sat down, hunched over, and locked arms more tightly. By then, the tear gas was so strong our eyes couldn't open. One by one, our heads were jerked back from the rear, and pepper sprayed directly into each eye. It was very professional. Like hair spray from a stylist. Sssst. Sssst.

While Paul was in the thick of this mess, I was on my way to Washington, D.C. It was not until I landed that I first heard rumors that the World Trade Organization's meetings in Seattle might be canceled, not merely disrupted for a morning. I had known that a few old friends would be among those gathered in Seattle, hoping to expose the WTO's role in undermining endangered species protection and farmers' rights. But in the months prior to their demonstrations, I could feel how their frustration with the WTO was close to brimming over into anger and outrage.

No wonder: In every environmental conflict they had presented to the WTO's Dispute Settlement Body to resolve, its three judges had always supported business as usual and ignored their concerns about irreparable damage done to endangered species and their habitats. Activists were angry that 125 disputes affecting millions of workers in dozens of countries were all "resolved" behind closed doors by three male judges, whose individual votes remained off the record. Nevertheless, when Seattle exploded into riots, I was caught off guard. When food, farm labor, and equity issues were suddenly on the front pages of newpapers around the world, I was amazed. When hundreds of millions of factory and farmworkers finally realized that WTO delegates had a stranglehold on their livelihoods, I was relieved.

I suddenly recalled the prophetic conversation at an informal dinner I had attended some twelve years before, on the sultry western coast of Italy. I was consulting at the UN's Food and Agriculture Organization in Rome at the time, which had become the most important battleground for keeping traditional seeds in the fields of farmers, and free-ranging fish in the nets of fishermen. I assumed it would stay that way, but two of my dinner companions predicted that the battle would shift to a new organization that U.S. economists had begun to sketch out, one that would be given unprecedented power to break down barriers to international trade and investment, and to decide which countries had rights to certain resources. When this leviathan was finally unveiled as the World Trade Organization in 1995, it had somehow been granted the authority to overrule any country's health, safety, or environmental protection laws that potentially interfered with trade. Within its first four years, its policies had favored multinational corporations to such an extent that some of its own trade experts wondered whether they had helped create a Frankenstein. When these trade experts arrived at the Seattle airport in late November, it became clear to them that many labor and environmental organizations were also terrified by the monster they had made.

While they were arriving in Washington State, I was full of regrets, heading in the other direction across the continent, to Washington, D.C. By the time I arrived in the capital, there was already chaos in the air, and other E-mails informed me of friends gassed, jailed, or held for hours by the police, without being offered food or water. It was no token protest—more than seven hundred organizations were there to say no to the WTO, to halt its masquerading as the final international arbiter in all global decisions affecting our diets, our medicines, and our destinies.

Just six months before, *Science* magazine had reported that most Americans didn't care about the labeling of genetically modified foods and other technotrivia. But now there were fifty thousand Americans roaming the streets of Seattle, and the genetic-labeling issue was among those that vaulted onto the covers of every major newspaper and magazine in the world.

It was surprising to see how the media initially misjudged the depth of feeling and sophistication of the protesters. Most of the early reports from Seattle featured Oregon's rowdy anarchists, characterizing them as Luddites who spent their lives up in trees. National Public Radio interviewed a housewife dressed up in a sea turtle costume, who said that she didn't exactly know what the WTO had done to sea turtles, but was nevertheless against its policies. And the globalization guru of the *New York Times,* Thomas Friedman, called the demonstrators "a Noah's Ark of flat-earth advocates, protectionist trade unions and yuppies looking for their 1960s fix."

Actually, there was one similarity with the sixties that impressed me as well. When the police started to gas and beat the protesters, I felt the same shock and indignation that I did in 1968, when Chicago's Mayor Richard J. Daley let loose billy clubs, police dogs, and fire hoses on peace demonstrators. As pepper spray, tear gas, flares, and rubber bullets filled the air, it was painfully evident that the Seattle police, FBI, and Federal Emergency Management Agency were largely unprepared to deal with either the groups trained in nonviolent civil disobedience or the roving gangs of anarchists.

The majority of protestors present could hardly be classified as anarchists, protectionists, yuppies, or Luddites. Within the demonstrators' ranks were the most accomplished "green businessmen" in the country, the political engineers of the Global Biodiversity Strategy, the masterminds of the Slow Food Movement, and the leaders of philanthropic organizations most actively involved in supporting environmental justice, food safety, and cultural property rights concerns. The list of individuals jailed, gassed, interrogated, or held by the police read like a who's who of regional and multicultural movements toward sustainability: Doctors Without Borders, Paul Hawken, José Bové, Mark Ritchie, Randy Hayes, Anita Roddick, Jane "Butterfly" Hill, Jia Ching Chen, and Betita Martínez. That these leaders were ignored by most mainstream media reporters was conspicuous.

Even more outrageous was the coverage of Seattle by magazines like *The Economist* and *Business Week.* Their reporters claimed that opponents of biotechnology and free trade would so disrupt the global economy that more people would starve than ever before. These magazines typically did not give much space to the plight of the 35,000 people who *do* starve to death every day, but suddenly they were defending transnational food corporations with the claim that only further globalization would lead to adequate feeding of the world's hungry.

Fortunately most of the American and European public was not duped by such whitewashes. Consumers forced additional baby food companies to cancel their orders of grains and beans produced from genetically engineered crops. Farmers refused to plant them, and some companies agreed to pay premium prices for crops that were not genetically engineered. Europe and Mexico banned imports of corn products that included Bt varieties. Even Archer Daniels Midland shunned Bt corn. Monsanto and Seminis stock values plummeted. It seemed as though everyone except the biotechnology industry's most strident spokesperson, Val Giddings, had conceded that genetic engineering was a major ethical and political issue that Americans deeply cared about.

Within days the Internet was filled with new prognostications from analysts who track trends in world trade and power. On November 29, a business website, STRATFOR.com released its analysis that the WTO's own "participants are so divided that they could not even develop a formal agenda for the meetings . . . the fact is that the WTO is moribund. . . . Its failure is rooted in the fundamental reality of today's global economy: de-synchronization of regions of roughly equal bulk . . . the world's economic regions are completely out of synch. . . . That means that the creation of integrated economic policies is impossible. What helps one region hurts others."

Mark Ritchie of the Center for Food Security noted that:

> "inside the WTO, the old process by which the United States and the European Union cut a deal and then imposed it on everyone else is a thing of the past. . . . Almost all member countries, rich and poor, are insisting on a new process that is more inclusive and democratic. . . . At last, the Nobel-Prize-winning group Doctors Without Borders was able to lead an effective campaign to convince delegates to give special global exemption from intellectual property rights laws to reduce the costs of medicines essential for fighting AIDS and other epidemics that spread across borders.

As if that were not enough, a commentary by Russell Mokhiber and Robert Weismann in their "Focus on the Corporation" weekly column raised the stakes even higher: "WTO critics face a perilous moment. They must not be distracted by . . . substantive proposals for changing the WTO. . . . Instead, they should unite around an uncompromising demand to dismantle the WTO and its corporation-created rules."

Out on the streets of Washington, D.C., I desperately tried to spot the taxi driven by that Rastafarian prophet, Mr. Donahue. He was nowhere to be seen. Before Seattle had even simmered down, a friend at Department of Interior headquarters took me aside to alert me that shock waves from Seattle were still surging around the building. She told me she had learned that advisory responsibilities on biotechnology, trade, and environment issues had been taken away from Bill Brown, Secretary Babbitt's proindustry science adviser. Babbitt had hired Lisa Guide in the International Affairs Office to bring on six additional experts to reevaluate issues such as Bt corn and monarch butterflies. Mexico had already told U.S. diplomats that it would be keeping all genetically modified crops out of the country's fields until their ecological and economic impacts were thoroughly evaluated. Its environmental leaders had been incensed by American companies' claims that the decline of monarchs could only be linked to the destruction of the butterfly's wintering grounds in Michoacan, thereby downplaying all the impacts of herbicides, toxic pollen, and other agricultural manipulations along the U.S. portion of the monarch's migratory corridor. Apparently Secretary Babbitt, a personal friend of Mexico's environment secretary Julia Carabias, did not want to see a rift between U.S. and Mexican conservationists. His staff authorized Fish and Wildlife Service biologists to work more closely with the Environmental Protection Agency to investigate just what damage Bt corn might be doing to the country's twelve endangered butterflies. Washington was abuzz with discussions of what the Seattle protests actually meant, and how representative the protesters were of mainstream America.

A couple of weeks after leaving Washington, Laurie and I found ourselves in America's heartland once again, in St. Louis to celebrate Christmas with her family, and to visit with ailing relatives and friends. I was surprised how well informed her father, her uncles, and others there were about the global controversies surrounding the products Monsanto manufactured there in their midst. They reminded me that Monsanto headquarters was just a few miles away—the agricultural control tower that had attempted to capture four-fifths of the U.S. cottonseed market, and nearly half of the corn and soybean markets. One morning Laurie and I took a drive over to Monsanto's campus, where we got past its gates by telling security guards that we had an informal meeting with one of their public relations officers. Somehow the name of a single employee got us through the security checkpoint.

The campus was nearly deserted for the holidays, but that made it even more eery. Dozens of banners and signs proclaimed Monsanto's slogan: "Humanity, Health, and Hope." We strolled over to a massive sculpture in the plaza between Monsanto's administrative buildings, and read a placard describing the intent of the artist commissioned to create *The Branches of Promise*: "Using imagery from Nature, the sculpture represents the artist's view of the Monsanto Worldwide Family—strong, yet caring, diverse, yet unified. The sculpture is created of laminated glass. . . . Bonded with Saflex® interlayer, a Monsanto product."

One massive building was adorned with educational exhibits explaining how biotechnology enhances, enriches, and "provides" bio-diversity. A related Monsanto/Searle calendar of upcoming short course offerings encouraged high school science teachers to "learn how biodi-versity can provide a gateway to sustainability through the latest in pest management strategies." And while meeting Monsanto's scientists at the nearby hospitality suite, teachers could also "learn more about the con-nections between agriculture, food, and health and enjoy light refresh-ments." They were being trained to pass Monsanto's perspective on to schoolchildren, 4-H clubs, and scout troops. The entire program was designed by Monsanto so that educators could "Take a Closer Look at Beautiful Science."

But we could not take a closer look, to "discover DNA with Mon-santo's Look Closer Machine" or glance through its "Population Kalei-doscope." Since the PR person whose name I knew had not come in that day, we were locked out of everything else. All the buildings had multi-ple security measures in place, no doubt to guard company secrets prior to their being patented.

It was too bitterly cold to stay outdoors. We failed to find any scien-tists or educators who were willing to talk awhile inside, so we left the

Monsanto campus without hearing any "words of hope" from the staff. But when we picked up a local newspaper later, we read that some of Monsanto's own stockholders were furious with the corporation's administration for bungling its opportunities in agricultural biotechnology. Within weeks it had merged with one of the world's largest transnational pharmaceuticals, Upjohn-Pharmacia, and rumors flew that it would soon rid itself of all genetic engineering efforts aimed at food crops.

Our last night in St. Louis, I overheard Laurie explaining to her brothers how we had been spending the previous months seeking out local foods. Daniel and Ben listened silently but intently to their older sister's stories, apparently impressed by our diligence. Before Laurie could offer them our provisional definition of "local foods," Ben broke in with a question: "Have you thought about sharing with Gary one of our local food traditions here in St. Louis? Remember that eatery in Maplewood we used to go to after movies and parties?"

Daniel chimed in, grinning. "Laurie, you *have* to take Gary there, or you really haven't shown him what St. Louis cuisine is really like. When you come back from the hockey game tonight, drive down Big Bend past Clayton. . . ."

Suddenly Laurie was grinning as well, remembering the place they were speaking of. She turned to me: "They're right. You can't leave St. Louis until we eat there."

That night, after the Blues got their butts whipped by Nashville, Laurie drove us through the icy streets of St. Louis. Just after midnight, as we passed through a rather well-to-do neighborhood on the edge of Clayton, I began to look for local eateries.

"Are you sure the place will be open this late?"

"It was when I was in high school. I think it stays open into the wee hours of the morning."

I began to look around for jazz clubs, but then we passed out of the ritzy area into one that was visibly run down.

"There it is," Laurie announced as she drove into a well-lit parking lot in front of a little white building. A true temple of local foods it was not. Instead a sign proclaiming our arrival at White Castle glowed down on us. We had arrived at the Midwestern shrine to the greasy goddess of fast foods.

"Still the same old place. It's like walking back in time," she said as she walked toward the door.

I peeked inside the window. No temple. Maybe more like a haven for runaway teenagers, druggies, and drunks.

"C'mon in. Let's do some interviews. This is urban anthropology, sweetie."

We entered another kingdom. Although the first White Castle hamburger was sold in Wichita, Kansas in 1921, the company was well established in St. Louis by the time Laurie's father and mother grew up there. About the time Laurie was weaned, White Castle patented its famous tortilla-thin hamburger, the five-hole Slyder, and when she returned from Latin America to finish high school in St. Louis, the two-billionth burger was flipped onto a White Castle grill. As a young mother Laurie struggled to keep her son, Jeremy, out of the place after baseball teams, even though many of his friends were probably there downing an entire bagful of Slyders. Whereas her son had needed protection from such cravings, she hinted that perhaps I had become too pure in my food choices, and that a couple of Slyders might balance me out.

After coming in the door, my eyes had to adjust to the bright lights and pure whiteness surrounding us on every wall. Before I could even find the menu, I became dazzled by all the signs and video monitors bombarding us with messages. The first one I read was above the grill, right in front of where the cook was standing: THE DISCHARGE OF LARGE AMOUNTS OF WET CHEMICAL MAY CREATE HAZARDS FOR PERSONNEL.

But that was only the first of White Castle's ancient proverbs I would see. Many of the others spoke directly to our quest for spiritual and emotional peace: SATISFY THAT BURNING DESIRE WITH A SACK OF BURGERS, ONLY $4.10. Next to an artificial Christmas tree was a registry where anyone who came here on a religious pilgrimage could sign in: "Look who's got the crave." And finally, with the solemnity of a promise written in stone, there was the sign that carried the timeless White Castle vow: SERVING THE FINEST PRODUCTS FOR THE LEAST COST.

"*Psst,*" Laurie whispered to me. "We gotta order or they'll think we're plainclothes cops. The girl is getting impatient with us."

An African-American girl with a white hairnet on was tapping her fingers against the counter. "You want what?"

"I'll have a cheeseburger and some french fries with cheese. Hey, Gary, pay attention: Want to split an order of mozzarella cheese sticks?"

"No, I'm going traditional. I'll have a half dozen Slyders and a large cola."

"Be up in a second," the cashier said, taking my five-dollar bill and handing me back some change.

"Say, I was wondering something," I said, trying to catch the cashier's attention. "Have you ever met the owner of White Castle? I mean, does he ever come here?"

"That be Willie Graham. All this started by his great-grandfather in 1921."

"But have you ever talked with him?"

"Whatever," she said, plopping the bag of burgers down in front of us. End of interview one.

"You're not very good at this," Laurie whispered to me. "Go sit down over there, and watch what I do."

She strolled up to a small table where three black girls huddled together on one bench, with a black guy and a white guy on the other side.

"Got the time?" Laurie asked.

"Lady, there's a clock behind you," the white kid replied. "It's about twelve-thirty."

"*Twelve-thirty*?!" Laurie feigned surprise. "What we doin' up this late?"

The black girls giggled and huddled closer together. None of them had jackets with them, even though it was below freezing outside. "Gotta keep ourselves awake till three," one of the girls said, shrugging. The others giggled again.

As Laurie sat down across from me and began to eat her cheese-burger, I listened to the kids talk among themselves: "*Watch* that cheese stick, boy. It better not explode all over me!" one of the girls sassed.

"It's as sticky as that crap in your hair. You better lay off that hair gel, honey, all your hair be fallin' off."

I whispered to Laurie, "Your interview with them wasn't much longer than mine was."

"Well, I bet you didn't notice the drug deal going down in the women's bathroom."

"*What?*"

"When we came in, did you notice that there was a girl all wrapped up in a long scarf sitting at the far table? She had a bag under the table, and when the cashier was taking your order, she picked it up, took it into the bathroom, came out empty-handed, and left. A minute later another woman in a ski mask came in, went straight to the bathroom, came out with the bag under her arm, and then *she* left without buying a thing."

"I'm not interested in drugs other than burgers. I'm just here for the beef." Suddenly I felt myself dropping off into a semiconscious stupor. The Slyders had begun to do their magic in my stomach. It took me a while to get out my next sentence to Laurie: "Can we eat the rest . . . on the way home . . . go . . . to your folks' house?"

"I thought you had given up eating food on the road. Or don't Sly-ders count as food?"

"*Home,*" I pleaded with her, "before they slide right out of me."

"Then use the bathroom here."

"But what if there's another drug deal going on in there?"

As we got up and left, Laurie asked, "Are you sure I shouldn't buy a thirty-two-burger frozen pack for \$13.12? One time I did that leaving St. Louis on my way to Arizona, and it lasted me the entire way. . . ."

I never heard her finish the story. I was blacking out, falling dead asleep. Laurie had to guide me into the house as I sleepwalked to the bed. When she explained my condition to Ben and Daniel the next morning, they knew instantly what had happened: I had been taken over by the Crave . . .

Chapter Twenty-One

Hunting Quail and Stalking Scavengers

By the time the holidays were over, I had reached my saturation point with driving around cities, crowding into smoky restaurants, attending hockey games in coliseums and family gatherings in overheated houses. I felt claustrophobic and sun starved, just as plants do under such conditions, growing pale and etiolated. All I wanted to do was stay outdoors, in the boonies, every daylight hour available to me. I walked across mud-cracked stream bottoms as if they were filled with gold shavings. I filled my socks up with the barbed seeds of grasses and sticky leaves of blazing stars.

Quail hunting was my best excuse for staying outdoors and aloof. It didn't much matter to me whether I bagged any quail, but if I did, it would allow me to take another small step toward food self-sufficiency. Hunting was one more way of making the authentically local—as opposed to the White Castle (franchised) version of local—part of my everyday life. I needed to absorb whatever life and light the dead of winter could afford me, and was glad to breathe its cold, fresh air into my lungs as well.

My neighborhood is blessed with two species of quail. Gambel quail can be found there in abundance, and one covey roosts every night in my mesquite tree, feeding every morning on my garden's seedlings. The other species, the scaled quail, is less common, and also less prone to wander around my backyard. Both are challenging to track across mesquite grasslands, and both are good eating. They were my ticket to fly away from humankind each morning before work, and each afternoon until the sun went down, gaudy as a thin slice of Spam. With the winter sun low in the sky at these times, it backlit the shrubs with a silvery glow, and all the grasses had a golden glow. I stood there amazed amid their sparkle and shine, listening for the call of quail.

When I heard one of their call notes, I would murmur to myself, "Take quiet steps toward them. Little quiet steps. Make yourself disappear into the land. Quiet little steps."

I had spent a number of years as a boy practicing marksmanship with a .22, going to an Isaac Walton League shooting range nearly once a week. I continued to hunt with a .22 well into graduate school, but then a hunting buddy went weird on me, and I gave it up. While I was never opposed to hunting game for food, my wife at the time did not condone the sporting life, so I let my interest in game birds go dormant for a few years.

And then, curiously, I felt myself reaching the age that my father, my uncles, and their friends were when they first let a shotgun knock me onto my butt, and I fondly recalled their sportsmanly rituals and pranks. Unable to find where my now-deceased uncle's favorite shotgun had gone, I went out and shopped for a single-barrel twelve-gauge shaped like the one he had loaned me when I was young. I oiled it and tended it in memory of my father, Ted; my uncle John, and my cousin Fred, who was a falconer as well. I had lost touch with the kind of sporting life they had introduced me to, so I began to go out again by myself, hoping the feel for it would gradually come back.

Of course, I was seldom out on the range alone during hunting season. Well before the sun came up, I could see the silhouettes of other hunters, and hear their dogs, ambling along the ridges between me and the dawn. There were some fifty thousand of us in Arizona who got out hunting for quail each season, and most of us devoted at least five full days each year to this pursuit. After a wet summer and fall, we could expect to bag some 750,000 quail throughout the state. But after a year or two of drought, that number might be halved, and the hunting could become much more challenging.

I happened to be grateful for the dipping and peaking of game bird populations from year to year, because they forced me to look at the land in a different way. If I didn't see many quail out and about, I began to look for patches of heron's bill and sour dock, which were among their favorite foods. When I was casually hiking through the same area, I seldom paid close attention to where patches of these herbs occurred, or where there was heavy, shadowy cover. But whenever I go there carrying a shotgun, my eyes change their focus: Perhaps I begin to look at the shrub, herb, and grass cover more as a game bird would. And every time my eyes fully refocus, I bag a bird or two within minutes of homing in on the very habitat cues that the quail use to guide their foraging and roosting.

Perhaps it is not so much a game of making conscious choices as it is a sport of unconsciously picking up subtle cues. I hardly have developed a vocabulary for it, falling back on terms like *gestalt* to explain away what I sense to be the differences between two superficially similar microhabitats, differences in texture, color, and shadow that my words can't aptly describe. Suddenly I know when I've arrived: A covey of quail alights, and I turn my body so that the shots' trajectory crosses theirs. That's all I can say about the conscious part of it. I can ponder over what happened after the fact, but I seldom have time to think as the crossing becomes possible. I suddenly sense a minor movement in the brush, and give myself over to it, following it out. If I paused to think about it, the moment would be gone.

If the quail and the shot intercepted each other, I might go home with a bird in hand. If the moment was lost, the covey would break up and scatter itself through the shrubbery. Either way I am often left in awe: a still-warm feathered carcass clutched in my cold hand, or the explosion of fluttering wings as a dozen flushed-out game birds rise, then disappear before my very eyes.

After bagging a couple of quail, I walk back home, shotgun over my shoulder, pluck all the feathers from their cooling bodies, slit their stomachs to eviscerate their crops of seeds and innards. I remove their top-knotted heads and their feet. It takes me hardly two minutes to turn a Gambel or scaled quail into grillable meat.

However, it has sometimes taken four hours of basting the quail in balsamic vinegar, garlic, and lemon juice to bring out all of its flavors. If I quickly sear it, then turn down the heat and slowly grill or bake it, the quail holds all its juices inside but remains as tender as any meat I've ever eaten. A quail hardly needs to share a plate with much else to make a satisfying meal: A dollop of winter greens and *nopalitos* sauteed in olive oil; a few winter potatoes; a half cup of leftover white tepary beans baked into a miniature cassoulet.

After such a meal I am inclined to sit in front of the fireplace, read a tale of hunters from centuries past, sip some aged mescal, and drift off into a night of dreaming.

One morning, after fruitlessly stalking a particularly elusive covey, I came home, cleaned up and drove into work on a backcountry road. There was only one car in front of me the entire way. As we both rounded a bend in the road, I caught sight of a peccary bouncing off the front tire of the car and landing dead in the middle of the road. I dodged the fresh carcass, circled back, and picked it up—it was a collared peccary, or javelina. It had a little blood draining from one of its nostrils; otherwise it was intact.

Having heard that Arizona Game and Fish had relaxed its rules on the salvaging of roadkills, I placed the peccary in a large cooler in the back of the Blazer, then drove to a store and covered it with ice. I wasn't sure how to know if the scent glands or guts had ruptured and spoiled the meat, so I called a neighbor who had a permit for dressing wild game.

"Buddy, I just picked up a fresh roadkill and have it cooling. You mind if I bring it over tonight?

"You got a tag from Game and Fish already? You know, a permit for its release?"

"What? They need to okay it before you can butcher it?"

"Well, how would they know that you didn't poach it?"

"But I thought the rules had changed—that anyone could claim fresh roadkills."

"They've changed, but you have to call them and have them meet you at the scene of the kill before they'll release it."

"Can I call them now?"

"You'd better—just tell them you made a mistake and want to know what to do. In any case I'd best not touch it."

Disappointed, I called the Game and Fish hot line. The staffer's response was sympathetic, but he didn't encourage me to keep the meat.

"Sure, I understand why you'd want to pick up a peccary that you saw another car kill, but I'm sorry, you'd better not hang onto it. The way the law reads now, it's your own car that must take down the roadkill, and you have to call us immediately to get the permit."

"So what do I do now?"

"You've given us your name and number, and we know you picked it up without understanding the law. But it's best that you take it out in the desert and leave it there, preferably near the site where you picked it up."

And that is what I did. I dragged the carcass dozens of yards away off the county road, and laid it out on the ground to rot.

Although the javelina's meat no longer interested me, its return to the food chain did. I came back every day for a week, hoping to run into coyote scat, eagle feathers, or vultures circling. Day after day I'd return, and the javelina would still be there, intact.

Worse than my earlier disappointment over not getting to roast any javelina meat, I became disheartened that no scavengers came. No carrion feeders, no worms or flies. Perhaps the winter days were so cold that the carcass never got to stinking over the nine days of my vigil with it. But what if this meant something else was awry: that this land's ravens, eagles, and vultures were too few anymore to find and break down a carcass of this size. Perhaps they had been poisoned, scared away, or thinned out by the cold snap. But I felt as though the local food chain had been broken here. The rotters of flesh, the putrefiers, the decomposers had been cut out of the action.

If carrion feeders were having a hard time making a home on the range, then perhaps some Arizona ranches had become far too sanitized for my liking. It was getting to be time for me to see if the same trend was under way across the border in Mexico. I was hoping that roadkills there could still be eaten by coyotes, caracaras, wolves, Harris hawks, humans, or other scavengers of our ilk.

Chapter Twenty-Two

Mexico's Breadbasket of Toxins and Migrants

I had become a migrant worker, going the wrong direction compared with all the Mexican fieldhands moving northward through the fields on the *migra* at this time of year. They first picked harvests in frost-free Jalisco, Nayarit, and Sinaloa, before reaching Sonora, Arizona and California. Meanwhile, I started out in early February in Arizona, and worked south into Sonora, then down through the other states on Mexico's Pacific coast. I was traveling with two other biologists, revisiting places where migratory pollinators had once been seen, to determine whether or not they still resided there for parts of the year, or had vacated for good. Ironically many of the places we visited were near the home villages of the workers who had passed us as they moved northward, some of them going for just a season's worth of wages, some of them never to return.

Because we were biological detectives, we stopped and looked at nearly everything that interested us, living or dead: roadkilled doves being picked apart by vultures; caves filled with vampire bats where different kinds of nectar-feeding bats once lived; giant freshwater prawns sold by night-prowling teenagers who had plucked them from pools or streams running out of caverns and canyons. We searched everywhere for clues about certain partnerships that had come under assault. We wanted to find who or what (other than weather) had disrupted the interactions among migratory birds, bats, butterflies, and their food plants. We sought to confirm or deny reports of the manslaughter of entire cave faunas—bats, mice, salamanders, and spiders. Were they dynamited or burned into oblivion out of human fear, or did they abandon their roots on their own? We investigated alleged truancies or "no-shows" reported at other points along their flyways. Lesser long-nosed bats, rufous hummingbirds, and white-winged doves had been reported in decline, or absent altogether at former roosts. As we tracked them along their nectar trail down the West Coast of Mexico, I tried to assess how the food supplies of nectar and pollen were faring. But at the same time, I recorded how the human food supply was faring—most vegetables eaten in winter in the American West are grown in the Mexican West, and I wanted to understand the hidden expenses of that binational partnership.

Not even an hour after we crossed the Mexican border, we started to see road-killed coyotes and dogs, catered to by circling ravens, vultures, and caracaras—a good sign that feathered travelers had not been hunted or poisoned out. The warp and weft of one part of the food web were still connecting, but soon I realized that another part had been unwoven. Fields where Sonoran peasants had once practiced subsistence farming were now being filled with greenhouses. Hermetically sealed greenhouses were replacing the ancient fields where butterflies and buttercups, bean plants and bees, Sonorans and floodplain soils had interacted for centuries.

More accurately, farmlands were being developed into *cities* of glass houses—artificial environments where tomatoes, chiles, cucumbers, onions, squash, and green beans were grown in climatically controlled, industrialized conditions beyond the reach of wildlife. One complex owned by the Cris-P Produce Company added nearly an acre of greenhouses a month, and its empire already covered more than a hundred acres of prime floodplain land. This was Sonora's way of catching up with its neighboring state of Sinaloa, which traditionally produces the same amount of summer vegetables as Sonora does, but four times as much produce in the winter. The difference? Sinaloa was frost free, but two-thirds of Sonora still suffers from killing frosts. Sonorans must use greenhouses to stay in competition with Sinaloa's vegetable magnates, but even that seems to be a losing battle. While Sinaloa's field agriculture still employed about the same number of farmworkers as it did in 1993—the year before the North American Free Trade Agreement (NAFTA) went into effect—Sonora lost thirteen thousand jobs in its food production sector in the first five years after NAFTA was passed— nearly 32 percent of its agricultural livelihoods.

The reasons for this loss were more complex than the fact that several hundred workers sealed into a hundred acres of greenhouses can grow more tomatoes than several thousand farmers can on thousands of acres of land. While Mexico was now exporting hundreds of tons of its greenhouse tomatoes for the benefit of American consumers every winter, it was also importing cheaply produced (in some cases, government-subsidized) corn and beans from the United States. In fact, American corporations gained ten times more money selling corn to Mexico in 1998 than they did in 1993, demonstrating that their political support for NAFTA paid tangible dividends. The value of American bean imports jumped twenty-sevenfold over the same period. But the corn and beans formerly grown by Mexican peasants for local markets could no longer compete in the marketplace, and the peasants could not get rid of their harvests. Perhaps hundreds of thousands of Mexican farmers threw in the towel and let the fields lie fallow. But no one knows how many, for Mexican agricultural statistics atlases skirt the issue, reporting only that overall national crop production soared. The successes with greenhouses helped the U.S. and Mexican governments gloss over the loss of centuries of traditional agricultural knowledge, and thousands of years of cultural selection of regionally adapted seeds. Even though the buying power of Mexico's minimum-wage workers decreased between 1993 and 1998, NAFTA was still proclaimed a success.

South of Guaymas, Sonora, we entered the region once known as Mexico's Breadbasket, where wheat breeder Norman Borlaug won a Nobel Prize for feeding the world with the Green Revolution's hybrid crops. Like greenhouse tomatoes, these were crops that were no longer *precisely adapted* to the peculiar conditions of any particular place; instead they were widely adaptable, capable of being grown nearly anywhere agribusiness could provide them with ample doses of fertilizers, irrigation water, herbicides, and pesticides. There was still hybrid wheat in many of the fields, but once the Green Revolution's irrigation infrastructure was made available through government subsidies, many of the larger-scale farmers shifted from sowing wheat to growing vegetables for export. Portions of the Yaqui and Mayo River Valleys still produced grains for national consumption, but at great cost.

Until 1950 the Río Yaqui Valley was largely inhabited by Yaqui families living in rancherias out in the desert scrub. Those who grew wheat grew a variety known as White Sonora, good for making huge tortillas, a variety introduced by Spanish missionaries in the 1690s. From 1950 to 1990, thanks to the Green Revolution crop varieties derived from White Sonora that were bred to be more fertilizer responsive, yields per acre increased fourfold. The success was not simply due to sophisticated crop improvement schemes designed by plant breeders. It was jump-started by the equivalent of giving a teenage athlete a steroid shot: 250 pounds of nitrogen fertilizer were being added to each acre of already-nutrient-rich floodplain soils. Despite the great soil fertility developed over thousands of years of annual flooding of the Río Yaqui, the Green Revolutionaries were convinced that they needed to give Borlaug's mighty grain yields the ultimate liftoff.

So much urea and anhydrous ammonia were dumped on the fields that as the fields were irrigated, twenty-five to fifty pounds per acre leached out of the root horizon they were meant to enrich, and much of it contaminated the groundwater instead. Some of my friends at Stanford University—Pam Matson, Peter Vitousek, and Ros Naylor—began to look at this so-called breadbasket a decade ago, and discovered that it was "leaking."

Pam once explained to me what is happening: "We have lost the capital of hundreds of years of alluvial buildup in a matter of four decades. The farmers along the Río Yaqui have, in a sense, burned away the reservoir of organic matter that floods brought in over millennia. They don't have a prayer in the world of farming sustainably in the short run—they must import water as well as nitrogen from other landscapes—their fields are now so low in organic fertility."

And so the farmers of the Yaqui Valley now find fertilizers to be their single largest cost, amounting to 24 percent of their expenses during the cropping season. At the same time their pesticide use is tragically high, especially when so many Yaqui Indians live in or near the fields being sprayed. Yaqui families who work and live in these fields claim that pesticides are applied to some crops up to forty-five times during the growing season. Often, the barrels that once held toxic organochlorines and other chemicals are used by farmworkers to haul drinking water, or to bathe in. The many side effects of this exposure are now obvious in the disease rates of children born in the Yaqui breadbasket.

There are many danger signs that the Yaqui Valley growers' penchant for monoculture has put both their neighbors' health and their own crops in the danger zone. Their farmworkers' bodies are vulnerable to chemical assaults, and their crops are more and more susceptible to a variety of pests and diseases. As their farm landscape has become more monocultural, their wheat has become more vulnerable to diseases like the carnal bunt inadvertently brought into the valley by the Green Revolution's plant breeders.

As we passed field after field of diseased wheat growing amid weeds, I remembered Pam's words: "In a way, what they're doing—and as consumers, what we're doing—is homogenizing the landscape. We're losing the special places around us because we didn't see the invisible connections that bind them together."

And as we traveled away from the border, we saw that those connections were becoming unbound, severed, and frayed. While we went south, most of the folks we saw—in cars and minivans, on horses and on foot, were going north. They were fleeing Mexico's farm country, where the land had been eroded, the water contaminated, and the labor force underpaid. Since the passage of NAFTA and the flooding Mexican markets with U.S. and Canadian commodities, the poorest of the rural poor in Mexico have abandoned their fields and orchards, their roadside vegetable stands, and their cheese- and jam-making kitchens. They have put down their hoelike *coas,* their machetes, and their ladles. They have pulled up shop to tumble northward like uprooted tumbleweeds. As many as four million have ended up dispossessed of their land. Each year since 1988 about 150,000 displaced Mexicans—mostly farmers and farmworkers—have successfully crossed the border and taken up residence in the United States. But for every successful border crosser, many others have been apprehended and turned back. The intensity of apprehensions reached epic proportions during the period in February and March 2000, as I was tracking the pollinators down the Mexico's west coast. Between 180,000 and 220,000 Mexicans were caught near the border and sent back into Mexico.

"But for every one we catch, ten other dirt-poor Mexicans have been escaping us recently," one border patrol officer confessed to me. "Our vans and cycles pass by a canyon, and all of a sudden ten bushes stand up and continue their walk northward, looking for work." As we left Sonora, I kept looking out my car window at the run-down shacks built right next to the fields being sprayed and the ditches being filled with herbicides and fertilizers, the same ditches where families drink and bathe. Pesticide imports from the United States to Mexican fields had jumped by 50 percent in the first six months after the passage of NAFTA, and the number of pesticide poisonings suffered by farm laborers and their families also skyrocketed. When we passed through Sinaloa, we witnessed plane after plane spraying chemicals over fields of vegetables destined for U.S. markets, cave after cave dynamited for fear of vampire bats and *chupacabras,* the mythical animals that appear in Mexico whenever periods of political oppression and social unrest make *campesinos* fearful of everything seen and unseen. In Nayarit we saw thousands of acres that no longer grew grain for humans to eat but were dedicated instead to attracting waterfowl and doves for vacationing hunters from the United States to hunt. And in Jalisco we heard *jimadores*—the high-skilled horticulturalists of the tequila industry— grieve the loss of tens of thousands of agave plants their bosses had ignorantly planted with just one disease-susceptible variety of cultivated mescal. Fields with diseased plants and weeds were being burned all along the roadside, leaving blackened, barren, eroding earth in their wake.

But all the landscapes we passed through Mexico were not so dark, all the reports were not so stark. Before leaving Guadalajara, I read in the city's largest newspaper that Mexico had banned any import of Bt corn seed or foods from the United States until research was sufficient to prove that there would be no significant effects to wildlife or human health. I was relieved to know that the very nation that had given corn to the world was not about to let a toxic corn come back to haunt it or its monarch butterflies.

That said a lot about the Americas, it seemed: Mexico was lax in its regulation of pesticides, but could be a model for other countries in the way it exercised the "precautionary principle" to stave off the ill effects of GE organisms. To the north the United States had more pesticide regulations in place but needed to be challenged by other countries to exercise similar prudence in letting GEs loose on the world. The solutions to all these messes didn't all emerge from the same place; it was as though Mexico and the United States needed each other to keep each other's worst tendencies in check.

If there was a solution to the "food problems" of the American continent, it would no doubt emerge from some collaboration that spanned political and cultural borders. Hopefully it would be one that would help not only consumers and mainstream farmers but these marginalized folks as well, who were once farmers but now behaved like the migratory bats we were studying, following the blooms, then harvesting the fruits, each in their season. They were the very folks that produced much of what Americans ate to stay healthy during the winter months. If there was a way to link the plight of these people and their lands with that of our own, we desperately needed to demonstrate that link. Otherwise the rising tide of displaced, dispossessed, and culturally degraded lives would grow even higher.

For my particular food shed, it was painfully obvious that most problems were binational in nature, with pressures generated on one side of the border rippling across to the other. This might be just as true for the continent as a whole, for its shrimp trawlers and fruit pickers, its diabetes-prone and its cholesterol-crazed consumers, for its migratory bats and its monarch butterflies, but few of my friends living beyond the borderlands were convinced of this. I had to figure out a way to affirm that our food community had always spanned one sort of border or another, for it inherently involved several cultures and many species. There must be a way, I thought, to rebind, graft, or air-layer our disparate branches into one family tree, to make our connectedness bear fruit.

But I didn't immediately know what it was. So I meditated on this riddle, letting it settle deeply until the pieces fitted together in a manner I could not have consciously arranged.

Chapter Twenty-Three

The Desert Walk for Heritage and Health

Sometimes I have dreamed of engaging in something so simple and powerful that, had I done it by myself, its sheer power would have mowed me down and killed me. Even though such stray dreams still come to me on an episodic basis, they somehow become tempered by the act of having to describe them in full daylight, and by the pragmatic offerings of friends and loved ones. Still, I have awakened some mornings from dreams so outlandish that I must blurt them out to cool them off, as I did with Laurie one dawn before her eyes were fully open.

"I was walking all night long, looking for some kind of food that we once had all around us. You were with me, and we were out in the desert wilderness, looking under bushes for some kind of manna that I hadn't ever seen, but I knew that it was out there. Have you ever had that feeling?"

"Huh?"

"Looking for manna. You know it's nearby, you keep asking people about it, and they say, Yeah, it's out there. You're wandering around, crossing borders, and you keep feeling you're getting closer and closer to it. . . . Y'know, before the year is out, I'd like to be out wandering around like that. Maybe walk from the ocean down in Mexico back here to our house . . . searching for our food along the way. We could begin at one of the Seri fishing villages . . . then pass through cactus forests and fields where some of my O'odham friends live, then head on up through the grasslands and oaks. . . . Maybe we can't get everything we want to eat by foraging as we go, but perhaps we could cache foods from other seasons to pick up along the way."

As one of her eyes opened wide, looking somewhat terrified, the other eye stuck shut, not fully wanting to acknowledge what her ears had just heard. In her silence, I added, "Wouldn't you like to go along? When do you think we could pull it off?"

Fortunately, once awake, Laurie has a remarkable capacity to improvise on the spot. I think it comes from years of hanging out and jamming with kitchen musicians, including her father and older sister. That is, it was hard for her not to jump in and add a few riffs when someone else has started improvising.

"Sure I'll go," she sighed, "as long as we make it a *sacred* pilgrimage, like a walking prayer—a prayer for what healthy food means—how it is wrapped up in most social and environmental justice issues. We'll be pilgrims . . . for Just Food, Slow Food."

And then she sang out one more set of notes: "But why not take some of our Seri friends along with us?" She took a deep breath, then warbled again.

" I mean, why leave our friends behind when we leave their village? They could get a lot out of this . . . see how much effort it takes for the O'odham to deal with this huge diabetes problem, now that it has advanced so far. . . . Look at the Seri's own rate of diabetes; it's not a whole lot lower than the O'odham rate anymore. I don't know . . . it might help if they saw how it affects entire communities, not just individuals. . . . What do you think?"

Suddenly the original notion of a couple of us walking through the desert had become obsolete. I let it go. I played off Laurie's riff by adding my own: "That sounds fine, but let's invite some O'odham friends along as well. They could learn from seeing how the Seri still use so many native plants and animals as food and medicine. . . . And they have an ancient tradition of going back and forth from the Gulf of California on sacred pilgrimages. They would be sure to make it prayerful."

When that little brainstorming session took place one October day, neither of us could have imagined that six months later we would complete the last leg of a trek from the Gulf of California with more than 180 O'odham, Seri, Yaqui, Hopi, Latino, and Anglo pilgrims walking along with us. We were all slowly trudging along behind a handful of their elders, who were chanting out a riveting homecoming song: We had come home to the foods and medicines that could nourish us without depleting the desert around us, the desert we had walked through and camped in for the previous twelve days.

As I caught sight of several hundred people there to greet us at the end of our pilgrimage, I knew in my heart that the vision that had propelled us was no longer (if it had ever been) mine or Laurie's or that of any other person alone. What had happened to us was due to some collective affirmation that we all needed to reengage with the lands and the seas immediately before us, the deep traditions about them that could guide us. By renewing our contact with the power of the desert and the ocean, their foods and their medicines, their songs and their stories, we could be healed. And as we learned in conversations with others along the way, we were not the only ones who were opting for local foods and medicines rather than just accepting any "organic foods" or "natural herbal remedies," wherever they came from. We learned of www.local-harvest.org, an on-line guide for tens of thousands of other Americans who were actively seeking out fresh-food markets located as close as possible to their homes. As Karen Lehman and Julie Ristau declared in their manifesto for the Minnesota Institute of Sustainable Agriculture:

> When we buy local food, we are supporting community health: a network of farmers, food processors and fellow customers who live and work in our community, our regional landscape and our local economy. Personal health . . . and the health of the environment is at stake: Local foods do not generate the same pollution and waste the same energy as foods that are trucked, shipped or flown in from far away. . . . [We know when] we are protecting our wildlife habitats, our waterways, and workers who are also our neighbors.

Laurie and I gathered together such neighbors—fishermen and foragers from the Seri villages, farmers and basketmakers from the Papago Indian Reservation, seed savers from Native Seeds/SEARCH, schoolyard gardeners from the Ha:shañ charter school. We joined together for a collective journey to see how our health stemmed from the very wildlife habitats, croplands, and cultural communities that surround us. We went out to see how badly those habitats, fields, and communities had been injured and how that had something to do with our own injuries and maladies. We tasted what each community we passed through called their "local food," and we took a hard look at how it was produced. We learned how to step together, covering one long desert mile after another, until 240 miles had been completed and celebrated. It was then that we realized we would be dedicating the rest of our lives in one way or another to restoring our communities to fuller health.

And so we called it the Desert Walk for Biodiversity, Heritage, and Health, a multicultural pilgrimage fueled by native foods and medicines, prayers, and songs. We unabashedly spoke about what ailed us; one O'odham pilgrim broke the silence by telling how he had felt doomed to a premature death when he first found out he had diabetes. And then younger, ‸‸‸ ‸‸ fishermen admitted that they had once thought only other tr‸‸‸‸ ‸‸‸‸‸d from diabetes until they were diagnosed themselves with t‸ ‸‸‸ ‸‸ ‸liction.

‸‸‸ ‸‸‸ ‸‸‸fore our departure, Laurie's research about Seri diabetes was fea‸‸ ‸‸ in the *Boston Globe*. Under a half-page color picture of Seri elder Luis López sternly, quizzically, looking down on us, Sy Montgomery's story reported the rising rate of adult-onset diabetes among the Seri—which was rapidly approaching the O'odham community's dangerously high prevalence of aberrant blood sugar and insulin levels—and my studies of desert foods as means to control the damaging dynamic of those. Laurie had found that in the Seri village farthest from fast-food outlets, diabetes was slowly rising. There was little difference in the susceptibility of those with 100 percent Seri ancestry, and those with one or more grandparents of O'odham ancestry.

But in the village, where fast foods were more pervasively replacing traditional foods from the desert and sea, those individuals with O'odham ancestry were more prone to diabetes. This is not surprising, since the O'odham (Pima and Papago) now suffer the highest incidence of diabetes of any ethnic population in the world. While her study suggested that fast foods aggravated these peoples' susceptibility to diabetes, my collaborations with nutrition scientists demonstrated that certain native desert foods protected them from diabetes in the first place, slowly releasing glucose and increasing insulin sensitivity so that the food's energy was accommodated without stressing the pancreas.

Sy had seen firsthand what any Seri homemaker was up against when she went to the local grocery store hoping to find nutritious foods for her family: The shelves were stocked with sugary Zucaritas breakfast cereal, Instant Lunch noodle soup, and giant plastic bottles of Coca-Cola [while outside] a 5-year-old chewed a marshmallow candy."

But by the time we had walked our 240 miles, we had put considerable distance between ourselves and those Zucaritas and Coca-Colas. We had feasted on boiled venison, baked rabbit, and grilled corvina, tomatillo consommés and squash soufflés, tepary bean burritos wrapped in mesquite tortillas, freshly picked and lightly steamed lamb's-quarter, purslane, tansy mustards, and cress. We had guzzled down ocotillo blossom tea and prickly pear punch, mistletoe and Mormon tea. We had been presented gifts of organpipe cactus jam, stewed pumpkin, and pinole to eat, and creosote bush salve, jojoba oil, and damiana tea to lessen our aches, pains, blisters, and bruises. Our desserts had ranged from chia seeds soaked in cactus juice, to pit-roasted mescal. We had walked right past stores full of sodas and beers, chips and cupcakes, knowing that they seldom take away our thirst and hunger. Instead we gathered around campfires at night, listening to personal testimonials of hardships, and rising to dance with one another as fiddlers, drummers, rattle shakers, and singers moved us to our feet.

Then, up and walking once more the next day, we bore witness to what was happening to the land, both good and bad. It was a slow walking meditation on where we've been, what we've ignored around us, and what we have yet to see. Any of us can fall into this reverie when we walk along for mile after mile.

Think of the highway that you have driven over the most times in your life. You recognize certain hills and trees, certain fields or orchards, as "landmarks," as if they exist for no reason other than to tell you how many miles you have gone and how many you have yet to travel.

But on one hill that you have passed dozens of times, there grows an oddly crested saguaro cactus that you have passed by but missed all these years, and an old Indian man tells you that it has a special power, so he sings to it. Its blooms are hardly discernible at even forty miles an hour, but now you know where it is, and can look next time for its fruit. As you walk, you notice a hackberry tree, and you taste its berries, they are more sugary and tart than any other. Next, on a farm hidden down in a small valley, you meet a seventy-year-old widow who knows how to prepare a dozen medicinal teas from the plants growing wild alongside her irrigation ditches. And ahead, perched high in the mountains near the border, lies an orchard abandoned fifty years ago where the fruit trees still stand like statues, reminding us that their roots once tapped into a

⌣pring. It is the last place in the Americas where a particular kind ⌣ apricot persisted, one which a missionary from Trent, Italy, had sent from his hometown three centuries ago.

"Ohhh," I moaned over and over again as we walked, "What I have missed by moving so fast."

And I moaned again each afternoon as my feet became so tired that I had to give them to the entire community to keep them moving. Each evening we dedicated ourselves to the care of one another's feet, as if they had become community property, as if they were the tangible manifestation of the spirit we shared with one another. We shed our boots or running shoes and our socks, and dried our sweaty, slightly puffy soles out in the wind. We put our neighbor's feet into our laps, looking for blisters, bruises, thorns, and infections. We popped the ballooned-up ones with pins and slathered them with creosote grease. We cut out moleskin curlicues to fit in between their toes to keep the burning sensation in their soles from becoming even more inflamed.

We spent five, sometimes ten minutes at a time holding in our hands the feet of another who might have been a mere stranger yesterday. Now we knew how their toes curled, how flat or arched their feet were, and whether they grimaced with the pain or remained stoic as we performed minor investigations and operations. Now we not only knew where they stood in the desert, but how they did it. It was our feet that first brought us together as a group. We blessed and caressed one another's feet and never took our own for granted again. It was our feet, not merely our minds and our hearts, that would eventually carry us across the border, and back home.

More than any other moment, I remember the instant we crossed the border, that 150-year-old line that has worked to divide our food shed in two, separating river from ocean, deep-sea fisherman from hinterland forager, Mexican from American, Seri from O'odham, me from you.

Around one in the afternoon the day before, I heard singing ahead of me and saw that the pilgrims had set up our shade ramada on the roadside. As I climbed up out of one last wash and leveled out once more, I caught sight of the sacred peak of the O'odham, Baboquivari, which stood on the *other* side of the border. The mere sight of this familiar face made me happy, but I soon learned that it had made the O'odham jubilant.

"The very moment Danny saw Baboquivari," Tony remembered, "he began to sing one of its songs. I joined in, others joined in; it was like we knew we have come home."

The pilgrims sat in little groups facing the peak, talking quietly. The camp table held a full spread of baby squash, mesquite tortillas, cooked wild greens, tepary beans, *chiltepines,* and elderberry tea. But those of us who knew Baboquivari were filled up in another way, cognizant that the most unimaginable stretches were behind us. The peak would then become a near-constant landmark, a reminder that we were all on sacred ground.

That final morning in Mexico, our bodies understood that we would be stepping across the border, and even those Seri youth who had never even seen the international boundary had some image in their mind of what our crossing might be like. I could not remember breakfast once it was done; I could not remember packing our bags. From the start of the day, the very act of simply walking was superseded by the notion that we would be walking across, and that somehow made our journey more political than it had seemed before.

As we reached the little bordertown of Sasabe, Sonora, we began to walk as slowly as we could, our anticipation building and building. Baboquivari reappeared when we passed a hill, and it was such a splendid view that I asked Danny to tell the Seri about the peak. I translated for him.

"It is the place where our Creator lives, the one we call I'itoi, and there is a cave below the peak we call I'itoi Ki, for it is his home," he began. He told how you must leave an offering for I'itoi if you go anywhere near the cave mouth, as his people once did to gather plants that grew abundantly there but nowhere else. He spoke of the wild onion, *I'i-toi siwol,* the one that Diann Peart had returned my way nearly a year ago, and of a parsniplike root, *sa:d,* which the Seri knew by another name but used just as well. As Danny and Tony sang one last song to the sacred mountain from the Mexican vantage point, three elderly women came up to us and blessed us.

"You are the pilgrims, the ones we heard about on the radio show from Caborca, no?" And they welcomed us, blessed us again, and wished us luck on our way. We could hardly wait anymore, and so we began walking in double file, hoping that everyone who had wished to had arrived at the line by now. Danny and Tony started up singing, thumping their staffs on the ground. We all shuffled behind them, pacing ourselves like the masked dancers in the indigenous passion plays held throughout Sonora and Arizona.

As we started up the last hill before the border, we saw several O'odham women, including Tony, Terrol, and Avery's mothers, Danny's wife and mother-in-law, singing on the roadside and shaking their gourd rattles. Cameramen began to appear everywhere, and even the customs officials were there to welcome us, waving like children, as if they'd never witnessed such a sight. I was so caught up in the rhythm of the music that someone had to nudge me to get me to look up at the ridge running parallel to us. There, moving at the same speed we were, were a half dozen Mexican hikers, intending to cross the border at the exact same time that we did, when the customs officials and border patrol were most distracted. They were in plain view to anyone whose eyes wandered toward the eastern horizon, but all eyes were on us.

That was when little things began to go wrong: No one could find the bag of bread we had brought along for the borderline communion; the digital camera was accidentally locked inside a van, as were its keys; when they were rescued with another set of keys, the camera was dropped on the ground, and like the rest of us, had trouble focusing for a while. But then the singing smoothed everything out, and a dozen cameras flashed as we reached the grated cattle guard that served as a boundary line between lands, people, cuisines, caloric opportunities, and destinies. Onlookers clapped while we cheered and posed for pictures.

Suddenly our friends from the other side appeared with an armful of the breads we had chosen to break on the border, not for nourishment but for catharsis. We had chosen Pan Bimbo and Wonder, the loaves of foul air and feeble constitution. They were the "foods that had come out of Nowhere," that had lured us in with empty promises, that had seduced us like the whores and studs of a bordertown brothel, that had dazzled us with the glitter of their baggage but left us feeling hungry and heartbroken, cheapened and cheated, diseased and dirty. They were the loaves that had doped us into forgetting what truly had nourished us over the course of our lives. Suddenly, as if he were an exorcist sent to drive away the devil, Adolfo the Seri elder howled out a song, and dozens of us saw the bread at our feet and realized what we must do. We leaped high then came down hard on what stood between us and the sacred earth. We stomped and danced until we flattened those plastic-wrapped globs of doughy airbread into the ground, right on top of the borderline. Some danced the *pascola,* while others hooted and hollered, jumping up and down until the pale, empty loaves were beaten flat as tortillas.

Pan Bimbo and Wonder Bread were the perfect manifestations of the vacuous nutritional promises of the industrialized food that had sold our health down the river. I heard echoes of the jingles from my youth, how such facsimiles of bread could "Build Strong Bodies Twelve Ways." They had popped up and spread across the Americas in the thirties, replacing ashcakes, stottycakes, and johnnycakes, baguettes, biscuits, and bagels, focaccias, puglieses, and pitas, hand-shaped tortillas and dark, seedy harvest loaves of all shapes and sizes with a phantom of one standardized size, machine knifed into equally thick slices. A white bread for white America, which sooner or later became so symbolic of the dominant culture that Mexican restaurants would see Americans sit down at their tables, and remove all corn and wheat tortillas, replacing them with a dozen slices of Bimbo.

"They are as substantial as foam." El Indio smirked, picking up the flattened carcass of a Bimbo loaf after the dancing was done. "*Pan de espuma.*"

As the bewildered customs crew let us pass, I knew that however many more miles we had yet to walk, we had broken bread in an altogether unprecedented sense, by accepting no substitutions for true communion with one another and this sacred land.

On our last night before we ended the pilgrimage, we had that true communion: venison and cottontail, posole and pumpkins, beans and whole-grained breads that the O'odham villagers of San Pedro had lovingly made for us. O'odham and Anglo, Seri and Latino were leaning up against one another, quietly weeping as each participant offered prayers and proverbs of thanksgiving. The leader of the O'odham youth, Tony Johnson, stood up among us, then scanned the room, looking into the many faces all around him.

"We started this walk ten days ago down at the ocean. Started out, walked all the way. I was afraid that we weren't going to make it. We did. I did. It wasn't because of any strength that I had that all of you don't have; it was because of the people who are here with me. Yes, the people right here. O'odham. The Desert People. *Alive!* That's why I walked; I believe we are not dead.

"Understand what I'm saying? *We're not dead!* There are people who say we might as well be dead because we're diabetic, that we'll die young anyway; they also say we're dead because some of us are alcoholics. But walking from Mexico to here, I didn't see any dead Indians. We're alive, we may look dead tired, but we're alive."

There was some laughter, but others were still weeping. I felt a rush of relief wash across the room. It was out on the table: All these folks had been told that diabetes was in their genes, there was little they could do about it, that they should be resolved to a limited life. And Tony, on behalf of all the pilgrims, was standing tall and calling that a lie. A lie from deterministic scientists who had spent hundreds of millions of dollars trying to find the elusive gene that caused Indian diabetes, instead of helping people with ways to live a rich life that included savory native foods and plenty of exercise out in the desert they loved.

"And all of you O'odham kids out there, don't ever let them tell you that you can't make it. . . . Look at all these people who have walked, all these people who have helped, all these people who are willing to support you, to bring you to places that you never thought you could go to. . . . I was afraid that we weren't going to be able to make it back. But we made it through again, because of everybody out there that was praying for us. Even those who may have never set foot on the road with us, those people prayed and believed in us, believed we could make it.

"You know, when we were so far away, and we missed home, it felt like we didn't know where we were going, we didn't know where the next road was going to lead to. The only thing familiar to us, the only thing that made us feel at home, was our songs, the ones that come from our *O'odham himdag,* our traditional way. And I realized that no matter where we were, wherever we go in this world, if we have our songs . . . our language . . . we'll always be home."

"So kids, no matter where you are in this world, no matter where you go, always remember that home is just a few miles over those hills, where your people are. That's where your strength is, where your people can feed you the good food. And that's what is going to keep you moving over all those dirt roads, those cliffs, those valleys. That's where the Creator is, and if it wasn't for him, we wouldn't be here today. I just want to thank our Creator and everyone else who helped us for giving us all that good food, that strength."

I remembered how the O'odham words for "healing," "wildness," and "wholeness" came from the same root: *doa,* "to be wildly alive and healthy." We had walked all the way down to those roots.

It was the very last afternoon of the twelve days that something altogether remarkable appeared before us. It was a white-tailed deer, a fawn, unfazed by our presence, standing in the middle of the road as it wove through a mesquite bosque. White-tails were relatively rare in those parts compared to mule deer, but no matter; this one was as intrigued by our presence as we were by hers.

"*Maaso!*" the Seri cried, using the word they had borrowed from their Yaqui neighbors. It referred to the deer that they became in their *Danza del Venado.* They were humbled by its presence. None of the vans moved for a minute or two, until the fawn slid into the mesquite cover alongside the road and disappeared from sight.

Two hours later, as we slowly stepped together for the last mile of 240, that deer appeared again, as symbol spilled out to bind us together. The cadence of our walking arm in arm shaped our movements, and no one could say a thing for a while; we simply listened to Danny and Tony sing, and watched the saguaros slowly being passed on the road-side. Then Amalia glanced back and noticed that Terrol was in the row behind us, clutching Tristan and Frances's hands, Marlene along with them. She leaned toward me and asked, "Will you translate something for me that I want to say to that Papago boy who doesn't want to die of diabetes?"

"Yes, Amalia, wait. Terrol, Amalia is trying to say something to you."

She closed her eyes, held on to me even tighter, and began to speak in a mix of Seri and Spanish: "Tell him that I remembered this dream when we saw that little deer in the middle of the road."

As she whispered a sentence into my ear, I translated. Then another, and another.

"For the last two nights, I have dreamed of deer that had nearly died. A doe and her fawns, they are coming at last into a dense patch of their favorite foods, and it saves them. They are here happily eating, the danger of dying is gone. They will not die for lack of good food, nor will they be killed. They will live. They have come to a place in the desert where there is enough nutritious food to keep them going a very long time. Tell him that."

I glanced back at Terrol, whose eyes were like desert springs flowing with joy. A half second later, as I turned my head around, we were suddenly home.

Epilogue

Yes, I lost eight pounds or more during the walk, and as expected, my HDL/LDL ratio improved, confirming that all of those fiber-rich native foods probably do have the health benefits that our clinical studies suggested earlier. But walking has its health benefits, too. And foraging. And praying. And singing. And laughing. And community building.

If the native foods are worth eating only for their value in reducing blood sugar and cholesterol levels, we might as well just extract their soluble fiber-making genes and insert them into some easy-to-grow, easy-to-prepare nutraceutical packaged food. But they are also good for the land and good for our souls. I have come to love their flavors, even though friends still remind me that some are acquired tastes. I don't doubt that they are right, since I still serve meals at my table that my friends and family don't have the guts to eat. But their acceptability to consumers is not really what is keeping them from being more widely embraced and adopted.

The real bottleneck to the revival of native, locally grown foods is a cultural—or more precisely, a spiritual—dilemma. If we no longer believe that the earth is sacred, or that we are blessed by the bounty around us, or that we have a caretaking responsibility given to us by the Creator—Yahweh, Earth Maker, Gaia, Tata Dios, Cave Bear, Raven, or whatever you care to call him or her—then it does not really matter to most folks how much ecological and cultural damage is done by the way we eat. It does not matter whether we ever participate in the butchering of our meat, the harvesting and grinding of our grain, the foraging and drying of our herbs. Until we stop craving to be somewhere else and someone else other than animals whose very cells are constituted from the place on earth we love the most, then there is little reason to care about the fate of native foods, family farms, or healthy landscapes and communities.

I continue on, adding to my dooryard garden, harvesting what I can from the wildlands around my home, raising minor breeds of turkeys and planting native seeds. The percentage of food that I get from local sources will no doubt vary over time, but I'm sure it will never return to the abysmally low proportion it was before I began my modest experiment. I cannot go back to ignoring where I am situated in the food chain, that cascade of energy that can be shunted in the direction of regeneration or in the other direction, toward desolation row.

Whenever I have doubts about whether all this effort has been worth it, I go out to the wilds beyond my backyard and taste a fruit or flower freshly plucked from a tree or vine. My mouth, my tongue, and my heart remind me what my mind too often forgets: I love the flavor of where I live, and all the plants and creatures I live with.

Cornucopia of Native Foods Eaten within the Sonoran Desert/Gulf of California Foodshed

While many of these species are abundant and easy to harvest, obtaining permits and other permissions may be necessary to sample a few of these foods legally; the author does not condone or recommend illicit taking of these organisms merely for eating pleasure.

Wild Plant Foods

Amaranth greens, barrel cactus fruit, cardon cactus fruit, chiltepines fruit, chainfruit, cholla cactus fruit, cholla cactus buds, damiana tea, emory oak acorns, epazote greens, hackberry fruit, ironwood seeds, mescal leaves and heart, mesquite pod flour, mexican oregano leaves, misteletoe tea, ocotillo blossom tea, organpipe cactus fruit, prickly pear cactus fruit and pads (nopalitos), piñon nuts, purslane greens (verdolagas), saguaro cactus fruit, saiya roots, soapweed yucca blossoms, sow thistle greens, watercress, and wolfberry fruit.

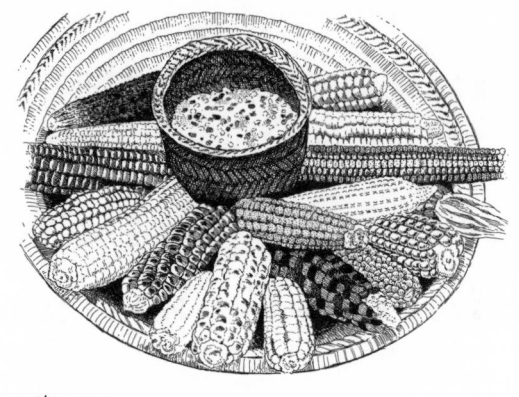

native corn

Cultivated Plant Foods

Amaranth grain, big cheese squash, ancho chiles, serrano chiles, cushaw squash, jalapeño chiles, mescal leaves and heart, prickly pear fruit (tunas) and pads (nopalitos), pumpkin, pinto beans, Sonoran panic grass, squash blossoms, sixty-day corn, and tepary beans.

Wild Animal Foods

Antelope jackrabbit, Audubon's cottontail, black-tailed jackrabbit, black-tailed shark, blue-eating crabs, "china" clams, "chocolate" clams, corvina, curve-billed thrasher, diamondback rattlesnake, flounder, freshwater crab, Gambel quail, grasshoppers, halibut, javelina, lobster, Mearns quail, marlin, Mexican barracuda, mourning dove, mule deer, mullet, northern mockingbird, piebald chuckwalla, "Pleasure" oysters, royal clams, sole, tiger rattlesnake, yellowfin tuna, white clams, white-tailed Deer, white-lined sphinx-moth larvae, and white-winged doves.

Domesticated Animal Foods

Duck, goose, and turkey.

Further Reading

Berry, Wendell. *Farming: A Handbook.* Orlando, Fla.: Harcourt Brace, 1970.

Buchmann, Stephen, and Gary Paul Nabhan. *The Forgotten Pollinators.* Washington, D.C.: Island Press, 1996.

Calvino, Italo. *Under the Jaguar Sun.* Translated by William Weaver. Orlando, Fla.: Harcourt Brace, 1986.

Center for Public Integrity. *Unreasonable Risk: The Politics of Pesticides.* Washington, D.C.: Center for Public Integrity, 1998.

Clark, Robert. *Our Sustainable Table.* San Francisco: North Point Press, 1990.

Cooper, Ann, and Lisa M. Holmes. *Bitter Harvest,* New York: Routledge, 2000.

Davidson, Alan. 1999. *The Oxford Companion to Food.* Oxford, England: Oxford University Press, 1999.

Eggers, Linda, ed. *The Spam Cookbook.* Atlanta: Longstreet, 1999.

Friedman, Thomas L. *The Lexus and the Olive Tree.* New York: Anchor Books, 2000.

Goodland, R. and D. Pimental. "Environmental Sustainability and Integrity in the Agriculture Sector. In D. Pimental, L. Westra, R. F. Noss, eds. *Ecological Integrity.* Washington, D.C.: Island Press, 2000.

Gray, Patience. *Honey for a Weed.* New York: Prospect Books/Harper & Row, 1986.

Groh, Trauger, and Steven McFadden. *Farms of Tomorrow Revisited.* Kimberton, Pa: Biodynamic Farming and Gardening Association/Chelsea Green, 1997.

Harrison, Jim. "Why I Write, or Not." *Zoetrope: All Story* (1998) 1: 41–42.

Jackson, L., and P. W. Comus. "Ecological Consequences of Agricultural Development in a Sonoran Desert Valley." In R. Robichaux, ed., *Ecology of Sonoran Desert Plants and Plant Communities.* Tucson: University of Arizona Press, 1999.

Lappé, M., and B. Bailey. *Against the Grain: Biotechnology and the Corporate Takeover of Your Food.* Cambridge, Mass.: Common Courage Press, 1998.

Meadows, Donella. *The Global Citizen.* Washington, D.C: Island Press, 1991.

Mellon, M., and Jane Rissler, eds. *Now or Never: Serious New Plans to Save a Natural Pest Control.* Washington, D.C.: Union of Concerned Scientists, 1998.

Mills, Stephanie, ed. *Turning Away from Technology.* San Francisco: Sierra Club Books, 1997.

Nabhan, Gary Paul, and Paul Mirocha. *Gathering the Desert.* Tucson: University of Arizona Press, 1985.

Nabhan, Gary Paul, "Nectar Trails of Migratory Pollinators: Restoring Corridors on Private Lands." *Conservation Biology in Practice* 2 Vol. 1 (Winter: 2001): 20–27.

Pellegrini, Angelo. *The Unprejudiced Palate.* San Francisco: North Point Press, 1984.

Safina, Carl. *Song for a Blue Ocean.* New York: Henry Holt, 1997.

Shand, H. Human *Nature: Agricultural Biodiversity and Farm-Based Food Security.* Ottawa, Canada: Rural Advancement Fund International, 1997.

St. John, Primus. *Communion: Poems 1976–1998.* Port Townsend, Wash.: Copper Canyon Press, 1999.

Teitel, Martin, and Kimberly A. Wilson. *Genetically Engineered Food: Changing the Nature of Nature.* Rochester, Vt: Park Street Press, 1999.

Thoreau, Henry David. *Wild Fruits: Thoreau's Rediscovered Last Manuscript.* Edited by Bradley P. Dean. Washington, D.C.: Island Press, 1999.

The author is grateful to the journalists, scientists, and editors of *Orion, Slow Food, Resurgence, World Watch, Science, Nature, Atlantic Monthly, Agriculture and Human Values, BioScience, HortScience, Chefs' Collaborative Newsletter, Fortune, Business Week,* the *Wall Street Journal, HerbalGram,* and the *Seed Savers Exchange Summer Edition* for brief quotations from the many articles they publish on these issues.

Sustainable Food Organizations

Local Harvest
OceanGroups, Inc.
Santa Cruz, CA
Web site: www.localharvest.org

A nonprofit venture to sprout and grow a definitive and reliable directory of small farms and their products nationwide, to attract local supporters.

Chefs Collaborative
282 Moody St., Ste. 21
Waltham, MA 02453
(781) 730-0635; fax (781) 642-0307
E-mail: cc2000@chefnet.com
Web site: www.chefnet.com/cc2000

A dynamic coalition of restaurateurs and chefs involved in advancing the use of locally grown, sustainably produced foods and boycotting swordfish and other destructive harvests.

Oldways Preservation and Exchange Trust
266 Beacon St.
Boston, MA 02116
(617) 621-3000; (617) 421-5511
E-mail: oldways@oldwayspt.org
Web site: www.oldwayspt.org

A food history group promoting healthy eating, encouraging sustainable food choices, and preserving traditional foodways.

Slow Food U.S.A.
P.O. Box 1737
New York, NY 10021
E-mail: pmartins@slowfood.com
Web site: www.slowfood.com

A gastronomic movement ideologically and sensually engaged with regional, traditional foods.

The Center for Food Safety
660 Pensylvania Ave. SE, Ste. 302
Washington, DC 20003
Web site: www.icta.org

A nonprofit organization promoting sustainable agriculture, fighting for strong organic standards, and protecting consumers from the hazards of genetically engineered foods and pesticides.

Center for Rural Affairs
P.O. Box 406
Walthill, NE 68067
E-mail: infor@cfra.org
Web site: www.cfra.org

One of the most effective groups in working with family farmers to maintain their economic and ecological sustainability.

Sustaining People through Agriculture Network (SPAN)
Columbia, MO
Web site: www.agebb.missouri.edu/sustain/span

A Midwestern network to sustain family farms and communities, with an annual conference in Columbia, Missouri.

Just Food
625 Broadway, Ste. 9C
New York, NY 10012
(212) 677-1602; (212) 674-8124

E-mail: justfood@igc.org
Web site: www.justfood.org

One of the most eloquent groups regarding ethical relations between farmers, farmworkers, and consumers.

Bioneers
Collective Heritage Institute
901 W San Mateo Rd., Ste. L
Sante Fe, NM 87505
(505) 986-1644
E-mail: chisf@bioneers.org
Web site: www.bioneers.org

A think tank with an annual conference on advances in green economics, alternative medicines, and natural foods.

Seed Savers Exchange
3076 N Winn Rd.
Decorah, IA 52101
(319) 382-5590
Web site: www.seedsavers.com

The oldest and most active group in preserving heirloom vegetables, fruits, flowers, and rare breeds throughout the world.

Rural Advancement Fund International
P.O. Box 640 and 655
Pittsboro, NC 27312
(919) 542-1396; fax (919) 542-2460
E-mail: rafiusa@igc.apc.org
Web site: www.rafiusa.org

An international, nongovernmental organization dedicated to the conservation and maintenance of sustainable traditions of agricultural biodiversity.

Native Seeds/SEARCH
526 N Fourth Ave.

Tucson, AZ 85705
(520) 622-5561; fax (520) 622-5591
E-mail: info@nativeseeds.org
Web site: www.nativeseeds.org

A multicultural group that conserves, distributes, and documents the adapted and diverse varieties of seeds, their wild relatives, and the role these seeds play in cultures of the American Southwest and northwest Mexico.

American Livestock Breeds Conservancy
P.O. Box 477
Pittsboro, NC 27312
(919) 542-5704
Web site: www.albc-usa.org

A nonprofit organization that protects genetic diversity in American livestock and poultry.

Community Farm Alliance
624 Shelby St.
Frankfort, KY 40601
(502) 223-3655
E-mail: cfa@kih.net
Web site: www.communityfarmallliance.com

A group supporting farmers in society.

American Farmland Trust
1200 18th St. NW, Ste. 800
Washington, DC 20036
(202) 331-7300
E-mail: info@farmland.org
Web site: www.farmland.org

One of the most effective groups in establishing conservation easements and other strategies to protect the cohesiveness or rural landscapes, not just single farms.

Conservation Beef

304 Main St., Ste. 11
Lander, WY 82520
(877) 749-7177
Web site: www.conservationbeef.org

One of the broadest coalitions of ranchers using alternative, conservation-oriented techniques to produce range-fed beef.

Council for Responsible Genetics

5 Upland Rd., Ste. 3
Cambridge, MA 02140
(617) 868-0870
E-mail: crg@gene-watch.org
Web site: www.gene-watch.org

A think tank that sponsors public debate on implications of new gene technologies.

Sea Web

1731 Connecticut Ave. NW, 4th Fl.
Washington, DC 20009
(202) 483-9570
Web site: www.seaweb.org

Sea Web, a project of Pew Charitable Trusts, is a nonpartisan, public-education initiative designed to raise awareness of ocean issues and diminishing sea foods.

CSAS of North America

Northeast Sustainable Agriculture Working Group
P.O. Box 608
Belchertown, MA 01007
(413) 323-4531
or Indian Line Farm
57 Jugend Rd.
Great Barrington, MA 01230

(413) 528-4374
E-mail: nesfi@igc.apc.org
Web site: www.umass.edu/~umext/csa

A networking organization assisting existing, aspiring, and potential CSAs.

Land Stewardship Project
2200 4th St.
White Bear Lake, MN 55110
(612) 653-0618
E-mail: bdevore@landstewardshipproject.org
Web site: www.landstewardshipproject.org

A project working to sustain small farms and promote conservation practices in the Upper Midwest.

Pesticide Action Network of North America
49 Powell St., Ste. 500
San Francisco, CA 94102
(415) 981-1771
E-mail: panna@panna.org
Web site: www.panna.org

A watchdog group on pesticide abuse which also offers alternative food production strategies that minimize pesticides.

Center for Sustainable Environments
P.O. Box 5675
Northern Arizona University
Flagstaff, AZ 86011
(520) 523-0637
Web site: www.nau.environment.org

A research group producing a sustainable foods directory and other benefits for growers on the Colorado Plateau.

Index